Chasing
Ghosts

Other titles of interest from Potomac Books, Inc.

Insurgency and Terrorism: From Revolution to Apocalypse,
Second Edition, Revised
By Bard E. O'Neill

War of the Flea: The Classic Study of Guerrilla Warfare
By Robert Taber

Prodigal Soldiers: How the Generation of Officers Born of Vietnam
Revolutionized the American Style of War
By James Kitfield

Through Our Enemies' Eyes: Osama bin Laden, Radical Islam,
and the Future of America, Revised Edition
By Michael Scheuer

Soldiering: Observations from Korea, Vietnam, and Safe Places
By Henry G. Gole

Chasing
Ghosts

Unconventional Warfare
in American History

John J. Tierney Jr.

Potomac Books, Inc.
Washington, D.C.

Library of Congress Cataloging-in-Publication Data

Tierney, John J. (John Joseph), 1940–
  Chasing Ghosts : Unconventional warfare in American history / John
J. Tierney, Jr.
     p. cm.
  Includes bibliographical references and index.
  ISBN 1-59797-015-8 (hardcover : alk. paper)
  1. Guerrilla warfare—United States. 2. Counterinsurgency—United
States. 3. Special forces (Military science)—United States. 4. Military
doctrine—United States. I. Title.
U240.T59 2006
355.3'430973—dc22

                                                                2006004221

Printed in the United States of America on acid-free paper that meets the
American National Standards Institute Z39-48 Standard.

Potomac Books, Inc.
22841 Quicksilver Drive
Dulles, Virginia 20166

First Edition

10 9 8 7 6 5 4 3 2 1

This book is dedicated to Beatrice and to our children, Monica, Lauren, and John.

Contents

Illustrations

Preface

This is a history book that covers wars lost in memory while remaining based upon issues that have resurfaced since 9/11. The subject, generally speaking, can be described as "strategic culture," the particular concept of conflict as defined by a nation's worldview and geopolitical position. Both of these factors combine to shape the strategies and tactics that are used in waging war against enemies. Since strategic culture is generic, these choices tend to repeat themselves. The insurrection in Iraq has been active since the summer of 2003, and even if it ends tomorrow, it can already be compared to a number of other insurgencies in American history.

Specifically, the subject under review here is unconventional warfare, with its various synonyms: "irregular," "guerrilla," "partisan," "low-intensity," "people's," "revolutionary," etc. Over the past several years military professionals have used the concept of "asymmetric" warfare to define unconventional threats. While each synonym contains different nuanced meanings, the commonality among the meanings gives rise to a strategic culture almost totally opposite from conventional, or "regular," war.

This study will concentrate on those unconventional conflicts that involved Americans as prime combatants, both as insurgents against outside invaders and as counterinsurgents against irregulars. Instances such as the 1947–49 Greek civil war, in which America gave only aid and advice, will be assessed as secondary but critical models for counterinsurgency in its conceptual dimensions.

The Iraqi conflict began as a conventional firepower battle for regime change. This aspect was both brief and highly successful. The regime changed almost immediately, as President Bush declared with the words "mission accomplished" on May 1, 2003, but the aftermath provoked an insurrection against the occupation by segments of the population and outside sympathizers. Condemning these segments for employing terror, or complaining that they are aided from the outside, may satisfy our own conceptions of strategic civility, but it fails to address the problem. The use of both terror offensives and mercenaries has been standard operational procedure in unconventional war throughout history. Radical Islamic fighters use suicide bombers as tactics, a cruel method by any standard. But one might ask the citizens of 1945 Dresden or the sailors facing Japanese kamikaze raids if Iraqi insurgent tactics are a unique kind.

There are significant differences between the Iraqi insurrection and, for example, the Viet Cong or the Irish Republican Army (IRA), but all three are alike in their unconventional methods. Their operations reflect the strategic culture of the weak, the guerrilla, which is derived from tactical and psychological circumstances totally different from the conventional, battle-driven combat of powerful military forces. In Iraq since 2003 we have been waging war on *unconventional* terms, which are generally ill suited for an outside infantry. This, at least, is what history has taught. We need to adjust to such lessons, but as both contemporary and distant history has determined, such lessons are slow and painful. The larger history is the story of this book.

The differences between the two main modes of war will be examined in more detail in the text, but I mention them now in order to set the stage for the remainder of the book. Admittedly, distinctions in kind and circumstance exist throughout history and no two wars are identical. But I have made the case here to highlight the *similarity* among insurgencies and the differences between these unconventional war types and regular or conventional war.

This is a study of unconventional warfare in American history, before Iraq, and the lessons that can be derived from these past experiences should better inform the public and policymakers. Public debates about how to combat the Iraqi insurgency have generally not addressed similar historical cases. Current arguments and appeals generally focus on support for the troops as a patriotic duty, or the size and strength of the occupation force, the degree of armor allotted tank and truck, or the possibility of conscription. These are all aspects of war in its traditional mode, the one understood by most Americans. While such points have a compelling and obvious logic, they should not be the central issues. The nature of the war and the appropriate strategic and tactical response should be the focus of inquiry.

Similarly, the questioning of strategy should not be equated with disloyalty. On talk shows even the bare suggestion of dissent or questioning often results in pointless screaming matches. The controversies surrounding protestor Cindy Sheehan reflect this specter of Americans arguing past each other on street and sidewalk. Those truly interested in the *strategic* issues involved should consult such journals or forums of thought as *Military Review, Parameters,* or *National Strategy Forum* and stop wasting the country's time by either posing as patriots or looking for traitors.

As a historian, my opinion on Iraq is influenced very closely by the past and bears only a transcendent relationship to the situation on the ground. Like most Americans, I know very little about Iraq, do not speak its languages, and have never been there. But I recognize the relationship between past and present and believe that events of the past can be studied and applied wisely. I submit this record in the hope that it will broaden the debate and play a constructive role for achieving American interests in the larger war on terror and future unconventional conflicts.

Briefly, unconventional warfare exists within a largely *political* or *cultural* environment in which offensives against the status quo, or foreign armies, are derived from political causes and where the weapons of war are used in unorthodox ways to enforce political obedience or discipline. This results in guerrilla and civil war, rather than "battle" as generally understood, but this mode of combat can be even more brutal and unforgiving than orthodox combat involving armies or navies. In unconventional warfare, terror and ambush are routinely employed for a political contest involving civilians, not soldiers, and this contest ultimately will decide the political allegiance and fate of the people at large. In such an essentially political situation, nonmilitary pacification strategies should logically prevail. How earlier Americans reluctantly came to this same conclusion is a primary focus of this study. I will also emphasize the cultural and political manifestations of unconventional war as much as the military, stressing the pressures brought upon decision makers by public opinion and war-weariness.

If there is to be a debate on the future of American military "transformation," then it should at least involve the correct *definitions* of warfare. This engages strategic culture, and as I hope to demonstrate, the American strategic culture is, at best, disdainful of unconventional war. Fighting an unconventional enemy requires improvisation and reactive tactics against a kaleidoscope of shifting conditions, rather than an orchestration of efficient strategic movements, which a conventional military would prefer.

The historical approach developed here will suggest strong parallels between past and present that, in my own view, are too compelling to ignore. Readers are invited to share this history and to determine its relevance for themselves. Occupation policies and insurrections against outsiders go back as far as recorded history, as do frustrations by the outside army. The British discovered this in the American War of Independence, as did Napoleon in Spain with his intervention of 1808.

The American record is bipartisan and spans both the party and ideological spectrums. Colonial soldiers in the eastern forests used Indian tactics in an irregular strategic setting. Probably the first U.S. counterinsurgency was fought in the Revolutionary War between Loyalists and Patriots. The Florida war against the Seminoles in the 1830s was led by Andrew Jackson and Martin van Buren, both Democrats. James K. Polk, an original "expansionist" Democrat, absorbed (a willing) Texas and occupied Mexico. The notion of "Wilsonian" missionary zeal is traceable to the occupation policies of Woodrow Wilson and the Democrats in Mexico and parts of the Caribbean. The Republican William McKinley occupied the Philippines in 1899, and his successor, Theodore Roosevelt, had to finish the counterinsurgency there (later calling it his "heel of Achilles"). The isolationist Republican Calvin Coolidge sent thousands of Marines into Nicaragua in 1926, only to see them withdrawn later by another Republican, Herbert Hoover.

Few, if any, of these interventions, presented a noble image of U.S. foreign policy or of the country's political virtues. In most cases, the occupations distorted U.S. values, despite virtuous intentions to transform political life and equally energetic restructuring of the host country's social infrastructure. Most of the interventions produced intense domestic dissension and protest. In some cases, absolute censorship prevented information from reaching home. Success in restoring order in the Philippines in the early 1900s came at a very high price: nearly five thousand U.S. soldiers killed in combat (five thousand more from disease) and over two hundred thousand Philippine civilians killed. The image of the American soldier likewise suffered. Court-martials against officers occupied media attention, and the infamous "water cure" against Filipino prisoners of war produced a national outrage. The ideal of political conversion to democracy did not catch on either. Major campaigns of political supervision in Central America and the Caribbean, including close U.S. monitoring of national and local elections, failed utterly in reducing civil unrest and disorder. The United

States created a Guardia Nacional in Nicaragua to help fight the guerrillas, but after ten mutinies, the Marines had to lead most of the fighting themselves. After decades of occupation, U.S. officials finally could not restrain their frustration. By 1928 the assistant secretary of state cabled, "I fervently hope that we will have no more elections in Latin America to supervise." By 1932, after twenty years of an American attempt to bring democracy to Nicaragua, he wrote that it would be "preferable to run the risk of revolutionary disturbances now and let the strong man emerge without further waste of time."

Such frustrations sprang primarily from the nature of the conflict and differences in political culture rather than from any political or party principles. The clash between such mismatched cultures and modes of combat often brought out the worst in America's political image. The same holds true today. A picture is worth a thousand words, and the photographs of Iraqi prisoners on leashes or those of bombed-out Fallujah, seen by millions worldwide, are images of America, not Iraq. These may have been inspired by "military necessity," but in a paramilitary war that concept might well mean strategic defeat.

As the following chapters will demonstrate, similar image problems beset earlier American operations against insurgents. And the problem remains dominant today. *New York Times* journalist John F. Burns, reporting from Baghdad on November 20, 2005, summarized the cultural disparities present today that can be traced to the earliest clash between differing strategic cultures:

> To a great extent, the American story in Iraq has been one of a profound clash of cultures—of invaders who came with a belief that they could transplant the virtues of democratic bargaining and a civil society that secure the vital interests of all, only to be confounded by what Iraqis themselves often describe as the culture of Ali Baba, the mythical villain of Baghdad. In that culture, maneuver and guile, secrets and untruths, terror and treachery are, too often, the coin of the realm for deciding who gets wealth and power.

This book is not intended to offer prescriptions to solve the Iraqi problem, but it should add a valuable perspective from history's judgment. Two of the case studies in the text, for example, involve similar problems faced by American authorities in the Philippines. In the first, the Philippine insurrection at the turn of the twentieth century, the United States sent an overwhelming conventional force but supplemented it with another "army" of civilian political and technical specialists, led by William H. Taft. After nearly half a century of supervision and administration, the United States finally granted independence, in 1946. The second case occurred almost immediately afterward, when a small team of Americans led by air force general Edward Lansdale used police tactics and a superior political strategy, championed by the brilliant Philippine defense minister Ramon Magsaysay, to eliminate a Communist-backed insurgency in less than two years.

Details of these case studies can be found in this book, and I will not presume to judge the longer-term results of the impact of the United States on the Philippines. But the stark contrasts between the extremes of conventional power and occupation versus a campaign based upon political/psychological warfare might suggest the range of options available to the United States now and in future situations. Before making judgments on the present or future, one might first want to appreciate the historical record. As George Santayana once wrote, "those who do not remember the past are condemned to repeat it."

Acknowledgments

I acknowledge the first debt of appreciation to my colleagues and students at The Institute of World Politics, Washington, D.C., especially to IWP president John Lenczowski, for providing an indispensable atmosphere of collegiality and intellectual stimulation. Alexander C. Hoyt shepherded the manuscript through a number of channels until he found the right publisher. At Potomac Books, Don Jacobs facilitated publication and both Lisa Camner and John Church spent hours applying their creative skills as editors. Finally, I want to remember the late Lewis H. Gann, my real mentor in this field, who wrote a masterful short book on guerrilla war but, more important, was my friend at the Hoover Institution and one of the twentieth century's greatest historians. I alone, of course, am responsible for the content of the book.

Introduction

The first public indication that something had gone wrong, that the swift battle triumph in Iraq did not end the war, came on July 16, 2003, when the American military commander in Iraq, Gen. John P. Abizaid, declared that the enemy was engaging in "a classical guerrilla-type" campaign against over 130,000 American occupation forces. This revelation abruptly changed the dynamics of the entire operation and, as attacks and casualties mounted during the ensuing months and into 2005, forced the Bush administration to scramble for new answers to what was a problem as old as warfare itself, i.e., the clash between "irregular" and "regular" conceptions of conflict. By mid-October 2003 Secretary of Defense Donald Rumsfeld was challenging his staff, in the famous leaked memo, to "think through new ways to organize, train, equip and focus to deal with the global war on terror. . . . We lack metrics to know if we are losing," with the admission that the struggle in Iraq "will be a long, hard slog."

Such a "reality check" was long overdue, but the reappraisal cannot hide the fact that the administration found itself blindsided against the emergence of a nascent insurrection opposed to the presence of an American army inside Iraq. The United States had, in fact, become a "foreign troop," and even the most cursory reading of history should have been sufficient to warn against the potential problems derived from this simple reality. Instead, the administration deceived itself into thinking that the initial glow of a brilliant military triumph had produced, in the president's words, a "mission accomplished." True, the U.S. military had triumphed over Iraq's, but the triumph was superficial and equally misleading.

The word "guerrilla," like the companion term "insurgency,"

recalls the early stages of the Vietnam War some forty years ago, but the deeper history of the word, and the U.S. engagement against guerrillas, is part of an American past that remains largely obscure to the public and, apparently, to its leaders as well. If the ghosts of past insurrections have returned to haunt us in Iraq, we have nobody but ourselves to blame for the ignorance of our own past or for the presumptions that brought us to these dilemmas in the first place.

We are far from the first to discover this problem. It is ancient. The current American scenario in Iraq has hundreds of precedents throughout history. A recent example was the effort by the British to quell the rebellion in Malaya during the 1950s. As James E. Dougherty of the University of Pennsylvania once wrote, even the British army, with centuries of experience in colonial wars, was forced, as Rumsfeld has been today, to devise new tactics, almost from scratch.

> During the first two years of the war, the British relied almost exclusively on conventional military measures to put down the rebellion. But they gradually realized that the orthodox modes of warfare taught at Sandhurst were not applicable against an elusive jungle foe who was bent on protracting the conflict as long as possible. . . . By early 1950, the British had recognized the fact that they were making little or no headway against the MRLA [guerrillas]. They began to devise new approaches, which required a fuller strategic perspective of the situation.[1]

This problem has afflicted American armies throughout history as well. *Without exception*, there is not a single case from U.S. history in which an infantry, either by doctrine, equipment, or tactics, was prepared at the outset to fight an insurrection when faced with such a challenge. In each case, surprise turned into shock and anger and tactics had to be improvised through frustrating trial and error. The current imbroglio in Iraq, seen from this perspective, has a deep and logical historical pedigree, available but ignored. "There is nothing new under the sun" (Ecclesiastes, 1: 9), but, often, the light blinds the observer.

The point of this book is to relive the record of American engagements with unconventional warfare from a critical, even cynical, perspective. I cannot imagine viewing the subject in any other framework. With the country mired deeply in Iraq, and with the announced plan to transform the political culture of the entire Arab Middle East, Americans are again awakening to the realities of foreign occupation. As historian David P. Evans once labeled the British in America despised by the colonists as "a foreign troop,"[2] we should at least try to appreciate the implications of this label if we intend to change regimes and impose democracy where it never existed. Obviously, many dissidents within Iraq view American soldiers as unwelcome guests, and, regardless of their beliefs and human qualities, they have defined *us* as the problem. *We* need to know this, and *we*, Americans, need to have a perspective on the problem. The alternative is to remain in a cultural and strategic time warp, which, by some criteria, is where we are at the moment. Often the messenger is as unwanted as the message, and thus, I am submitting this book with the foreknowledge that its central message may be unwelcome and distorted in certain quarters and its empirical basis challenged. Nevertheless, I stand on the historical record as it developed and will allow this evidence to stand or fall on its own.

The experience in the 1990s brought home many of the unpleasant—at times tragic—results of U.S. policies seeking certain of the announced objectives of occupation: democracy, stability, justice, freedom, prosperity, etc. Such objectives, of course, are noble and appeal to traditional aspirations of public order, national security, and morality, but they almost always come at high risk and often at great cost. Eventually, Americans will decide if the costs of occupying Iraq are worth the sacrifices, but it is also to be hoped that the trials and errors will be worthwhile and that, rather than distracting from the larger effort, the Iraqi intervention will promote the destruction of global terror.

The death of eighteen Americans and the quick withdrawal from Somalia in 1993 brought the costs of intervention home to Americans, and the lesson was not lost on the Clinton administration. Subsequent interventions into Haiti and the former Yugoslavia, particularly the air campaign over Kosovo and the occupation of Bosnia (ongoing), have not carried the burden of American casualties.

Iraq has been different and offers a more familiar pattern of history's insurrections: quick military success on the surface, which masks hidden and sullen resentment, which, in turn, leads to ambush, disorder, and often enough, guerrilla warfare. The notion that the Iraqi irregulars do not represent the "people" of the country, but only a faction, offers little solace, since the greater patterns of resistance to occupation exemplify similar internal divisions. It does not take a united population to sustain a guerrilla war, only a fraction. The American Revolution itself was supported by only about one-third of the colonial population, and it would have done the British little good to condemn their opponents because they represented only a certain percentage.

Nor does the United States solve the problem by denouncing the hidden enemy as "thugs" or "killers." Many certainly are that, but U.S. intelligence has revealed very little information to the public as to the political, nationalistic, or ideological composition of the opposition in Iraq, and until they can be described with more precision, the presumptions that they are motivated only by greed and wanton bloodlust may be self-deceptive and, in the long run, do more harm than good to the overall military effort. To understand the political personality of the enemy is a strategic necessity, but sadly this is not the first time in history that guerrilla-insurgents were misjudged or underestimated. In fact, this failure has formed a pattern of history. The temptation to denounce guerrillas as merely "bandits" or "criminals" has long attended the American conduct of counterinsurgency. In Iraq today, thugs and Saddam loyalists fight with their own logic and purpose, however twisted these may be to the mentality of Western-schooled intellectuals.

This book examines the causes and results of military interventions and occupations by a "foreign troop." The first section starts with the perspective of America as the *occupied party*, in both the Revolution and the Civil War, when Americans themselves suffered occupation at the hands of British "redcoats" and Union army "bluecoats" inside the Confederacy. The second section turns the tables 180 degrees, to cases in which U.S. troops were the *occupiers*, both at home against Indian tribes and overseas against guerrilla armies aroused against the presence of the American infantry. The study will start with a fundamental premise, perhaps obvious to military specialists, but not so obvious to the general public and—judging from our recent history—equally distant from the perspective of critical decision makers. This premise underpins the study and will reappear throughout the text in many forms. As stated by Samuel P. Huntington over forty years ago, the use of guerrilla operations has never been a major American strategic priority.

Guerrilla warfare has not been an American forte. Guerrillas played a significant role in our eighteenth-century revolutionary war, when we were the underdog and the intervention of an outside power was necessary to secure victory. They also played a somewhat less important role on the southern side in the Civil War. In most of its wars, however, the United States has not had to rely upon guerrilla warfare. American experience with guerrilla warfare has been limited by the strength of American arms. The United States has been able to mobilize overwhelming economic and military power and to bring it to bear directly on the enemy, attacking him not where he was weakest but where he was strongest, because we were stronger still.[3]

A corollary to this premise is the acknowledgment of a significant pattern of occupation throughout American history, which itself constitutes a clear and definitive logic in strategic behavior, and regardless of the outcome of the present Iraq War, that conflict has already demonstrated the essence of this historic cycle. Even under the most optimistic of circumstances, i.e., a stable and democratic Iraq within a reasonable time frame, the United States is already committed to a protracted and lengthy protectorate. This will necessitate ground forces, making the United States an outside occupying force, even within an imposed democratic polity. This also resembles a historic pattern that has led to unforeseen results, much worse in every case than the original expectations. To be sure, much good in areas of social reconstruction was accomplished in most cases, but the price was always high, both in lives and treasure. By the terminal point of each episode, decision makers were nearly unanimous in their relief to be out.

Thus, while irregular war has occupied an important part of the American historical experience, this record has been largely buried by the experience of great-power wars. The American political culture has overwhelmingly regarded guerrilla war as dishonorable and has associated one of the guerrillas' main tactics, terrorism, as the worst human scourge, despite the application of terrorism throughout recorded history. This means that much of American political culture is strategically "ahistorical," a problem that allows very little perspective from which either to make policy or to judge it properly, leaving much of our reaction frozen in a conceptual time warp. That is to say, nearly *everything* seems unique, or as the administration repeats over and again, "entirely new." The 9/11 attacks were truly "unique"; terrorism as a strategic weapon is ancient.

These case studies of past U.S. interventions, before 9/11, were all "small war" situations, involving backward, impoverished areas of the globe, unfamiliar to Americans and governed by relatively primitive tribal chiefs or regional dictators ("thugs"). None of these involved a major U.S. national interest in objective terms, but the demands and requirements of each occupation seemed to grow proportionately as the years went by. In sum, they developed their own intrinsic importance, which can be seen as conforming to the definition of "quagmire," i.e., "a bog that recedes when stepped upon." Clearly, the present war against terrorism is a critical national interest, with U.S. survival possibly in the balance. Notwithstanding this essential distinction, the occupation of Iraq and the resulting insurrection contain many of the familiar patterns of occupations that echo from the pages of American history.

Without discrediting good intentions and productive results in many areas, the theme of the book will emphasize the problems and difficulties of counterinsurgency and occupation. The historical record will show a shift in mentality from a robust enthusiasm at the beginning of each occupation, and confidence in the military to "get the job done," to a continuous and nagging decline that often led to a mood bordering on desperation and the urge to abdicate the responsibility at any cost.

The experience of the American army in counterguerrilla warfare has proved time and again that infantry soldiers using conventional war tactics are the *least propitious* outfits to bring an insurrection to a quick and efficient conclusion. The British also discovered this reality in the swamps and rolling hills of North Carolina during the American Revolution, just as the Union army did in its long and frustrating quest to arrest the Confederate partisans led by John Mosby in northern Virginia.

Infantry tactics instinctively adopt the form of total war in the pursuit of elusive and hidden guerrillas, and this can succeed, but with tremendous toll. In 1779, for example, George Washington initiated a campaign to break the alliance between Iroquois Indians and the British. When Washington's soldiers found it impossible to bring the Indians to battle, he went after their means of subsistence. Thousands of Iroquois dwelling houses were destroyed in a scorched-earth manner and whole crops were uprooted; these tactics ended the Iroquois alliance with the British army. In a similar manner the American infantry destroyed the terrain of the Florida swamps in the Seminole War of the 1830s, coaxing the final surrender of that tribe. Union general Philip Sheridan attacked insurrection in the Shenandoah, but only by destroying the livestock and farm structures of the inhabitants who had supported the Confederate partisans. The army did the same against the *insurrectos* of the Philippines at the turn of the last century, just as the British were occupying South Africa with "blockhouses" to starve the population into submission. The U.S. Marines rounded up whole sections of Haiti and the Dominican Republic in the early twentieth century with miles of "cordons" in their irregular engagements of that era. In the initial stages of U.S. intervention in Vietnam, this same tactic was defined as the "strategic hamlet" program, a conventional response to unconventional war.

The result of such conventional strategies against irregulars has been demonstrated so consistently over time that there almost appears to be a form of "dialectical" logic to the process. The end product is, by any definition, total warfare against the population that, of necessity if not conviction, invariably supports home forces against outsiders. Mao Tse-tung called this phenomenon the "sea" in which the "fish" (partisans, guerrillas) survive; President Bush alluded to the same reality as "draining the swamp" of those who "harbor" terrorists. Whatever neologism is used, it seems universally valid that regular-force strategies as employed by infantries and conventional units invite total war with populations that irregulars depend upon for survival. The theory is near-universal: destroy the base of survival and you have destroyed the guerrilla. The Philippine insurrection between 1899 and 1902 exemplified this reality to the American army, and as acknowledged nearly a century later, it has since become an accepted primer in counterguerrilla theory. As identified in 1986 by the Joint Army–Air Force Low Intensity Conflict Project (JLICP), the Philippine insurrection offered the essential model for a conventional force engaged against guerrillas:

> The lesson learned from this experience is that military power can be effective against a guerrilla force which has the support of the population. Victory, however, required the political will to employ total control over the population and the government. This early American experience dramatically demonstrated a classic example of security/PRC [populace and resource control]. The insurgents were first separated from the population by strict security measures including resettlement, curfews, and an early forerunner of "free-fire" zones. The relocation of the populace, combined with food denial operations, resulted in defeat of the insurgency.[4]

But history has also demonstrated, with greater logic, that streamlined police-style units, using superior intelligence and native forces combined with attractive political tactics, are usually the most efficient and lasting means of operations for defeating home-based partisans. But, as the British discovered in Malaya, such conversions have invariably developed through improvisation or trial and error.

These patterns have repeated themselves in cycles throughout U.S. history, and in reporting this record, my own role is that of historian and messenger. It is my duty to chronicle history as a matter of fact, without prejudice. The narrative will let the story tell itself, often in the words of the participants themselves, who judged the results of their own best intentions. In the process, I have taken great pains to avoid any form of personal critique of civilian decision makers and, especially, to avoid personal assessments of the character or professionalism of military personnel, who did their duty as instructed and as the popular culture determined.

Although the historical record is available, it is not widely appreciated, nor have most applicable lessons been fully absorbed. Throughout most of U.S. history the subjects of insurgency/counterinsurgency, terrorism/counterterrorism have been unpopular and avoided. The legend of warfare in American history has been an almost exclusive preserve of the professional soldier, a belief that armed conflict was organized only against other military forces in the field, at sea, and later, in the air. From official perspectives, both political and military, guerrillas and irregulars were seen almost exclusively as "bandits," "criminals," or "terrorists," beyond the pale of civility. There is great truth in this generalization, but it is also self-deceptive insofar as it denies the armed opponent any political or nationalistic credential or motive. On the other side of the political spectrum, the profile of the guerrilla/terrorist has been romanticized by leftist propaganda, which portrays such characters as political Robin Hoods. But, like the persona of the late Che Guevara, the terrorists' "progressive" image masks dark, totalitarian personalities.

From both sides, thus, Americans have rarely appreciated the full significance and content of guerrilla warfare. The greater military history and legend of America, especially given the experiences of world war, have developed an autonomous image of conflict, defining war as the province of mass mobilization and firepower exercised on behalf of nation-states. Official U.S. Army strategies have always stressed heavy equipment, artillery, linear tactics, firepower, and concentration for attack against enemy cities, industry, and other vital conventional targets. A 1939 army field service regulation, for example, trained the American infantry to wage war in the classic, direct campaigns made famous by Ulysses S. Grant and the Union army. This was then, and is now, the epitome of the American "way" of war:

The ultimate objective of all military operations is the destruction of the enemies' armed forces in battle. Decisive defeat breaks the enemy's will to wage war and forces him to sue for peace which is the material aim. [5]

In the Civil War and in both world wars, the infantry was the backbone of the American military, joined in World War II, Korea, and Vietnam by the greatest naval and air power in history.

This faith and optimism in the quality and power of the American war machine is also present today, as the infantry attempts to police Iraq. Such qualities, as well, are demonstrated by the history of America's strategic "culture." Summarized in 1941 by the military historian Maurice Matloff, the strategy aimed at Germany and Japan reflected many of the same currents that led to successive and brilliant victories over Saddam Hussein's army, both in 1991 and 2003.

[The U.S. was] already disposed to think in terms of meeting the German armies head on—and the sooner the better. Here was the kernel of the American theory of a war of mass and concentration, in keeping with the traditional "sharp and decisive" war leading to the defeat of the enemies' armies. It reflected American optimism, confidence in its industrial machine and material resources, disinclination to wage a long war of attrition, and faith of the military in quickly preparing for a large citizen army for offensive purpose.[6]

World War II was fought on the American side by an industrial and managerial superiority that overwhelmed both Germany and Japan. In the war of mass machines the United States was clearly far ahead of any competitor. This "prodigy of organization," as Churchill called it, was "an achievement which the soldiers of every other country will study with admiration and envy."[7]

By the end of the war, the United States had mobilized over twelve million men, and in 1945 the American military machine was the most powerful single force ever developed in history. But it was war production, the industrial base, that created that machine in the first place and that, according to military historian Hanson Baldwin, "was the greatest advantage which we possessed over our enemies in the Second World War."[8] This tradition carried into the Cold War that followed. The bitter experience of fighting a "limited" war in Korea left Americans in no mood to repeat the experience. Eisenhower's strategic doctrine of "massive retaliation" reflected the nuclear version of the same temperament for the pursuit of war with the greatest mobilization of resources within the shortest possible time. This tradition, as it developed, had no room and little patience for the type of guerrilla insurrection associated with criminals. But this was soon to change, forced by circumstances.

Airpower, based upon the Strategic Air Command (SAC) and medium-range missiles, remained the essential pillar of deterrence policy throughout the 1950s. By the time of the Kennedy administration, intercontinental-range missiles (Polaris, Titan, Minuteman) formed the basis of the strategic force, which by 1962 had achieved a decisive lead over the Soviet Union. But almost at precisely that moment in time a new revolution in strategic doctrine was beginning to call into question the faith and confidence that Americans had always placed in their military machines.

From the defeat of the French in Vietnam in 1954 to the victory of Fidel Castro in Cuba in 1959, a new wave of armed aggression against Western positions, including those in Africa and the Middle East, had exploded upon the world scene. Revolutionary guerrilla communism, in its many political hues and disguises, had presented a new face of warfare as a unique challenge to the Western image of conflict. Days before the inauguration of John F. Kennedy as the thirty-fourth president, Soviet premier Nikita Khrushchev seized upon the movement of global revolution to announce his bold support of "wars of national liberation," which, he predicted, were historically destined to strangle and surround the global bases of capitalism without the use of a single nuclear missile. The Cold War had taken a sharp turn toward insurgency and terror.

President Kennedy, long before George W. Bush, adopted an aggressive and flamboyant, personalistic style of leadership against what was also defined, for his time, as an altogether "new" type of conflict. Kennedy introduced and popularized the concept of "unconventional" (guerrilla, irregular) war in the American lexicon. Like Bush today, Kennedy plunged his own charisma and the full weight of the presidency into the effort to rid the world of the threat of revolutionary terrorism and insurrection. He wrote the foreword to a popular Marine Corps book on the subject (T. N. Greene, *The Guerrilla—and How to Fight Him*, New York: Praeger, 1962) and kept a copy proudly displayed on his desk. He supported the Special Forces and helped make the green beret symbolic of the shift in U.S. military emphasis. He once flew to Special Forces headquarters at Fort Bragg to review the troops. There he witnessed the latest in U.S. training and technology against the worldwide guerrilla threat, including one soldier with his own personal helicopter strapped to his back, who literally flew over the treetops in mock combat. Technology would continue to instruct the predominant methodology in the American arsenal of counterinsurgency tactics.

Although U.S. cities and populations were never at risk in wars of national liberation, a war fever reminiscent of the present conflict against terror swept the country. Almost overnight, the public and media became obsessed with the unique nature of the challenge. A flood of publications on guerrilla war and terrorism rushed into print, prompting one reviewer to write that

> where once there were only one or two books about it there are now over a dozen. They march across the shelf in variety and confusion, trampling the same ground several times over when they are not treading on each other's feet. . . . What had been a tame subject became a hot one.[9]

Administration spokesmen Robert McNamara, Dean Rusk, Walt Rostow, McGeorge and William Bundy, Maxwell Taylor, William Colby, etc., all joined in. They lectured across the country and in Congress to prove, as Presidential Assistant Rostow put it, that "The United States has a role to play in learning to deter guerrilla war, if possible, and to deal with it, if necessary."[10]

The personalities mentioned above, plus their contemporaries who brought America into Vietnam, are mostly dead or forgotten. The most popular collective hearing they received was in *The Best and the Brightest* by David Halberstam, a penetrating insight into the gradual shift from buoyant optimism to sinking despair as the Indochinese "quagmire" dominated the country year by year. Yet, if that generation had absorbed the lessons that American history had already presented, *before* their own time, historical repetition in the case of Vietnam might well have been avoided or at least circumscribed.

Today, in the setting of the war against terrorism, many of the same features—psychological, cultural, strategic/military—that accompanied the historical American exuberance in foreign policy settings have returned. History has caught up with us once more. The suggestion here is not the precise repetition of history but a less ambitious notion that historical patterns are stubbornly cyclical, given the presence of parallel factors in both internal and external settings. In this regard, the following chronology of the occupation of Iraq (in parentheses) can be identified as similar to the greater historical pattern described in this book:

● the existence of an enemy who will not "play by the rules," i.e., the appearance of an "unconventional" opponent requiring an entirely different response (9/11);

● the deep American tradition to transform foreign policy goals into great crusades symbolized by lofty political goals (Bush doctrines);

● translation of this belief into the idea that democracy could and would be introduced into the local political culture through U.S. occupation policies (same);

● the faith and optimism in the capacity of the conventional military machine in mastering the situation through battle victory ("mission accomplished");

● disappointment and frustration in the light of an irregular "backlash" (Rumsfeld memo);

● surprise and improvisation on the ground in the search for the best options against terrorists and guerrillas (U.S. tactical reappraisals);

● public disapproval if the effort to bring results continues without visible end (approval ratings decline, dissension mounts);

● final resolution: either withdrawal in the face of failure or translation of the occupation into a form of total war against the enemy and his support (yet to be determined, either exit strategy or "drain the swamp").

In the setting of the contemporary war against terrorism, especially the occupation of Iraq, these elements have already appeared in the strategic/political setting, in one way or another. The essential point remains that there does, indeed, seem to be a cyclical pattern when a "foreign troop" occupies distant countries. This does not necessarily determine outcomes, tactics, strategies, resolve, or any of the other imponderables that exist in specific locales. All it suggests is a logical outline of comparison, which, if understood, might provide greater wisdom upon the subject than improvisation, speculation, and eventually, frustration bordering upon dismay. This task, one might think, should not be too ambitious, nor should it be considered presumptuous to recall Santayana's dictum, referred to above.

During the early stages of the Vietnam War, as noted above, a number of books and articles on the subject of unconventional warfare, with all of its attendant nomenclatures, appeared in the United States. These quickly became "lost" to history, pushed aside by the escalating conventional war, including ground troops and airpower, plus the daily rendition of body bag counts that dominated American culture throughout that long period of time. The aftermath of Vietnam submerged the memory of the initial optimism of "Camelot" in a sustained collective effort to forget. But not entirely. Perhaps the most ambitious effort to remind the public of the nature of unconventional war appeared in 1975, in Robert Asprey's massive, two-volume *War in the Shadows: The Guerrilla in History*.[11] Asprey included many sections on American history, especially Vietnam, but his focus was really world history, ancient and medieval.

Robert Asprey's research had the powerful advantage of widening the horizon of the subject by about four thousand years. This was ambitious but probably much more demanding than most American readers would appreciate. It is hoped that the present effort will help bridge that gap.

Although the subtitle of this book references the subject of unconventional or guerrilla war, a precise definition of these terms, and others associated with them, can be difficult. Strict boundaries between conventional and unconventional warfare, moreover, are often misleading—and there are ambiguities in language and meaning that make concise definitions almost impossible. At times, the two types of combat have simply been opposite sides of the same political-military coin.

Broad definitions, however, are relatively easy; the problem is in applying them to history and reality. The U.S. Department of Defense's *Dictionary of Military and Associated Terms* uses the following definition of unconventional warfare:

A broad spectrum of military and paramilitary operations conducted in enemy held, enemy controlled or politically sensitive territory. Unconventional warfare includes, but is not lim-

ited to, the interrelated fields of guerrilla warfare, evasion and
escape, subversion, sabotage, direct action missions and other
operations of a low visibility, covert or clandestine nature. These
interrelated aspects of unconventional warfare may be pros-
ecuted singly or collectively by predominantly indigenous personnel, usually supported and directed in varying degrees by
(an) external source(s) during all conditions of war or peace.[12]

A working definition of guerrilla war has been offered by Asprey:

[A] type of warfare characterized by irregular forces fighting
small-scale, limited actions, generally in conjunction with a
larger political-military strategy, against orthodox military
forces.[13]

A guerrilla, indeed, is a "soldier" in his own right, but a much different (i.e., "unconventional") one than what most of us assume a soldier to be. He fights, therefore, a much different kind of war. Guerrillas
live off the land and fight against stronger invaders who have taken
their towns and cities. They have to steal weapons or barter for them
from the outside. Their tactics necessarily emphasize surprise, ambush,
and retreat. A fixed battle is something guerrillas must avoid at all cost;
their methods seek to harass the opposing army, to embarrass the invader, and to frustrate him into clumsy mistakes.

Guerrilla war tactics, as described by Walter Laqueur, predate recorded history, but the first recorded mention of these can be traced to
the fifteenth century BC, when Mursilis, the Hittite king, complained
that "the irregulars did not dare to attack me in the daylight and preferred to fall on me by night."[14] Application of guerrilla war methods,
including the widespread use of partisans in the ancient Middle East
against the Roman Empire and in medieval and modern Europe, parallels the use of infantry and other features of conventional war
throughout history. Technically, the word "guerrilla" in Spanish means
"little war," and originated in 1808 in the "Peninsular War," when
Napoleon Bonaparte and 150,000 French regulars found their invasion of Spain and Portugal had become the first defined "quagmire"
of modern times. After years of impossible "sweeps" and chronic incapacity to end the rebellion, Napoleon's top commander, Maréchal
Bessières, described the tactical difficulties of history's first acknowledged guerrilla war:

The Emperor is deceived about Spain: the pacification of Spain does not depend on a battle with the English, who will accept it or refuse it as they please, and who have Portugal behind them if they retreat. Every one knows the vicious system of our operations. Every one allows that we are too widely scattered. We occupy too much territory, we used up our resources without profit and without necessity: we are clinging to dreams.[15]

The operational tactics of guerrilla war have changed little since (or before). Guerrillas are amateur ("unprofessional") soldiers; they rarely wear uniforms, and indeed, they depend upon anonymity for even bare existence. To be recognized would usually mean instant death. Guerrillas, therefore, are true citizen-soldiers. They blend into the population easily and can include women and children, as well as men who farm the land at day and raid the enemy's outposts at night. They fight amid the native population and depend upon the loyalty of their neighbors for their own lives. Disloyalty is punished severely, and enforced loyalty to the local cause can often be as brutal and as severe as the punishments inflicted by the outsider himself. By definition, guerrilla war has also been labeled "internal war" since it involves civilians within an established locale either fighting among themselves or against outsiders.

Geography is the guerrilla's ally, as much as it is the invader's enemy. Guerrillas know the land by heart; it is their home. They hide in the native mountains, swamps, jungles, farmlands, or urban sprawl, places where an outsider would seldom dare go. Guerrilla warfare is instinctive and generic; it comes naturally after the impact of foreign invasion or attack. It doesn't need academies to teach its methods and it doesn't need sophisticated weapons to be effective. Guerrillas can last on their own for years at a time, but they cannot force a military decision. Indeed, guerrilla armies can never "win" in a military sense, but they can help force a decision through harassment, intimidation, and frustration.

The history of twentieth-century revolutionary and guerrilla warfare movements has made unconventional conflict strategies a new and more important mode of war, much more numerous and powerful than in any previous time. The al Qaeda terrorist network, its many affiliates, and those states that harbor and finance terror represent the highest and most dangerous evolution of unconventional warfare to a point at which the survival of nation-states may hang in the balance. This

makes an appreciation of the subject, including history, tactics, and implications, that much more compelling. But there is a problem, and that
is the stubborn incapacity of the American political culture to appreciate the dimensions of this type of conflict. The sudden emergence of an
insurrection against the U.S. presence in Iraq, beginning in the summer
of 2003, has challenged an ingrained American cultural faith in the character and power of the military, along with an equal American incapacity to appreciate the nature and content of guerrilla/irregular warfare.

Nevertheless, the fact remains that unconventional warfare played
an important role in many conflicts in U.S. history, even though today
most of the guerrilla battles are nearly forgotten. American partisans
operated behind enemy lines in both the Revolutionary and Civil Wars,
but their efforts are far less known today than the great conventional
battles. There is, nonetheless, a romantic legend that still surrounds the
"forest warfare" of such irregular leaders as Andrew Pickens, Thomas
Sumter, and John Mosby, though the contributions of such men and
their forces, plus the true nature of these early American guerrillas,
have largely bypassed succeeding generations.

Apart from the Revolutionary and Civil Wars, U.S. troops waged
many campaigns against both native Indian irregulars and guerrilla
armies inside Latin America and in the Philippines. These all began
with standard weapons and operational plans and were initially conducted according to the tactics and logic of conventional war. Many
also sparked the same type of public controversy and military frustration that took place during the Vietnam War and that is slowly emerging from the Iraq experience. All of these operations eventually required
certain changes in field tactics, from the relatively slow and cumbersome movements of regular war to the more streamlined, mobile, and
flexible tactics of guerrilla war, including the use of native troops as
auxiliaries.

Guerrilla wars, however, have failed to capture the American
public's imagination. Most of them, to the contrary, were extremely
unpopular, a factor that undoubtedly has played a role in their relative
obscurity. The popular image of American warfare is deeply rooted in
the almost unbroken record of battlefield successes: Saratoga and
Yorktown, New Orleans, Gettysburg and Vicksburg, San Juan Hill,
Manila Bay, Belleau Wood, Normandy Beach, Midway, Iwo Jima,
Inchon, and now Operation Iraqi Freedom.

Against this background, Americans of the post-9/11 period would
do well to place the war on terrorism into a larger perspective, an intellectual spectrum that may actually help to gain an appreciation of the

nature of the enemy and the requirements for victory. In this sense it is appropriate to remember that the first major American military test against a great power was itself a revolution and includes original examples of revolutionary terrorism and guerrilla warfare.

The study of unconventional warfare in U.S. history begins properly with the American Revolution.

Part I

Home Frontiers:

TERRORISM, GUERRILLA WAR, AND THE AMERICAN CAUSE

The Colonial Heritage

The American "minuteman" who initially answered the call to arms against the British redcoat was no stranger to war. From the very beginnings of settlement, colonial Americans fought continuous wars against the forest Indians. They quickly discovered that Indian tactics included many features of irregular war: small units, loose formations, ambush, terror, raids against noncombatants, surprise, mobility, retreat, informal dress, etc. To combat the Indians, the colonials adopted the militia system, wherein volunteers would enlist for specific durations to protect against raids on their own settlements. But the militiaman in America was not a soldier; he was a farmer or a tradesman who emigrated, more often than not, to escape soldiering for the British army. What tactics the militia did use, moreover, were borrowed straight from the European heritage of linear formations designed for open plains.

By the end of the seventeenth century the American militia had proved itself useful as a defensive tool against Indian attacks on settlements, but as an offensive force of any duration or strength it was almost useless. Increasingly, the colonial militia came to rely upon allied Indian tribes to engage in forest warfare tactics. At the same time, colonists found themselves increasingly caught up in the endemic rivalries of the Old World for supremacy in the New World. In effect, these wars were global contests on both land and sea in which North America was a backwater theater. The first of these, known in America as King William's War, lasted from 1689 to 1697 and was waged throughout Europe, India, North and South America, and the Caribbean. In British North America, the French succeeded in making alliances with eastern Indian tribes who attacked the New England and New York frontier with torch and tomahawk. The town of Schenectady, New York, was virtually wiped out, but this seesaw, protracted contest ended in a territorial draw. The next of these wars, Queen Anne's War in America, was an even larger world war between a European coalition led by Britain and a French/Spanish global alliance. In North America, Queen Anne's War (in Europe, the War of Spanish Succession) saw the British win acquisitions in Canada (Nova Scotia, Newfoundland, Hudson's Bay area) but left the French in possession of Quebec and the entire mid-continent down to New Orleans. Spain was left still in control of both Florida and Mexico, including Texas and California. The third war, King George's War, was fought in America between 1744 and 1748 and saw no territorial gain by either side.

In each of these conflicts the bulk of the English settlers in America, residing from Maine down to Georgia, had no choice but to fight alongside the British, who regarded them as little more than pawns in the greater struggles for mastery of the political globe. As resentments mounted over succeeding generations, the American volcano finally began to erupt in the last of these wars, known in America as the French and Indian War, 1754–1763 (the Seven Years' War in Europe). This conflict engaged the largest geopolitical theater in world history to that time, including the entire European area, North America, the Philippines, Africa, and the high seas.

The war actually began in the New World, in the Ohio Valley, where the British enlisted large numbers of colonists to help them evict the French from what then could be called "middle America." Aided by Indian allies, the French fought the British incursions with savage fury on the frontier. The British drafted a company of 150 Virginians, led by a twenty-one-year-old surveyor named George Washington, to evict the French from outposts in western Pennsylvania and eastern Ohio. Washington's first armed encounter at Fort Necessity, below present-day Pittsburgh, resulted in abject failure. The Virginians were surrounded and Washington was forced to surrender his entire command, ironically, on July 4, 1754.

The next excursion was undertaken by the British army itself, which learned a lesson in forest warfare the hard way. Moving toward Fort Duquesne in southwestern Pennsylvania, the British general Edward Braddock marched his twenty-two hundred soldiers—dressed in full scarlet uniform—in a straight column through the dense woods and thickets. On the morning of July 9, 1755, this column was ambushed by a lesser force of about 250 French regulars and 650 Indians. Hiding behind the rocks, trees, and ravines of the landscape, this outfit handed the British their worst defeat in the New World to that time. The carnage was frightful. Of eighty-six British officers, sixty-three were killed or wounded. Braddock himself died of bullet wounds and the remnants of his men left the scene in what became a frenzied rout, which continued as far as fifty miles away. Washington himself, who was by then an aide to Braddock, had two horses shot from under him.

But the massacre near Fort Duquesne finally taught both the British regular and his American auxiliary the nature of guerrilla-style, forest warfare. Washington himself subsequently wrote that "Indians are the only match for Indians; and without these we shall ever fight upon unequal terms."[1] Braddock's defeat was never repeated, as American and British soldiers changed certain of their tactics to suit the terrain and nature of irregular forest war. They began using light, rather than heavy, infantry. They learned the value of concealment, surprise, mobility, and cover. They used scouts and skirmishers more than before. Many of their troops dressed in brown and green clothes, shaved their heads, and painted their skin to resemble Indians. They also formed "special warfare" companies, such as Maj. Robert Rogers' "Rangers."

Rogers, indeed, should be identified as the first authentic American guerrilla. A New Hampshire native, he grew up on the turbulent New England frontier and enlisted in the colonial militia when he was fourteen. In 1756, at age twenty-four, he was commissioned to lead independent companies of the British army in scouting and irregular missions. Although a typically independent partisan who often ignored orders, Rogers led a guerrilla war against French-Canadian regulars (*coureurs de bois*) and their Indian allies for three years in the dark and shadowy forests of upper New York. These operations provided valuable information to the British army and simultaneously harassed French outposts and Indian villages in both winter and summer campaigns. Rogers and his band of about seventy-five men—officially, the Independent Companies of American Rangers—fought on both ice skates and snowshoes during the winter, in reconnaissance and scouting forays deep within enemy-held territory. Authentic and original American partisans, each ranger wore a green leather uniform, carried a flintlock musket, powder, and shot for sixty rounds, plus a tomahawk and knife for close combat. Their knapsacks had sufficient food for two weeks. They operated principally between Fort William Henry on the southern shore of Lake George and Crown Point on northern Lake Champlain. The Rangers fought a number of violent encounters on behalf of the British, notably at Ticonderoga in 1757 and near Montreal in 1759, when they destroyed a major French and Indian staging area.

Rogers did not invent the ranger concept. Colonists had been using Indian tactics to repel the Indians themselves since the mid-sixteenth century. But Rogers codified the "Rules of Ranging" into twenty-eight distinct points and published them as a guide for operating in North American forest terrain. The essence of these instructions is point 28, an eighteenth-century version of the precise nature of unconventional warfare:

> If you cannot satisfy yourself as to the enemy's number and strength from their fire etc. conceal your boats at some distance, and ascertain their number by a reconnoitering party, when they embark, or march in the morning, marking their course as they steer, etc. when you may pursue, ambush, and attack them, or let them pass, as prudence shall direct you. In general, however, that you may not be discovered by the enemy upon the lakes and rivers at a great distance, it is safest to lay by, with your boats and party concealed all day, without noise or shew; and to pursue your intended route by night; and whether you go by land or water, give out parole and countersigns, in order to know one another in the dark, and likewise appoint a station every man to repair to, in case of any accident that may separate you.[2]

Rogers's men marched in single file so that one shot would not kill two of them. They were instructed not to shoot until the enemy was very close and were taught to disperse should the enemy outnumber them. They were told how to march in various conditions, including marsh, woodland, and along rivers, and how to attack from behind concealment. Rogers also formed an entire company composed exclusively of Indians. The British considered such unconventional tactics as "primitive" and "unsoldiery" but found them invaluable in frontier American warfare. By the mid-1750s the Rangers became the Crown forces' primary scouting and reconnaissance unit. Rogers expressed his mission as:

> from time to time, to use my best endeavors to distress the French and their allies, by sacking, burning and destroying their houses, barns, barracks, canoes, battoes, etc. and by killing their cattle of every kind; and at all times to endeavor to way-lay,

attack and destroy their convoys of provisions by land and water, in any part of the country where I could find them.[3]

After the French and Indian War, Rogers went to Britain but returned home during the Revolution, offering his services to the Continental army. Suspicious of his long absence and disdainful of irregulars by instinct, George Washington refused Rogers his commission. An embittered Rogers abandoned the Patriot cause altogether. After a brief and unsuccessful stint with the British army, including command of a Loyalist unit, he returned to England in 1780 and died, penniless and ignored, in 1795. His sad dismissal and passing as an expatriate remain symbolic of America's generic distrust of anything alien to the strategic culture of conventional warfare.

Nearly two centuries later the original American partisan received a belated renaissance. The 1940 movie *Northwest Passage* (with Spencer Tracy as Rogers) revived his memory. In 1942 the U.S. Army named its irregular units the "Rangers" and reprinted Rogers's 1757 training rules as tactical instruction against the German occupation of Europe. But Rogers's "rules" were being used against Western interests before the world war. Ironically, Mao Tse-tung's revolutionary war treatise, *On the Protracted War* (1934), seized the essence of guerrilla conduct against the Chinese Nationalist government even before the American army belatedly came to appreciate the brilliance within its own history.

Henri Bouquet was another prerevolutionary, unconventional American warrior. A Swiss native, Bouquet saw extensive service in Europe's wars before being recruited by the British to rally German-speaking militia of Pennsylvania against the French and Indians. Bouquet led expeditions against Pontiac's Uprising at Bushy Run, Pennsylvania, in 1763 and, in the following year, succeeded in driving hostile tribes away from the Ohio Valley along the Muskingum and Tuscarawas rivers. Promoted to brigadier general by the British, Bouquet was also hailed as a hero by the Pennsylvania Assembly. Grounded in the linear tactics of Europe's plains, Bouquet nevertheless adapted quickly to the forest warfare of North America. His instructions to other Europeans on Indian fighting were written in the early 1760s and show how the soldiers of that era viewed the New World military theater. As a primary document, its core is worth quoting at length:

Let us suppose a person, who is entirely unacquainted with the nature of this service, to be put at the head of an expedition in America. We will further suppose that he has made the dispositions usual in Europe for a march, or to receive an enemy; and that he is then attacked by the savages. He cannot discover them, tho' from every tree, log or bush, he receives an incessant fire, and observes that few of their shot are lost. He will not hesitate to charge those invisible enemies, but he will charge in vain. For they are as cautious to avoid a close engagement, as indefatigable in harassing his troops; and notwithstanding all his endeavours, he will still find himself surrounded by a circle of fire, which, like an artificial horizon, follows him everywhere.

Unable to rid himself of an enemy who never stands his attacks, and flies when pressed, only to return upon him again with equal agility and vigour; he will see the courage of his heavy troops droop, and their strength at last fail them by repeated and ineffectual efforts. He must therefor think of a retreat, unless he can force his way thro' the enemy. But how is this to be effected? His baggage and provisions are unloaded and scattered, part of his horses and drivers killed, others dispersed by fear, and his wounded to be carried by soldiers already fainting under the fatigue of a long action. The enemy, encouraged by his distress, will not fail to increase the disorder, by pressing upon him on every side, with redoubled fury and savage howlings.

He will probably form a circle or a square, to keep off so daring an enemy, ready at the least opening to fall upon him with the destructive tomahawk: but these dispositions, tho' a tolerable shift for defense, are neither proper for an attack, nor a march thro' the woods.[4]

Despite the adaptations made in certain tactics, however, neither British nor American soldiers in colonial times changed course in any fundamental way. The winning battles of the French and Indian War, Quebec in particular, were fought along classic, linear European lines. By 1763 the French were completely thrown off the North American continent. But the blend of Indian and guerrilla styles with European tactics made the later Revolutionary soldier a distinguished creature. Men like George Washington, Philip Schuyler, Francis Marion, Daniel Morgan, and others understood the tactical mixture that fighting in eighteenth-century North America entailed. They would use these fighting methods with great success against the British when the final test came.

The guerrilla (or "partisan") record of the American people in the Revolution is far less known than the great regular battles, such as Yorktown and Saratoga. Yet, American citizens fought as guerrillas in the same manner as the people of other countries when their own native land came under the heel of outside invasion. The rural South saw most of this action, but revolutionary and quasi-guerrilla terrorism affected the whole country, North and South, rich and poor, rural and urban. Indeed, the domestic and civilian terrorism among these first-generation Americans is probably one of the least known and most unsavory chapters of the American heritage.

-1-

Revolutionary Terrorism:
Whig vs. Tory

In the popular imagination the foe in the American Revolution is still the redcoat and the hero the backwoods rifleman. But to a large degree, the American Revolution was, in fact, a civil war between two groups of citizenry. This domestic war was waged between those loyal to the British (Loyalists, or Tories) and those who supported the Revolution (Patriots, or Whigs) and was an important element of the final victory itself. Unlike the military war, however, the internal war was *paramilitaristic*, combining guerrilla action with eighteenth-century terrorism that is still a classic example of the use of internecine violence for revolutionary political purposes.

The initial violence that occurred in Massachusetts was just the opening round in a long national campaign of revolutionary terror and unconventional strife. The resort to domestic violence, however, was at least partly a legacy from the colonial tradition. Between 1645 and 1760 there were eighteen domestic insurrections against colonial authority, six of which produced sustained violence. During the same period there were over seventy-five mob riots. In the years immediately prior to the Revolution, furthermore, the inclination of the Patriots to defy the British by independent actions greatly increased, with forty-four riots occurring between 1760 and 1775. By 1776 Americans were very accustomed to the use of violence to express their political grievances. The resort to mob action and terror against traitors in their midst was only a natural outcome of the specific revolutionary circumstances of the times. "Among the intellectual bequests of the American Revolution," one specialist has written, "has been the example that violence in a good cause pays, a lesson that has been well learned by Americans."[1]

On December 1, 1774, the Patriots succeeded in establishing the

Continental Association in the colonies. This proved to be the first major act to force public cooperation with the emerging revolt against British rule. Thereafter, conflict became inevitable. Citizens pledged not to buy British goods, and locally elected committees, usually dominated by ardent Patriots, enforced these pledges vigorously. The names of those who refused to conform, or of those who broke their word, were published in local newspapers and the offenders had to face social ostracism or other punishment. If the recalcitrant still refused to obey the edicts, brutality and violence were employed. In this respect, Massachusetts led the way.

The majority Whigs in Massachusetts had little patience with their domestic opponents. Mobs besieged both real and alleged Loyalists and forced the resignation of several who had accepted government positions. The Reverend William Clark, for example, described one such mob that terrorized his area of the state:

> a cruel and relentless mob of several thousands, have rose [sic] in arms at a time with the most hostile intentions against those who hold a place in government, nay, to such a pitch of madness have the people arrived that we are now forbidden not only to speak but to think.[2]

The intolerance against suspected Loyalists increased after the battle of Lexington in April 1775. Local Whig "committees of safety" went after Tories with a zeal and vengeance that surpassed even what they later demonstrated against the British. As has occurred in many other revolutionary conflicts, the fratricidal internal struggle often resulted in a hatred and viciousness usually reserved for the external enemy. Benedict Arnold, whose name is synonymous with "traitor," is still the classic villain of U.S. history, a much more notorious figure than even King George himself.

Relative to their Tory allies, the British in Massachusetts were aloof and secure, protected from attack after occupying the city of Boston. But outside the confines of Boston, Massachusetts Loyalists faced relentless persecution. Many had their property confiscated, others were confined to their homes, forbidden to leave until they recanted. Those fugitives who managed to reach Boston found safety at least but, as one historian has written, even there their torments were not over:

> Letters soon followed them telling of insults and threats to their friends that remained. Their private coaches were burned

or pulled to pieces, loads of the rich importer's goods were attacked and destroyed or stolen, and his effigy hung up in a conspicuous place in sight of his house during the day, to be burned or ignominiously treated at night. One had his riding horse, with saddle and bridle tarred and a human image on its back, driven through town with an infamous figure pinned on the image's breast. Others were frightened by finding incendiary letters that intimated terrible tortures for all Loyalists.[3]

As Americans, there were few distinguishable cultural issues between Whig and Tory. Tories remained faithful to the crown for a number of motives, ranging from birthplace (those born in Great Britain tended toward loyalism), occupation and position in society, the possibility of social or financial gain, nationality, or religion (Anglicans of New England were almost always loyal). The presence of British troops, furthermore, often flushed out formerly cowed Tories, while simultaneously restraining the Whigs. The long British occupation of New York City, for example, was undoubtedly an important factor in the Tory majority there. British occupation likewise influenced pro-Loyalist sentiment in Philadelphia, parts of New Jersey, Georgia, and South Carolina. Conversely, the lack of British strength in New Hampshire, Connecticut, Delaware, Maryland, and North Carolina encouraged Patriot support in those states.

The news of the Battle of Lexington gave Whigs everywhere great encouragement, however. In every colony but New York they quickly gained political control against the usually awkward and relatively sluggish Tory counterattacks. Tory conservatism contrasted sharply with the aggressive and provocative spirit of the revolutionaries. The Loyalists as a group preferred appeals to logic, rational persuasion, authority, and constitutionalism. But since the times were revolutionary, it was the Patriots, not the Loyalists, who were able to capture the momentum of American history. Bernard Bailyn has summarized the social and political failings that condemned America's Tories to be among history's all-time losers:

Committed to the moral as well as the political integrity of the Anglo-American system as it existed, the loyalists were insensitive to the moral basis of the protests that rose against it. They did not sense the constriction of the existing order, often because they lived so deeply within it, or the frustration it engendered in those who failed to gain the privileges it could bestow. They could find only persistent irrationality in the arguments of the discontented and hence wrote off all of their efforts as politically pathological . . . they were outplayed, overtaken, bypassed.[4]

Just as contemporary terrorists and irregulars often appear pathological or morally bankrupt to the rest of civilized society, so too did the Patriots to eighteenth-century Loyalists. In terms of organization and purpose the Patriots were more "extreme," and if for no other reason, they were more effective. Inside the internal war the Loyalists remained generally on the defensive, leaving the offensive initiative to the revolutionaries.

The Loyalists were also a numerical minority throughout the colonies, but not by very much. In some areas of the country, such as New York City, Long Island, Philadelphia, and portions of the Carolinas and Georgia, they constituted a majority. In other areas, notably in New Jersey, Delaware, Massachusetts, and Maryland, they formed an imposing percentage of the population. Only in the rest of New England and Virginia were they a decided minority. But, by and large, the Loyalists left the strategic and political offensive to their domestic opponents, hoping that the military superpower of Great Britain would be able to preserve the kind of America they wanted to live in. Yet, they too were often the initiators of domestic terror. In addition, nearly fifty thousand Tories served with the British army.

While Tory vengeance was not as comprehensive nor as organized as Whig warfare, the Tories wreaked havoc wherever they constituted a majority or wherever they were shielded by the British army. For example, one specialist has given this account of the Tory terrorist campaign in New Jersey:

> Much of the fighting done by the Jersey Tories was not orthodox, to say the least. They became so desperate, and often depraved, in their demeanor that they plundered friends as well as foes, warred upon aged persons and defenseless youths, committed hostilities against professors and ministers, destroyed public records and private monuments, butchered the wounded while they were begging for mercy, allowed prisoners to starve, and destroyed churches as well as public buildings.[5]

In this sense the American Revolution remains an excellent case study of the timelessness of terrorism as a form of quasi-military combat, separate from orthodox war but related and supportive. Although it took place in the eighteenth century, within a small, agrarian population, the distinction between irregular and regular operations was even then a pronounced feature of the collective mentality. The Patriots respected and understood the modus operandi of the British army, which represented warfare. But the Tories, who undertook subversive, back-alley, and "cowardly" tactics, were beyond the pale of warfare and represented an enemy who was nearly subhuman. While the Whigs initiated their own terror, they refused to countenance it when it was used against them. Such dual standards appear equally timeless in the terrorist versus military intellectual image and, as Claude Van Tyne presented it many years ago, help explain the unique vicious nature of terrorist, internal war.

> When the loyal militia had been organized, there fell to its unfortunate lot the performance of those acts of war which especially aroused the hatred of the Patriots. The small expeditions to burn and pillage towns and to annoy the Whig farmers were left to them. The great campaigns were recognized as legitimate warfare, and those who took part were recognized as honorable enemies; but the men who harassed and worried the country by petty attacks came to be hated in a most virulent way. Add to this the fact that, on the frontiers, they frequently acted in conjunction with the Indians and we may understand why a Tory was a devil in human shape in the eyes of the Patriots.[6]

Whig terror against their internal enemy often took the form of independent "vigilante" units, which fanned throughout the colonies in defiance of British authority. "Regulators" of prerevolutionary North Carolina, for example, plagued the British occupation and often took the law into their own hands, including using terrorism to promote what they defined as a just cause. By one account,

> The injustice of the government officials urged the regulators for justice. The once peaceful negotiators became violent, and lawless from the slowness of legal remedies taking place. The regulators refused to pay fees, and terrorized those who administered the law. They also disrupted the court proceedings. The regulators first tried negotiations; it was the injustice of the government officials that made them resort to violence. The

regulators intentions were not to terrorize the government officials, but only to find justice. The regulators fight for justice was a problem for royal Governor William Tyron, who wanted the regulators' revolt to stop.[7]

Persecution of the Tories took on a number of forms. Although there was a certain spontaneity connected with some of the earlier acts—particularly those of mobs—the pursuit of the Loyalists was soon covered with the veil of official sanction. In Whig-controlled areas, the machinery of local government was systematically geared toward a defeat of the Tories as political entities. The Massachusetts Patriots began organizing for revolutionary warfare years before the Declaration of Independence. As early as 1772 committees of correspondence were organized throughout the colony. A proliferation of committees soon enveloped all thirteen colonies in what amounted to a national and unified network of organized persecution.

By the time of the war, the committees had become the vehicles for enforcing even the most arbitrary measures against Loyalists. In many localities the committees constituted the only voice of public order. They took upon themselves the responsibility for exploring the extent of an individual's degree of support for the American cause. Freedom of speech was often suppressed, the liberty of the press was curtailed, and an organized campaign of general political repression was carried out. "What an engine," John Adams would later remark. "France imitated it and produced a revolution."

The adoption of the Continental Association by the Congress in 1774 gave the system of repression a national sanction, even though at the time it was still illegal. By prohibiting the importation of British goods, the association provided the raison d'être through which the locally chosen committees of safety and correspondence could function. In practice, the Continental Congress and the various provincial congresses issued general orders and passed laws, the execution of which was left to the local committees. If a majority of the committee judged that an individual had violated an edict of the association, that person's name would be published in the local newspaper. If he or she refused to recant, further punishments were meted out. A few Loyalists attempted to form their own counter-organizations, but these efforts usually failed. As Van Tyne has related, "wherever the Loyalists attempted to organize, they were set upon with verbal fury and the individual members exposed to the uncurbed rage of the mob."[8]

The legal basis for the persecution of Tories by the courts was

Congress's resolution of June 25, 1775, which defined treason as giving aid and comfort to Great Britain. The resolution permitted the revolutionary legislatures to specify further the nature of treasonous activity within their own jurisdictions. A number of them interpreted this resolution in the broadest possible terms. New Hampshire, for example, included as treason a personal belief in British authority. Other colonies outlawed a range of activities that were less than treasonous: undermining Patriot morale, acknowledging the sovereignty of the king, discouraging enlistments, etc. Prosecution of these and other crimes occurred when a specific complaint was filed against the suspect. Sworn statements were then collected, a hearing was held before a justice of the peace, followed by a public trial. Prison terms for convicted traitors were seldom longer than two years, and in practice, the courts preferred simply to confine the victim to his own home for a specified time.

In the internal war between Whig and Tory, neutrality was not permitted. All colonies passed at least one law requiring an oath of allegiance to the Revolution. Even those who were excused from taking the oath were often treated as if they had refused, and refusal was tantamount to the admission of guilt.

There existed a whole labyrinth of other laws that restricted the activities of the Loyalists. These varied from colony to colony, with the harshest laws usually coming from the colonies that harbored the largest and most active number of Tories. State legislatures passed bills, for example, that levied various fines against those who refused military duty, against the mere expression or publication of Loyalism, against the holding of public office by suspected Tories, etc. The displacement of convicted Tories into other colonies, or outside America proper, was also legitimized. Further punishment usually consisted of banishment or imprisonment. Sometimes the agents of the committee would arrive at night, followed by angry and shouting mobs that often numbered in the thousands. The purpose of these terrorist acts was not to kill the enemy but to convert him, or at least to elicit a public recantation. Suspected Tories had to endure rigorous interrogations, public ridicule, and the forced search and possible seizure of their homes and properties.

The category of personal, and frequently wanton, violence against the Tories provides some of the most telling examples of unconventional warfare in the Revolution. Most of these acts were committed under the cover of revolutionary—and therefore "official"—authorization. Often the excesses committed on both sides blended motives of personal antipathy and revenge with patriotism. The line separating the two was thin and frequently ambiguous and, to the victim, probably irrelevant. With passions on both sides reaching a fever pitch, it is not surprising that countless abuses often accompanied a nationwide system that, by its very definition, denied Tories the same rights that other Americans were simultaneously fighting for.

Across the colonies, campaigns of violence were waged, the patterns influenced by the regional balance of Whig and Tory strengths and the intensity of local feelings. In New Jersey, for example, Bergen County became what one authority has described as "a grim twilight zone of random violence and increasing insecurity."[9] In southern Connecticut and Long Island, a condition of near-anarchy prevailed. Tory raiding parties (the Queen's Rangers) played havoc with the Connecticut coastal towns, while Whig privateers plundered those on Long Island. Before the British reached New York City, Patriot vigilantes, such as the Sons of Liberty, rounded up and deported suspected Loyalists. These times, according to Van Tyne, "were months of terror for the Loyalists." He also writes that in parts of Pennsylvania "the Tories were cowed by a reign of terror."[10] During the first years of the Revolution, as recorded by another historian of the period, Howard Suriggett, "Pennsylvania was not a nation at war with another nation, but a country in a state of civil war." Suriggett went on to describe the terror that revolutionary warfare had brought to the banks of the Susquehanna:

> The sinister terror and suspicion which so cruelly attends civil wars enveloped the valley. Sounds on the road at night, heard through barred doors and windows, the hooded light in the field, were not made by friends or neighbors, but those who lived in lonely houses in bitter loyalty. . . . There was something fearful in every footfall. The lone valley, pictured by so many as an Arcadia, was in reality a cauldron in the hills, boiling with greed and violence and fear.[11]

In central Pennsylvania the internal conflict took on an even greater horror in 1778 when a group of over one thousand Loyalists and British regulars, plus warriors from the Iroquois nation, massacred 227 U.S. militia defending Wyoming, Pennsylvania (near Scranton). The resultant burning and plundering of neighboring settlements provoked a panicked withdrawal of thousands of local villagers in a refugee flight subsequently known as the "Great Runaway." This "Wyoming Massacre," as it was also called, became an instantaneous propaganda and political weapon in the hands of both Patriots and the Continental army.

The bravery of the outnumbered defenders and the savage cruelty of the enemy, especially the Indians, was often retold throughout the Revolution, in story, poem, and oration. The immediate reaction came from George Washington himself, who enacted a severe vengeance upon the whole lot of Tory and Indian enemy. The result was a classic, and still fairly unknown, case of revolutionary "counterinsurgency," an early introduction for Americans to the timeless character and circumstances of irregular warfare.

Intuitively, Washington seemed to grasp the magnitude of and solution to the problem, as many soldiers have against such opposition. His orders to Gen. John Sullivan and his forty-five hundred men were to defeat the Iroquois by eliminating their homes and crops, the essence of their existence. He called for the "total destruction and devastation" of Iroquois villages throughout the Cherry Valley of New York, so that "the country may not merely be overrun but destroyed." He urged Sullivan to act without restraint, "in a loose and dispersed way. . . . It should be impressed upon the minds of the men wherever they have the opportunity to . . . discourage and terrify their foes."[12]

Typically, the Iroquois retreated against the advance of Sullivan's three-pronged offensive, abandoning their villages but giving the Americans no opportunity for battle. But that proved their undoing and played directly into the soldier's strategy. Sullivan followed Washington's orders to the letter. In a campaign lasting no more than a month (August to September 1779), Sullivan discarded his large baggage trains and pursued the Indians relentlessly. More than forty Iroquois and allied Indian villages, including twelve hundred dwellings, were set to the torch, and at least 160,000 bushels of vegetables were confiscated in a campaign of total war against the enemy's population. General Sullivan later told Congress that there was "not a single town left in the country of the five nations." One of his officers, Col. Daniel Broadhead, bragged that "the wolves of the forest will have sufficient cause to howl as they will be quite destitute of food."[13]

George Washington is, appropriately, the "father" of his country and ranked by many experts as the greatest military leader in history. But to the Iroquois, who chose terrorist violence against settlements, he was a soldier of powerful, conventional armed revenge. To the Seneca chief Cornplanter, Washington was the "Town Burner," whose very name provoked "our women [to] look behind and turn pale and our children cling close to the necks of their mothers." Even in revolutionary America, guerrilla terror was synonymous with total war.

The American campaign of total war against the Iroquois nation in 1779 would be followed in parallel fashion by military commanders throughout the nineteenth century, against both Indian and Confederate irregulars. Similar tactics would be taken up again in the twentieth century whenever the frustrations of "chasing ghosts" exploded the patience and tactical training of professional soldiers. The result was total warfare as brutal and as comprehensive as that later waged from the skies by the technological brilliance of modern combat.

–2–

Southern Partisans vs. British Redcoats

G uerrilla warfare dominated the South, especially the Carolinas and Georgia, where strong pockets of Loyalists existed. During 1780 and 1781, for example, there were scores of ambushes and small-scale raids in South Carolina alone, with over four thousand casualties. Occasionally, set-piece battles occurred. There was one in 1779 at Kettle Creek, Georgia, where a force of four hundred Patriots led by Thomas Sumter surprised an even larger army of Loyalists and put them to rout, killing seventy. The aftermath of this battle, however, saw both Whig and Tory units lapse into the kind of quasi-war action that had been the dominant feature of the southern campaign from the beginning.

Neither side could fully protect its civilian population, and a ferocious guerrilla war spread throughout Georgia and the Carolinas. Areas thought to be under control quickly switched sides, as Loyalists and Patriots fought their own little battles of terror against each other and those suspected of favoring the opposition. In the South, anarchy reigned, and anarchy is the perfect breeding ground for revolutionary, guerrilla warfare.

In the northern theater of operations most of the military battles were conventional, with the notable exception of the guerrilla assaults under Horatio Gates against General Burgoyne's British army during the summer and fall of 1777. Burgoyne was marching south from the St. Lawrence River, hoping to link up with another British force and effectively cut off New England from the rest of the colonies. Gates pursued him in ambush all the way, finally gathering an army of seven thousand men that was able to match force with Burgoyne's. The result was the surrender of the British army at Saratoga on October 17, 1777, a battle of orthodox tactics but made possible by the unconventional methods of American partisans.

In the South, the partisan campaigns supervised by Nathanael Greene were much more important, particularly since the organized British forces had already taken both Savannah and Charleston and in 1780 had driven the Americans from the field in the battle of Camden, South Carolina. By that year, regular American resistance in the South had come to a virtual halt. But a new kind of opposition to the British arose in the form of the loosely organized guerrilla bands that were composed of native farmers who knew how to fight in Indian fashion and who had grown up in the rugged mountains and impenetrable swamps and woods of the Carolinas. These men were excellent marksmen and represent to this day the best examples of classic guerrilla warriors in American military history.

Both by temperament and environment, southerners were natural guerrillas. The rural setting, dense forests, and impenetrable, swampy interiors, combined with a subtropical climate, discouraged reliance on machines and linear tactics and, at the same time, promoted the utility of irregular war. The British domination of the coastal South, with a regular army encamped in cities, provided southerners with both the rationale and objective for irregular operations.

The problems the British had in attempting to pacify the North American colonies were common symptoms of regular armies operating against guerrillas in unfamiliar terrain thousands of miles from home. The geographic features of colonial America were made for unconventional operations. With a coastline of over fifteen hundred miles, in a poor and agrarian country that had few roads, the British found themselves in a serious tactical predicament. The thick forests and swamps of the Carolinas aggravated the difficulties of the redcoats, who had been trained to campaign on the relatively flat plains of Europe. Despite a population many times that of the colonies, and with vastly superior economic resources, Great Britain soon found itself bogged down in a distant war that had little popular appeal at home.

Nor were the British prepared for an extended war. Lord Sackville Germain, the king's colonial secretary, urged quick results. "As there is not common sense in protracting a war of this sort," he wrote, "I should be for exercising the utmost force of this Kingdom to finish the rebellion in one campaign."[1] It was not to be. After dispatching over thirty thousand troops, the British generals were forced to ask for reinforcements. But Patriots and partisans mocked British pacification efforts. Gen. William Howe summarized the British dilemma early in the campaign:

[T]he rebels get on apace, and knowing their advantages in having the whole country, as it were, at their disposal, they will not be readily brought into a situation where the King's troops can meet them on equal terms.[2]

As the Patriots' cause grew stronger in the South, they formed several types of military organizations, all of them irregular. Militias, which were controlled by local political committees, launched disciplined attacks on the disorganized Tories. Force was frequently applied by mobs, which acted without any pretense of authority. Volunteer organizations, such as those led by William R. Davie and William Lee Davidson of North Carolina, fought informal ambush wars. Both Davie and Davidson were ex-regular officers, the former a cavalryman, the latter a line officer who was with Washington at Valley Forge. Davie's guerrillas on horseback came to be known as "The Bloody Corps" for their brutality against Loyalists. Davidson was a Scotch-Irish Whig who combined with Davie to turn North Carolina into a beehive of irregular action against both the internal and external foe. Their sniping and harassing tactics in the last stages of the southern campaign forced British redcoat movements into long and frustrating delays.

The Battle of Moore's Creek, North Carolina, was typical of the early informal fighting in the South. In February 1776 a group of fifteen hundred men (mostly Scottish immigrants) crossed a bridge on Moore's Creek, unaware that over a thousand Patriots lay in hiding just on the other side. Up from their trenches rose the Patriots, and in a single volley they killed over fifty of the Scot Loyalists. Eight hundred more, in addition to hundreds of muskets, rifles, and swords, were rounded up in the ensuing chase. As a result, North Carolina remained firmly Whig.

During the fall of 1778, South Carolina and Georgia also came under Whig domination, even though their actual populations initially had pro-Loyalist majorities. As in the North, the Patriots were able to organize faster and better, they were more offensive-minded, and— lastly—they seem to have grasped the larger dimension of the political picture. In short, they were motivated by an ideological momentum that provided the political enthusiasm ("extremism") that has normally fueled the fires of revolutionary causes. The Patriots acted as if history was on their side, a powerful political advantage against the status quo, the Loyalist "cause."

Patriot irregulars in the last stages of the Revolution were eighteenth-century practitioners of the art of politico-military conflict. They used their own knowledge of the land, their common cause, tactical movement, and speedy intelligence to seize the initiative away from the Tories. The Loyalists were poorly armed and badly led. As soon as they tried an uprising, they were slaughtered or persecuted relentlessly.

In the southern theater, if the British Tories had had to contend with only the Continental army, they might have been able to win a victory by 1780. The American cause stayed alive in the South because of the action of its irregular forces, militia or partisan, who either acted independently or with the Continentals to force the redcoats north to Yorktown and final defeat. When the southern cause seemed lost due to British occupation of the key cities, the partisans of the interior swamps and woodlands spontaneously rose to save the cause.

Francis Marion, in his late forties at the time, became the symbol of American guerrilla resistance. A teetotalling Huguenot, Marion commanded a ragtag band of irregulars, including young boys and ex-slaves. They made their own clothes and weapons and shot their pistols with bullets made from pewter. Numbering no more than several hundred at its peak strength, Marion's force became skilled in night and dawn raids against British outposts. He and his men would ride as many as sixty miles at a stretch along the clay paths and marches of South Carolina in order to surprise a Tory or redcoat force. After the war, many of Marion's guerrilla paths became permanent roads. In one particular escapade, Marion surprised a British column escorting some 150 prisoners. The guerrillas swooped down on the column and freed the entire lot of Americans, an incident which made the "Swamp Fox" instantly famous.

Marion's irregulars made life for the British miserable. He was simply too clever to be caught. If there was a bridge to be crossed, he made his men cover it with blankets to suffocate the sound of the horse's hooves. His pickets were posted in the tops of trees and were taught a shrill whistle to warn of advancing redcoats. His camps, including "Snow's Island" and "Peyre's Plantation," were established deep within the South Carolina swamps. His men rode on horseback but fought on foot, usually in separate groups of three companies. If one base became threatened, he moved just as quickly to another one. This is what Lord Cornwallis wrote about Marion in December 1780:

> Colonel Marion had so wrought on the minds of the people, partly by the terror of his threats and cruelty of his punishments, and partly by the promise of plunder, that there was scarcely an inhabitant between the Santee and Pedee [rivers],

that was not in arms against us. Some parties had even crossed the Santee, and carried terror to the gates of Charlestown. My first object was to reinstate matters in that quarter, without which Camden could receive no supplies. I therefore sent Tarleton, who pursued Marion for several days, obliged his corps to take to the swamps, and by convincing the inhabitants that there was a power superior to Marion, who could likewise reward and punish, so far checked the insurrection, that the greatest part of them have not dared to appear in arms against us since his expedition.[3]

Clearly, to the British, Marion and his partisans were part of a larger terrorist riddle, which regular soldiers were forced to solve by improvisation, a problem that is central to the strategic culture of insurrection, then and now.

Thomas Sumter and Andrew Pickens were other South Carolina partisan leaders. Sumter, called the "Carolina Gamecock" by the British, was an independent-minded magistrate and farmer who lived in the Santee River country of central South Carolina. He also was a former Continental army officer who had served since 1776 as an infantry colonel. Neither a sound strategic planner, nor a man known to subordinate himself to higher authority, Sumter's best quality as a guerrilla was his stubborn tenacity (hence the nickname). After the British burned his plantation he gathered a force of other angry Patriots and set off on horseback against the invaders.

The South Carolina interior of Sumter's domain was dominated by marshland with little underbrush, combined with hard clay and sand, ideal for horseback warfare. The Gamecock was one of the best tacticians of mobile guerrilla surprise. He and his men operated independently and often without authority in swift and sudden raids on horse against both British and Tory foes. His stubborn independence, however, sometimes was as much of a problem to the American side as an asset. On several occasions he was also defeated by British troops, but he never left the field for long.

Andrew Pickens, a part-time guerrilla like Sumter, was most famous for his rout of the Loyalist army at Kettle Creek, Georgia. But by the spring of 1780, with the British in occupation of the urban south, Pickens, of necessity, also switched to rearguard ambush tactics. A somber elder of the Presbyterian Church, Pickens was a conservative, soft-spoken man. His guerrilla warfare reflected this orthodoxy in his temperament. To the Continental authorities, he was as much a regular soldier as he was a guerrilla. Indeed, he was always careful to coordinate his raids with the authorities, something that Sumter seldom bothered to do. Pickens described his fellow guerrilla Sumter this way: "He was self important and not communicative. I had little connection with him during the war."[4]

Daniel Morgan, another true partisan, was born in New Jersey and grew up in Virginia. As a youth he saw action in the French and Indian War and was with Braddock in Pennsylvania. The lesson he learned was not lost, especially when it came time for Morgan himself to lead American guerrillas against a new army of redcoats led by General Cornwallis.

In the early years of the Revolution, Morgan fought as an officer of a Virginia company. An experienced Indian fighter and rifleman, he became an excellent leader of the frontier light infantry of the Continental army. He took part in the invasion of Canada and was taken prisoner by the British after the American defeat on the plains of Abraham in Quebec. In August 1776 he joined the American army against "Gentleman Johnny" Burgoyne.

Morgan's skills as a forest soldier greatly helped to harass British columns in Burgoyne's march south from Canada toward Albany. Using Indian tactics, Morgan led five hundred riflemen against the British in a series of sniping and harassing operations. In the Battle of Bemis Heights, Morgan's men helped inflict severe losses on the enemy, who numbered five times those of his own men, and drove Burgoyne toward Saratoga and surrender (1777). After a year of inactivity, Morgan was summoned in 1780 by the newly appointed southern commander, Nathanael Greene, to begin partisan operations in the Carolinas. Tall and physically strong, with awkward speech habits, coarse manners, and homespun clothing, Daniel Morgan was ready for the job.

So was Greene. This Quaker Patriot from Rhode Island had overall responsibility for military action against the British in the South. "Guerrilla warfare" was an unknown term in those times but Nathanael Greene instinctively understood what was necessary. Appointed southern commander in October 1780, but at heart a Continental officer, Greene nevertheless realized that the British were in a dominant military position in the Carolinas. All he had left, for the moment, were the partisan armies that had formed under Marion and other native leaders. Greene intuitively used these guerrillas as his lever for the ultimate ejection of the British redcoats. Nathanael Greene, more than any other individual, can be credited with the success of American partisan operations. He supervised the entire southern theater, and he blended partisan and conventional operations so brilliantly that, within a year, the British army was finished as a military force in North America.

Greene's improvisation came from his strategic common sense. He turned his conventional weaknesses into advantages. "There are few generals," he once wrote, "that have run oftener, or more lustily than I have done. But I have taken care not to run too far, and commonly have run as fast forward as backward, to convince the enemy that we were like a crab, that could run either way."[5]

Having no military experience before 1776, and accustomed to conventional operations in the North, Greene still made the American "crab" a monster to British regulars in the southern theater. Partisan activity began in earnest when he assumed command.

The leaders of the American guerrilla resistance under Greene, all southerners like Marion and Morgan, were veterans of the Indian wars of the 1760s. They learned their small war tactics on the job, and years before the British arrived to fight against them. They used smoothbore rifles, pistols, muskets (with buckshot), and sabers, mostly homemade. Their appearance was rustic and ragged, and effected general ridicule from the Continentals and British alike. But their tactics and skills succeeded. Their marksmanship ("aimed shooting") was unknown to a British army trained to fire in volley standing up against massed opponents of linear columns. Their retreating tactics defied clumsy British counterattacks.

But the American irregulars also had their problems. Enlistments were informal and sporadic, and often guerrilla troops would change sides at will. There was periodic discontent in the ranks, a lack of money and arms, and on several occasions, actual defeat in battle. By the war's end, the British were beginning to learn the guerrillas' ways too, and were becoming equally adept at stealth, speed, and mobility in pursuit.

Despite the tactical success that the southern partisans had, the American Revolution was by no means a guerrilla movement writ large. Guerrillas were not professional military in the sense that they hoped to remove the British from North America. More often than not, they were locals motivated by a revenge against the atrocities committed by British regulars against their homes and persons. In one infamous episode, over one hundred American prisoners were slaughtered mercilessly by troops under the command of Col. Banastre Tarleton. In another case, a combined British-Loyalist army burned a swathe fifteen miles wide and seventy-five miles long through South Carolina. Shops and barns were burned, houses looted, and even the cattle and sheep were bayoneted. As John Shy has written, the result was anarchy: "[N]either side had the capability of fully protecting its supporters among the civilian population, and a ferocious guerrilla war spread throughout South Carolina and into Georgia and North Carolina."[6]

Aided by the presence of Greene's Continental army, southern partisans managed to wage a strategy of guerrilla war, a campaign that lasted through 1780. With the announcement of Greene's position, the irregulars of the South now had a chance to turn their uncoordinated and sporadic ambushes into a coordinated plan toward victory. To have even a slight chance of winning, the guerrilla needs the nucleus of a regular force. With the arrival of Nathanael Greene and his mixed bag of Continentals and irregulars, the hope of winning the war suddenly came alive.

In 1780 and 1781 there were hundreds of guerrilla skirmishes in the back areas of the lower South. The exact figure is unknown. But with the destruction of the Continental army and the disappearance of governmental authority, the Revolution in the South grew progressively unconventional, i.e., it became guerrilla war. Cornwallis's operational rear zones were vulnerable to ambush, and Marion, Sumter, and other American irregulars took full advantage of this. Content to hold what he thought were the key areas of South Carolina, Cornwallis began his invasion of North Carolina in the autumn of 1780. This historic decision took the British one giant step toward final defeat.

Cornwallis's left wing was composed of Loyalist and volunteer troops. Led by Maj. Patrick Ferguson, this army foolishly lost contact with Cornwallis and was forced into a major battle at King's Mountain, an elevated plateau thirty miles west of Charlotte. Facing a superior force of fifteen hundred frontier partisans, Ferguson and 157 of his troops were killed on October 7, 1780. Even before he saw the Carolinas, Nathanael Greene was presented with a surprise victory. On December 2, Greene arrived in Charlotte and formally took command. He set about immediately to put the partisan pieces together for a coherent victory plan.

Within a month, the irregular leader Daniel Morgan gave Greene a second welcome at a cattle-grazing area called "The Cowpens." Fewer than half of Morgan's men were partisans; the rest were militia and Continentals. But Morgan employed all the elements in a classic conventional military victory. Using riflemen as an advanced front, he lured Tarleton's combined Tory legion and British regulars into a trap. After the first volley, the riflemen retreated over a hill in the rear to reorganize in conjunction with four hundred better-disciplined Continental troops. Tarleton mistakenly took Morgan's retreat to be real, but it was only a feint. The Tory legion and the British regulars who followed them were quickly enveloped on both sides and were cut to ribbons. Morgan's men killed 110 enemy and captured over seven hundred in the greatest single victory of the normally unconventional southern theater.

But Morgan's men didn't stay around long enough to savor their win. With regular British troops after them, Cornwallis set out north toward the Dan River. The British general was now determined to beat Morgan at his own game. He disposed of the cumbersome wagon trains and heavy equipment that European armies normally carried and turned his orthodox army into a mobile striking force. Amid heavy rains, swollen rivers, and the dense forests of North Carolina, the great chase between Morgan's riflemen and the British army commenced.

Cornwallis never caught Morgan, although he came close several times. The Americans joined with Greene in central North Carolina, with the British hard on their heels. Greene then moved farther north, across the river into Virginia while Morgan stayed behind. Plagued by chronic back pains, Morgan never saw action again. For the British, the chase across North Carolina was an arduous experience. Cornwallis lost 250 men from sickness and desertion. He didn't have sufficient supplies or boats to continue against Greene and had to give up the chase at a town called Guilford Court House, in north-central North Carolina. There he met a rejuvenated American army under Greene, who had quickly returned from Virginia on March 15, 1781. Using tactics he copied from Morgan's win at The Cowpens, Greene took a fourth of Cornwallis's force before his army was chased from the field.

For the British, the victory at Guilford Court House was classically pyrrhic. While Cornwallis was exhausting his men chasing Morgan and Greene, Pickens had seven hundred partisans ambushing his rear lines. Greene went back and forth between North Carolina and Virginia, like the "crab" he said he would be. His movements, in retrospect, were reminiscent of the famous statement on guerrilla war made by Mao Tse-tung centuries later: "[E]nemy advances, we retreat; enemy halts, we harass; enemy tires, we attack; enemy retreats, we pursue."

After Guilford Court House, Greene moved into South Carolina and dispersed his several guerrilla bands around the colony. Sumter was sent to the Camden area, Pickens went south toward Georgia, and Marion, along with the famed partisan cavalryman "Light Horse" Harry Lee, moved to disrupt British communications with Charleston. With a new aggressiveness, the American irregulars moved to bring the enemy out into the open. In a particularly innovative tactic, the cavalry-man Harry Lee dressed his officers in the forest green uniforms of the notorious British colonel, Banastre Tarleton, who was already known to give no quarter to prisoners. In the presence of captured British officers, Lee succeeded in convincing Loyalist farmers that he was, indeed, Tarleton himself. The Loyalists led the disguised American "greencoats" to their militia headquarters, whereupon Lee's men slaughtered ninety of them on the spot. Not a man of the American irregulars was lost in this great unconventional *ruse de guerre*. By March 1781 the guerrillas had taken the initiative in the American Revolution.

Within less than a year, the British (now led by Lord Francis Rawdon) were virtually out of the entire southern theater, with the exception of a small strip between Charleston and Savannah. The combination of guerrilla raids against British forts, plus Greene's tactical achievements in a series of battles proved to be too much for the conventional eighteenth-century redcoats. Although the British army was better trained and equipped to fight in orthodox style, the patient and unconventional operations of Nathanael Greene and company exhausted their abilities. Not only were they outnumbered and on the defensive, but the reservoir of Tory support that they had hoped for was simply put out of action by Whig partisans.

The American irregulars struck at the British fort system in South Carolina, beginning in April 1781. Marion and Lee took Fort Watson and Fort Matte, after which Marion's men drove the British garrison out of Georgetown. Sumter did the same at Orangeburg, while Pickens went into Georgia and took Augusta. Lee then stormed Fort Granby, as interior South Carolina became a scene of rampant disorder before the defeated invaders. For his part, Greene involved the British army in a series of inconclusive but important battles at Hobrick's Hill (April 25), Ninety-six (an unsuccessful siege, May–June), and at Eutaw Springs (September 8). While Greene's army failed to defeat the British in any of these battles, his relentless pursuit of Rawdon proved to the British that the southern campaign was becoming unwinnable. "We fight, get beat, rise, and fight again," Greene proclaimed after being replused at Hobrick's Hill.

In a remarkably short period of time, the combined regular and partisan strategy of Nathanael Greene and his armies had reversed the entire military picture of the American War of Independence. Although Greene became a partisan by necessity, he also intuitively recognized the inherent limitations of irregular warfare. Whenever the occasion presented itself, such as at Eutaw Springs, Greene abandoned guerrilla tactics in pursuit of the orthodox battle. Ideally, he would have preferred to chase the British from the South with an overwhelming force of regulars. Even for his mobile operations, such as reconnaissance and harassment of enemy flanks, Greene preferred light infantry and regular cavalry units.

In all, despite the reliance upon guerrilla operations when they were required, and despite the success generated from these operations, the leaders of the American Revolution were anything but guerrilla chieftains. The military character of the war was overwhelmingly conventional. A full-scale partisan war was never advocated by either Congress or by any important military leader. Washington and other American leaders were extremely wary of allowing the war to become in any way a social revolution. In many cases, the guerrilla and terrorist raids were generated by their own momentum and were conducted without official sanction. Indeed, they were sometimes discouraged by the leadership as a direct challenge to discipline and authority. "Let officers be men of sense and sentiment," Alexander Hamilton wrote, "and [the] nearer the soldiers approach to machines, perhaps, the better."[7]

The thousands that were killed, wounded, or left homeless by partisan and terrorist raids, however, reflect the extent of savagery that the "other" war inside the Revolution came to be. The cruelty and pillage between Whig and Tory, guerrilla and soldier, was everywhere so great that a British chaplain was moved to write,

> These Americans so soft, pacific, and benevolent by nature, are here transformed into monsters, implacably bloody and ravenous; party rage has kindled the spirit of hatred between them, they attack and rob each other by turns, destroy dwelling houses, or establish themselves therein by driving out those who had before dispossessed others.[8]

Not until the great Civil War did Americans turn on themselves this way again. Then, as in the Revolution, Southern partisans took up the guerrilla's cause against an outside army of "bluecoats" from the North. But even after the Civil War, the fever of the irregular campaign in the Revolution stayed embedded in the South's memory. One military historian, Jac Weller, wrote of his boyhood memories in Georgia, "This writer can recall vividly the meaning that 'Tories' had in Georgia when he was a boy in Lee County in the early 1920s. They were hardly human, worse than 'Yankees.'"[9]

With the American victory at Yorktown in October 1781 the British cause was hopelessly lost. As in the defeat of the French army at Dien Bien Phu in Vietnam (1954), the formalities of conventional war decided the issue, but the unconventional struggle went on. In eighteenth-century America the hatred among Loyalists and Patriots was too deep to bring peace to the countryside. For two more years an ugly irregular struggle continued between elements of the British army that remained, their Tory allies, and Greene's partisans. Persecution of Tories was, in many cases, worse than before, especially in areas evacuated by the British. With the withdrawal of the king's regulars, the remaining Loyalists (about four hundred thousand) were completely at the mercy of the victorious Whigs. Many Tories chose exile in England, Canada, and the Bahamas. Those who remained behind had to face legalized repression, confiscation of their property, and wanton ambush.

Nevertheless, America was again at peace with itself, at least formally. By 1790, anti-Tory legislation was stopped, although personal bitterness continued well beyond. Gradually, those Tories who remained began to re-enter American society. But the end of the Revolution did not see the end of unconventional warfare in the United States. The eighteenth century ended on a note of civil violence and division, which spilled over into the nineteenth century.

The American partisans who waged war in the South during the Revolution played a significant role in the ultimate victory, but the War for Independence was won by soldiers on battlefields. Nonetheless, partisans helped sustain a legend of the American soldier as a rustic, leather-clad backwoodsman, hiding behind trees and rocks and picking off the enemy at will with his accurate rifle. The idea persisted, in textbooks and popular mythology, that the American soldier was a true partisan, a nonprofessional volunteer who employed irregular methods by choice.

This was largely inaccurate in the Revolution, but still the image prevailed. Later military conflicts, including the War of 1812, the Mexican War, and the Civil War, came to elevate technology, firepower, and the infantry to a position of supremacy in the American military tradition, a position they have retained to this day. During the Civil War, as in the Revolution, partisan warfare was only adopted reluctantly, and with little enthusiasm, by the political and military hierarchy of the times. The fact that irregular war and terror were employed in the first place remains a lasting testament to the appeal of such methods in the political and strategic atmospheres of anarchy and desperation. Still, the image of the American partisan persisted, particularly in the Robin Hood-style legend of such men as the Gamecock, Daniel Morgan, and the post–Civil War "outlaws" such as the James brothers and Cole Younger. In their earliest incarnations, Americans proved that such tactics were indeed universal in human behavior.

The Civil War, like the Revolution, would furnish another great arena for partisan military operations in the American South.

-3-

Gray Ghosts vs.
Union Bluecoats

The guerrilla campaign in Virginia was the most important and the most authentic in terms of guerrilla "theory." It was led by John S. Mosby, who became the most famous partisan of the Civil War and today still ranks as one of the most resourceful guerrillas in U.S. history. Mosby was a twenty-eight-year-old lawyer from Bristol, Virginia, when the war began. Slight, weighing only 125 pounds, he began the war as a cavalry officer. Assigned to Gen. James "Jeb" Stuart's staff, Mosby quickly grew restless for more action of his own. By nature a partisan, he soon developed a reputation for audacity and quick thinking. With an unusual flair for publicity, he requested a commission in 1861 to operate independently behind Union lines, ahead of a brigade of Partisan Rangers. The request was eventually granted, but not without much soul searching from reluctant Confederate headquarters.

With the Union army encamped in most of northern Virginia, and Washington surrounded by a string of armed fortifications, the Federals were poised for a full assault on Richmond. In the interior of the state, however, armed bands of men were being hastily organized to harass Union outposts, rail lines, and detached groups of Yankees who happened to stray from their units. In addition to Mosby, the names of Turner Ashby, Harry Gilmor, Elijah White, John Imboden, John "Hanse" McNeill, and scores of others were about to make Virginia a hotbed of partisan unrest. Throughout the mountainous areas, where artillery and regular warfare were practically impossible, guerrilla warfare became the only recourse, and these irregulars were as proficient as any in history. But when they looked to Richmond for official endorsement, the first reaction was disappointing.

To mid-nineteenth century America, including the South, guerrilla war was still a dishonorable form of combat. Many of the best Southern officers were West Point graduates, and the military tradition of the South was nurtured in the best of professional characteristics. As early as June 1861, General Lee advised against irregular action, as did Confederate president Jefferson Davis. There the matter rested until March 1862, when the Virginia General Assembly passed an act authorizing the organization of ten companies of partisan rangers of one hundred men each, to fight in the parts of Virginia overrun by Union armies. The state assembly was, nevertheless, careful to avoid the stigma of officially endorsing guerrilla war or insurrection. The partisans were strictly under the control of the governor and were placed under the jurisdiction of the local Confederate army whenever they operated within its territory. The act also stipulated that the partisans should conform to the rules and customs of warfare, "provided the enemy on their part shall conduct the war according to the usages of civilized war."[1]

Reality was soon to mock such naive legalisms. Throughout Virginia, local groups of desperate guerrillas fanned out on their own to intimidate the invading armies. They cut telegraph lines, burned railroad cars, and so disrupted Northern communications that Union military leaders had no choice but to turn their attention from the main force effort. General McClellan complained that "individuals and marauding parties are pursuing a guerrilla warfare, firing upon sentinels and pickets, burning bridges, insulting, injuring and even killing citizens because of their Union sentiments and committing many kindred acts."[2] The guerrillas were fast becoming more than just a nuisance; they were beginning to tie up thousands of Federal soldiers needed for the regular war against the Confederacy.

Gen. John C. Fremont commanded the Union Mountain Department in western Virginia, which included a main railroad line of the Baltimore and Ohio. Unnerved by constant irregular attacks against this line, he feared that systematic guerrilla warfare was becoming an imposing reality of the Virginia theater. Fremont issued a general order to commanders of posts and troops in the field to fight the guerrillas in their own style, through mobility, surprise, and severity. He brought in the "Ringgold" cavalry from Pennsylvania, in the hope that these rough farmers would be able to operate against the Virginia irregulars on their own level. Fremont also invited in a group of Kansas "Jayhawkers" who had previously fought with him against rebel partisans in Missouri. These farmers and laborers bore the name of "Jessie Scouts" (after Fremont's wife). They frequently wore Confederate uniforms to confuse the enemy and were used against the advance of the Southern army as spies and as counterguerrillas.

Neither Pennsylvania nor Kansas soldiers, however, did the Northern cause or Fremont much good. The Kansans, in particular, aroused the Virginia population so much against Yankees that they helped cause Fremont's resignation from the Union army. They came apart as an organization and, typically, began to prey upon the civilians of the locale. They set about a campaign of lawlessness so notorious that most were either driven from the state or arrested and placed in local jails.

By mid-1862 the guerrilla problem in Virginia was reaching serious proportions. Enlistments in the irregular forces were increasing in number. These forces attracted the daring, the adventurous, and the notorious, to whom regular army life appeared boring. Routine advertisements in the newspapers and flyers made flagrant appeals, with constant promises for a break from the tedium of army life for "all enterprising men" to join the irregulars. Virginia was approaching a state of guerrilla insurrection, against the best wishes of its government.

The Virginia guerrilla units acted on their own, with or without official sanction from Richmond. The fact that the assembly had at least formally endorsed a regulated set of partisan rules of warfare was probably irrelevant to the units' codes of combat. Guerrillas are by nature spontaneous and sui generis, seldom governed by legalistic prescriptions. So they were in the state of Virginia, where John Mosby roamed free during most of the Civil War.

Mosby's raids against the Union army were prime examples of the best (or worst) in American unconventional operations. He towered above all the other rebel partisans, in the range of his operations, in the publicity he received, and in sheer daring. Perhaps the most famous of Mosby's exploits was the capture, alive in his bed, of the Union general Edwin Stoughton. Asleep in his quarters at Fairfax Court House, barely twelve miles from Washington, Stoughton was rudely awakened at 2 a.m., with Mosby's pistol leveled at his head. The rebel guerrilla and his men had crept through Union lines undetected, to bring back as prisoner a prize catch. This was in March 1863. The event soon brought Mosby to national fame. But he was already a seasoned guerrilla warrior, with more years of active fighting ahead of him.

In classic guerrilla style, Mosby led his irregular unit as an adjunct of the regular units. With an average force of five hundred men, using mostly pistols and other small arms, he made occupation a hell on earth for Union armies in Virginia. During the three years of Mosby's partisan raids, he and his mounted guerrilla troopers attacked Union forces, including stores and railroads, on over a hundred occasions (the exact figure is unknown). Every week brought a new surprise against the Northerners. He ranged a broad area of Virginia, including Alexandria, Fairfax, and Loudoun counties near Washington, D.C., the moun-

John S. Mosby, America's greatest irregular leader, was nicknamed the "Gray Ghost" of the Confederacy for his stealthy sabotage operations behind Union lines. *Library of Congress*

tains and valleys of the Shenandoah, throughout the B & O rail line, and in the rear of Grant's army near Fredericksburg. Federal cavalry sent out after him usually came back empty-handed, and on several occasions Mosby's men dismounted, ambushed, and defeated their pursuers. One such example occurred at Dranesville in early 1863, when the rangers were trapped at a farm but fought out of it, killing twenty-five Federals and taking eighty-two prisoners.

Mosby's reputation was enhanced by his small physique and flamboyant dress. Mounted on a white steed and wearing a wide-brimmed hat topped off with a large plume, he looked and acted the part of the romantic guerrilla. His men rode the best horses and dressed alike. Their fighting outfits consisted of a gray felt hat with one side fastened with a rosette and the other with a black feather. The legend of the "guerrilla shirt" reflected the dress of these Southern partisans. They wore dark jackets and gray pantaloons, set off by a yellow cord on the seam.

While Mosby was the best known, he was not the only Virginia partisan leader. Scores of other irregular outfits complemented his efforts, sometimes in coordinated raids, but usually on their own. "Swamp Dragons," Elijah White's "Commanches," John McNeill's "Rangers," "The Mocassin Rangers," and other equally colorful units fanned out in the South against the invading Union armies. Turner Ashby was a guerrilla even before Mosby. Enraged by the death of his brother at Yankee hands, this brash, black-bearded, and handsome bachelor vowed eternal revenge. An aura of mystery surrounded Ashby during his short life as a Confederate partisan. His dashing manner and the white charger he rode were matched by the daring elusiveness of his warfare. He seemed to be forever taunting Union soldiers to attack him, only to suddenly disappear at the last minute to canter up the crest of a distant hill. Most of Ashby's legend grew after his death; a large part of it was doubtless exaggerated. But there was enough truth to support the fictions. Ashby was killed in action in June 1862, the first of the Southern partisan chiefs to so die. Had he lived, he might have succeeded Mosby as the folk hero of the rebellion. As it was, the silhouette of his mounted figure crested on a Virginia ridge was legend enough to spur hundreds of others like him to join the partisan cause.

One of them was John H. "Hanse" McNeill. McNeill was in his late forties at the time he entered the war, the father of three boys. A prosperous farmer and one of the nation's leading experts on cattle breeding, McNeill gave up farming in 1861 to form an independent partisan unit of his own—McNeill's Rangers. His favorite weapon was a double-barreled shotgun loaded with buckshot, which he preferred to use at close range. For three years his rangers operated in the backwoods and mountains of Virginia, tearing up telegraph lines and raiding Union sentinels. McNeill also cooperated with the Confederate army in Pennsylvania and with Jubal Early's cavalry raids in central Virginia. In October 1864 McNeill and one hundred rangers attacked one of Sheridan's supply lines in the Shenandoah Valley. In the exchange of fire he was mortally wounded, and he died five weeks later. His place was taken by his son, Jesse, who finished out the war as the head of McNeill's Rangers.

Harry Gilmor was a Virginia partisan who worked closely with both McNeill and Elijah White. Son of a prosperous shipping family of Scottish background, the twenty-four-year-old Gilmor joined Turner Ashby's partisans early in the war. There he teamed up with the twenty-nine-year-old White, who owned a large farm near Leesburg. Both men formed their own guerrilla units after Ashby's death, and both survived the war and became partisan legends in their own right in the protracted internecine struggle against the powerful Northern army. They derailed trains, stole scores of horses at a time, robbed stores, killed Federal soldiers, and took prisoners; all of this with a relative handful of guerrillas against thousands of disciplined regulars. The Northern military command had no plans to combat guerrillas operating in its rear and flanks. The Union made do with improvisation, but it was never able to erode the guerrillas' tactical ability, despite massive assaults against the Virginia population wherein Mosby et al. derived their support.

The North tried, from scratch, every known method of stopping guerrilla war. But West Point had no textbooks on coping with such a fleet and nigh-invisible enemy. The effort taxed the imagination of the Union officer corps, including Grant. At first, the guerrillas of Virginia were underestimated, which is a common problem for conventional soldiers. When Philip Sheridan took command of the middle Virginia theater in 1864, he was beleaguered with suggestions as how to rid the area of the hornets' nest of partisans, certainly numbering no more than two thousand.

General Rosecrans requested twenty thousand troops to combat the two thousand partisans, an early example of the ten-to-one ratio so familiar to Americans of the Vietnam War era. His request was denied. Another innovation was made by Gen. George Crook, who later used his ideas against Apache Indians. Crook wanted to get rid of Mosby with a band of one hundred handpicked men, led by Capt. Richard Blazer, who had experience fighting Indians in the West. Blazer's unit was organized in mid-1864, but the effort fizzled out before any serious results could be scored. Another effort organized a group of Yankee soldiers to serve as spies among the Confederate partisans. These "Sheridan's Robbers," as they came to be called, were carefully selected, wore rebel gray uniforms, and rode freely within the confines of the partisan neighborhoods of Virginia. But they soon revealed a greater propensity for stealing and drinking than for intelligence gathering. This Northern ruse de guerre came to absolutely nothing.

Clever as these schemes may have been, they were hasty and ill conceived. There was nothing in orthodox U.S. military history to prepare Union officers to fight Southern guerrillas systematically or deliberately. In October 1864 the *New York Herald* reported that "The intervening country between Harrisonburg and Winchester is literally swarming with guerrillas, and only a force of considerable strength can pass up and down the pike."[3]

The guerrilla problem had presented Northern officials with a unique military issue, apparently insolvable. To find an answer to the question of guerrilla warfare, the Union turned to a legal authority, Professor Francis Lieber of Columbia Law School. Lieber's recommendations were as studious as they were irrelevant. He published the results in a book entitled *Guerrilla Tactics Considered With Reference to the Laws and Usages of War*. Lieber introduced the guerrilla concept to the military and traced its origins, especially in Spain and Greece. A partisan, in Lieber's studied view, was "part and parcel of the army and, as such, considered entitled to the privileges of the law of war, so long as he does not transgress it."[4] Such legalisms dismissed the stark reality of guerrilla warfare in America and contributed to the stubborn incapacity of authorities to appreciate modes of conflict beyond their own.

With thousands of Union soldiers tied up protecting person and property against Virginia irregulars, Grant and Sheridan turned to desperate measures indeed in 1864. They went directly against the population, having failed to stop the partisans themselves, in early American efforts to "drain the swamp." By this time, the North was beyond compromise on the partisan issue; the war was winding to a conclusion. In a dispatch to Grant, Sheridan confessed his frustration against the guerrillas: "I know of no way to exterminate them except to burn out the whole country and let the people go North or South. If I attempt to capture them by sending out parties, they escape to the mountains on fleet horses."[5]

Grant agreed that the whole country had to be burnt out. In a telegraph to Sheridan he issued the following orders, with President Lincoln's permission:

Give the enemy no rest, and if it is possible to follow to the Virginia Central road, follow that far. Do all the damage to railroads and crops you can. Carry off stock of all descriptions, and Negroes, so as to prevent further planting. If the war is to last another year, we want the Shenandoah Valley to remain a barren waste.[6]

In another message, Grant went beyond the recommendations of Dr. Lieber, as well as those of his predecessors in command. "When any of Mosby's men are caught," he wired, "hang them without trial."[7] The counterguerrilla effort had taken on a new horror.

Those who paid the price of this horror were the inhabitants of the Shenandoah, who had harbored partisans for over three years. Sheridan went after them with a terrible devastation. He made the whole country from the Blue Ridge to the Northern border untenable for man or beast. More than two thousand farms went up in smoke. Thousands of cattle, plus thousands of horses and sheep, were herded away. Many of these animals were slaughtered on the spot, just to show retribution. A Confederate officer who witnessed the aftermath wrote later,

I try to restrain my bitterness at the recollection of the dreadful scenes I witnessed. I rode down the Valley with the advance after Sheridan's retreating cavalry beneath great columns of smoke which almost shut out the sun by day, and in the red glare of bonfires, which all across that Valley poured out flames and sparks heavenward and crackled mockingly in the night air.[8]

On Sheridan's instructions, Gen. Wesley Merritt did the same in Loudoun County, near Washington. Merritt had two brigades of cavalry, and they destroyed the area entirely. He brought back almost six thousand head of cattle, one thousand hogs and over five hundred horses. The smoke from his pillage blanketed the entire county, but he still could not find the partisan enemy. In his wire back to Sheridan, he confessed, "it was found next to impossible to come in contact with any guerrillas, as they avoided even the smallest portions of the command."[9] Gen. George Custer also took his toll upon the population. His Fifth Michigan Cavalry destroyed almost all of the buildings in the vicinity of the Shenandoah River near Castleman's Ferry. In his own words, Philip Sheridan left the Shenandoah residents with "nothing but their eyes to weep with." He also is said to have remarked cryptically, "The crow that flies over the valley of Virginia must henceforth carry his rations with him." To the people of Virginia, guerrilla and counterguerrilla war came as total and unrelenting conflict, no less so than many of the more well-known and notorious atrocities of the twentieth century, the alleged age of total warfare.

Caught between guerrillas and soldiers, the citizenry in the middle of unconventional war has little choice but to suffer. The people of Civil War Virginia were no exception. By the last years of the war, Southern officials were beginning to doubt the wisdom of their earlier endorsement of the partisan rangers. Most of the violence done to Southern citizens had been caused, at least indirectly, by Northern counteractions. Worse, the partisans had frequently taken it upon themselves to ruthlessly uphold the law, an effort which aroused many Southern patriots to question their cause as much as it did Northern loyalists to flock to Union colors. The terror conducted by the rangers against the blue-clad enemy was sometimes inflicted upon innocent bystanders as well.

On too many occasions, the partisan leaders proved unable to control their own men. The very nature of guerrilla service, furthermore, often attracted thieves and other outcasts to whom regular army life offered little chance for looting. In their zeal to obtain popular support the guerrillas frequently went too far against their own population. Some of the men robbed Southern stores and plundered settlements. Heavy drinking bouts led to fighting and outlawry. Confederate general Henry Heth, who commanded the District of Lewisburg, accused the guerrillas of being "more ready to plunder friends than foes."[10] By 1863 the Confederacy was already discouraged by the effects of partisan service. In a report to President Jefferson Davis, the Confederacy's secretary of war James A. Seddon concluded that,

> The permanency of their engagements and their consequent inability to disband and reassemble at call precludes their usefulness as mere guerrillas, while the comparative independence of their military relations and the peculiar awards allowed them for captures induce much license and many irregularities. They have not infrequently excited more odium and done more damage with friends than enemies.[11]

The guerrillas also discouraged stragglers from the Union army, which in Southern military circles meant more regular soldiers in Northern divisions. To both North and South, guerrilla warfare was fast becoming a scourge. Confederate general Jubal Early, a cavalry officer who appreciated mobility, was outspoken, at the end, against the contribution of the Southern irregulars. "The fact is," he cabled," that all those independent organizations, not excepting Mosby's, are injurious to us, and the occasional clashes they make do not compensate for the disorganization and dissatisfaction produced among the other troops."[12] General Lee, himself a skeptic from the beginning, never changed his mind on the independent guerrillas. "I regard the whole system," he wrote, "as an unmixed evil."[13]

-4-

Outlaws and Guerrillas on Civil War Frontiers

The disrepute that partisans were beginning to have within the losing Southern cause was small compared to their reputation in the Western theater. The anarchy that existed in Kansas and Missouri produced unconventional warfare, engulfing that region in a full-scale insurrection, on a level that never existed in Virginia. In the West, there was no vestige of stability; it was literally every man for himself. In the Western theater, regular armies rarely encountered each other in the field; the area was wide open for irregular and terrorist ambush.

The political difficulties of this area predated the Civil War by several years. The term "Bleeding Kansas" was familiar to Americans throughout most of the 1850s. The central issue there was slavery. Northern abolitionists, backed by Horace Greeley and a fanatical eastern press, pushed for a massive settlement into Kansas to ensure its future as a "free" state. Missouri was a Southern frontier state, mostly populated by descendants of the Old South. Slavery was important to the state's agricultural economy, and most Missourians grew infuriated by the infusion into neighboring Kansas of thousands of Northern abolitionists.

Between 1855 and 1860 the Kansas–Missouri border was in flames and in a condition of political near-anarchy. Gangs of armed men from Missouri invaded Kansas, occupied Lawrence, and looted settlement towns. Led by John Brown, who was later killed after the raid at Harper's Ferry, Virginia, free-soil Kansans advanced into Missouri and murdered and destroyed on their own. Slave-stealing, arson, and looting became commonplace on both sides. This created the perfect conditions for guerrilla warfare, especially when the Union army came to occupy Northern Missouri in 1861.

To the residents of Missouri and Kansas, the Civil War had actually been raging for many years before secession. Almost unique to the Civil War of 1861–65, and completely different from the battlefield tactics of most of the regular war, the western conflict was led by partisan cavalrymen, outlaws, and desperate opportunists. William Quantrill, Frank and Jesse James, "Bloody" Bill Anderson, "Little Archie" Clement, Coleman and James Younger—all have become figures of notoriety in U.S. history. But much less known were their careers as rebel guerrillas amid a political and social turmoil that gave them little choice but to fight as partisans. Most of them were in their teens and early twenties at the time. The warfare they waged was as unorthodox as it was independent. The guerrilla theater in the West was removed from the main theaters of the Civil War and quickly degenerated into little less than mayhem and looting. But the residents of the two states saw themselves as waging a total guerrilla struggle for the political future of the region and against the equally brutal reign of Yankee occupation.

In the West, Missouri in particular, the irregular conflict erased the thin line between combatant and civilian and between soldier and guerrilla, and it was often impossible to distinguish between sides. Southern partisans frequently wore Union uniforms, while Union soldiers sometimes posed as partisans. Lines were blurred and the degree and nature of the violence was random. The struggle destroyed the fabric of society and culture and undermined established values. Confusion at the highest levels attended the leadership on both sides, as the insurrection grew beyond the control of either one. This was the closest Americans ever got to a true "people's war," in which the conflict developed spontaneously by, for, and against the people. Lincoln himself once explained his frustrations on the nature of conflict in the western theater:

Thought is forced from old channels into confusion. Deception breeds and thrives. Confidence dies and universal suspicion reigns. Each man feels an impulse to kill his neighbor, lest he be first killed by him. Revenge and retaliation follow. And all this . . . may be among honest men only. But this is not all. Every foul bird comes aboard and every dirty reptile rises up. These add crime to confusion. Strong measures, deemed indispensable but harsh at best, such men make worse by maladministration. Murders for old grudges . . . proceed under any cloak that will beat cover for the occasion.[1]

In his study of the Missouri civil war, Michael Fellman has summarized the true nature of the partisan beast that had grown within the American psyche. Calling it "the worst guerrilla war in American history," he noted that

normal expectations collapsed, to be replaced by frightening and bewildering personal and cultural chaos. The normal route by which people solved problems and channeled behavior had been destroyed. The base for their prior values—their 'moral structure'—underwent frontal attack. Ordinary people, civilians as well as soldiers, were trapped by guerrilla war in a social landscape in which almost nothing remained recognizable or secure.[2]

Missouri irregulars began when Confederate general Sterling Price issued a call, in November 1861, for insurrection against the Northern army. His units burned bridges and tore down telegraph and railroad lines. Gen. Henry Halleck, in command of Union forces, ordered the strictest countermeasures. He considered the Missouri partisans beyond the laws of war and ordered their immediate execution when caught. To his friends he wrote that he believed the local country was as hostile to his army as Mexico had been during the war there. The outrages his men perpetrated on the population of Missouri drove the likes of Quantrill and the James brothers into hated opposition. Gen. John Pope, who organized one of Halleck's military districts, held every citizen personally responsible for the destruction of railroads in his area. He forced the civilian population to do all their own guard work and made them pay for all damage done by Price's guerrillas. He formed "Committees of Safety" to supervise the job, a tactic reminiscent of the Revolutionary War Patriots. If a town refused to cooperate, Pope's Illinois and Kansas troopers marched through it, burning and looting as they went. Soldiers got drunk at local saloons; farmers in the fields were shot on sight. All of Northern Missouri was in outrage. The pro-Union railroad agent cabled Secretary of War Edwin M. Stanton that Pope's tactic was "enough to drive a people to madness, and it is doing it fast."[3]

Western Missouri was a classic case-in-point. A group of Kansas volunteers, led by the U.S. senator from the state, James H. Lane, had crossed into Missouri to rout the local population. "Lane's Brigade," as it was called, turned into little more than a looting expedition. As they marched, they destroyed and took most of the available property with them. Osceola was put to the torch, citizens were shot at random, and a million dollars' worth of property was "liberated." When Lane, the "Grim Chieftain," left the town, Osceola had ceased to exist.

Another Kansan notorious to Missourians was Dr. Charles R. Jennison, who formed the Seventh Kansas Volunteer Cavalry, commonly known as the "Jayhawkers." Composed mostly of horse thieves, the Jayhawkers marched through western Missouri towns unopposed in late 1861. Jennison was a favorite of John Brown and an equally dogmatic abolitionist. To the horror of Missouri residents, he outfitted an entire company of Negroes, led by an ex-slave and dressed in Union blue. For Missourians, this raised the specter of a possible slave rebellion. The Jayhawkers raided and murdered at will, going as far east as Independence.

The Northern militia units stationed in Missouri often committed the same type of offenses against civilians as Jennison, Lane, and company. As the guerrilla war grew in intensity after 1862, Union tactics grew to be equally ruthless. Most of the officers and men were from Kansas, Iowa, and Illinois, and most of them lacked discipline and experience. They were often forced to live off the land in Missouri because they lacked subsistence, a fact that forced them to loot neighborhood farms and stores. By 1862 all of Missouri appeared ripe for insurrection, and the young partisan leader William C. Quantrill capitalized on this.

Quantrill came to be the symbol of guerrilla resistance to the Union army in Missouri. He also came to symbolize murder and pillage, and by the time he was killed in 1865, at age twenty-seven, his reputation as a dashing figure had largely vanished. Quantrill's career as a guerrilla was violent and short. Born in Ohio, he taught school for a short while before drifting west. When the war broke out he saw brief service with General Price but deserted in November to begin his own independent warfare. At five feet nine inches tall, with reddish hair, he projected an outward sober and quiet manner, but Quantrill's calm outward appearance belied an internal rage. Almost completely amoral, he was one of the most ferocious and dangerous men of the Civil War. For three full years, Quantrill and the guerrillas who later formed out of his parent unit waged ceaseless unconventional warfare against the populations of Missouri and Kansas and the Northern army. Of all the partisans in American history, perhaps none was more ruthless or controversial than Quantrill.

Quantrill's skill with pistols and his cold-blooded determination to drive the Yankees from Missouri were combined with a keen intelligence. He was a natural leader, and while he was riding high, his men followed him religiously. He seldom had more than three hundred in his outfit, but they were able to tie up thousands of Union soldiers, who were forced to constantly guard logistics and communications lines and to ferret out the elusive and mounted irregulars. Since they knew the country intimately, the guerrillas were able to operate in numerous small units, so that they could ambush the superior Federals and quickly disperse on the fastest horses in the region. They were fed and protected by the sympathetic population; those not sympathetic were forced into helping.

Many of Quantrill's men sought personal revenge. Eighteen-year-old Cole Younger's father was killed by the Union. Fourteen-year-old Riley Crawford watched Jayhawkers take his father from his home and shoot him on the spot. Crawford joined Quantrill and vowed to kill every Yankee he came upon. This he did until he himself was killed two years later. The James family received brutal treatment from the Northern army, a fact which forced nineteen-year-old Frank and seventeen-year-old Jesse to start their careers as partisans and outlaws. "Bloody" Bill Anderson became Quantrill's most notorious compatriot. Anderson's sister had been killed when a women's prison building collapsed because Union soldiers, it was believed, had purposely made the building structurally unsound. The event may have caused Anderson to go insane; he quickly thereafter rose to become a ruthless leader, with near-satanic tendencies. Anderson got his reputation by giving no quarter to Union soldiers or their sympathizers. His behavior—marked by wild screaming and hysterical outbursts during battle—became so intense and emotional that he gained a deserved reputation as a homicidal maniac.

There is no official count of the number of skirmishes between the several guerrilla bands of Missouri and Northern soldiers, nor is there a credible body count, but armed contacts probably numbered nearly one thousand, with several times that number killed or wounded. The Kansas–Missouri border scene was anarchy in the extreme. Persons and property were continually attacked by both sides. The guerrilla-counterguerrilla struggle may have been remote from the main conflict back east, but to the people of the western theater it was full-scale insurrection and, therefore, total war.

Throughout 1862 and into 1863 Quantrill's raiders ran wild in the districts of western Missouri. Their numbers grew daily. They robbed mail escorts, ambushed Union patrols, destroyed railroad cars, and openly shot up riverboat steamers. The guerrillas had an elaborate system of espionage and communications around the whole area. They knew in advance where Union patrols were and how many men were in them. The following account by a Union cavalry officer, made in June 1862, describes the style of warfare so common to Civil War Missouri:

> We had proceeded some 10 miles when I learned that some of Quantrill's men had been seen in the vicinity. I proceeded very slowly and cautiously, with six men riding by file as an advance. They had proceeded only a short distance when they were fired upon, 2 of them being killed on the spot and 3 dangerously wounded. I was about fifty yards in the rear with 18 men. We charged in the brush and routed them and then dismounted and searched the brush, and fired at them a number of times. I do not know what their loss was, as I had to leave to take care of the mail.[4]

In August 1862 a large force of Quantrill's partisans routed the Union army at Independence, capturing the town. This was a major blow to the Union, for it indicated the reality of a serious insurrection. From Independence, Quantrill raced across the Kansas plains, with several columns of Federal cavalry hot on his heels. The partisans swept through Olathe, Kansas, and captured the garrison of 125 soldiers. On October 17, Quantrill entered Shawneetown, where his men burned, looted, and murdered at will. When they left the next day, Shawneetown, was erased from the map, not a building had been left standing.

At this point, Quantrill's partisans had developed a romantic reputation for being daring. Their great audacity, their ability with the Colt revolving pistols (some carried as many as eight at a time), and their peculiar dress all added to their mystique. Quantrill's men wore what came to be termed a "guerrilla shirt." Made in the fashion of the western cowboy, this outfit was cut low in front and slit narrow to the waist, where it was joined by a rosette. With giant pockets, the shirts ranged in color from brilliant red to butternut brown. The guerrillas wore wide-brimmed hats and rode the best horses they could steal. Few of them had beards; many were simply too young to shave.

The romantic legend of the partisans, however, soon gave way to reality. As news of their terrible deeds spread, they came to be feared by civilians as much as they were by the Union soldiers. The destruction of Lawrence, Kansas, in August 1863, finally exposed the reality of Quantrill's cutthroats. Lawrence was the center of abolition sentiment in Kansas, a town of about two thousand. At dawn on August 21, a force of 450 partisans led by Quantrill raced into the main street. What took place that day, until nine in the evening, was a massacre that had few parallels in American history. About 185 buildings were razed to the ground, $2 million of property destroyed, and most of the adult males shot, stabbed, or clubbed to death on sight. "Kill every man big enough to carry a club" were Quantrill's last instructions. The Lawrence bloodbath was the epitome of irregular warfare in the western theater, and it also marked the highpoint of Quantrill's murderous career.

This illustration of the massacre in Lawrence, Kansas, which ran in *Harper's Weekly* in 1863, depicts William Quantrill and his raiders as they sack the town and murder the inhabitants. *Library of Congress*

The aftermath of Lawrence shocked the entire nation. President Lincoln demanded an explanation. The populace of the border area fled to safety; by 1864 there were neither people nor animals in sight for miles. The Northern command stepped up its pursuit of the partisans and clamped down even tighter on the Missouri population. Martial law was vigorously enforced.

The Confederate leadership also came to realize that partisan cruelties were having a reverse effect on their own war operations. Many Confederate leaders denounced Quantrill in no uncertain terms. Attempts were made to discipline his men and integrate them into regular divisions, but these all failed. When Quantrill was chased out of Missouri, he went to Texas, where his men continued to loot and kill. Gen. Henry McCulloch, CSA, wrote to his superiors regarding Quantrill:

> Quantrill will not obey orders and so much mischief is charged to his command here that I have determined to disarm, arrest, and send his entire command to you or General Smith. This is the only chance to get them out of this section of country, which they have nearly ruined, and I have never yet got them to do any service. They regard the life of a man less than you would that of a sheep-killing dog. Quantrill and his men are determined never to go into the army or fight in any general battle, first, because many of them are deserters from our Confederate ranks, and next, because they are afraid of being captured, and then because it won't pay men who fight for plunder. They will only fight when they have all the advantage and when they can run away whenever they find things too hot for them. I regard them as but one shade better than highwaymen, and the community believe that they have committed all the robberies that have been committed about here for some time, and every man that has any money about his house is scared to death, nearly, and several moneyed men have taken their money and gone where they feel more secure.[5]

By 1864, Quantrill's guerrilla band began to come apart at the seams. His absence from Missouri caused defection in the ranks. Bill Anderson and Archie Clement branched out on their own in a series of pillage operations, which they had learned so well from Quantrill. Many of the partisans had taken to wearing stolen Union uniforms, which confused both soldier and civilian no end. Union patrols had to devise an elaborate system of badges, passwords, and signals, but many of the partisans learned these and used them as well.

Despite the loss of control by Quantrill himself, the independent partisans continued their maneuvers in Missouri right up until the end of the war. The units led by Bill Anderson were the most notorious during the last year. Union dead were found mutilated and scalped, some with bizarre notes tied to their bodies. By the middle of 1864 Northern Missouri was, again, under a reign of terror. On the evening of September 26, a band of two hundred Confederate irregulars, led by Anderson, looted and terrorized the residents of Centralia, executing a number of them. Union congressman William Rollins barely escaped death by giving a false name and hiding in a hotel. The following day Anderson's guerrillas stopped a Union steam train in Centralia, taking 150 prisoners and executing twenty-two soldiers on the spot. The same afternoon Anderson ambushed a Union detachment commanded by Maj. A. Johnston. The major and his entire command were quickly annihilated, their bodies mutilated. In less than twenty-four hours Bill Anderson's rebel guerrillas had destroyed Centralia and killed over 150 Union soldiers.

But the death of Anderson, in October, ended this particular menace. By early 1865, guerrilla fever had dissipated. Those partisans who remained became flagrant outlaws, killers, and bank robbers, occupations that they, like Jesse James, would follow for years after the war. For these men, the Civil War never really ended.

Guerrilla warfare also took place in Kentucky and Tennessee. Although the regular Confederate armies had been driven from both states, the absence of a sizable Union force (except in southern Tennessee) permitted the growth of unconventional operations. Two men led these diverse forces. The first was John H. Morgan, a cavalry officer of the Confederate army who was commissioned to organize partisan units in 1862. Morgan was thirty-five years old, six feet tall, mustached, with bluish-gray eyes, a light complexion, and a steady and determined personality. He was known before the war as a great marksman and a generous, fun-loving Kentucky horseman. But the Civil War turned Morgan into a resolute guerrilla chieftain. He gave no quarter to those who questioned either himself or the Southern cause. When a trooper once refused to obey an order, Morgan killed him on the spot with his revolver.

Morgan's first action of any consequence was his invasion of Kentucky in the summer of 1862. With twelve hundred armed partisan horsemen behind him, Morgan wanted to become the liberator of Kentucky and to start a move to bring the commonwealth formally into the Confederacy. He denied that he was a guerrilla, hoping to avoid the stigma of the term. "Everywhere the cowardly foes have fled from my avenging arm," he proclaimed. "[M]y brave army is stigmatized as a band of guerrillas and marauders. Believe it not, I point with pride to their deeds as a refutation of this foul assertion."[6]

Morgan's actions, however, revealed his army as a true irregular outfit. He did a brisk recruiting business among the young men of Kentucky, who proceeded to dash about the state systematically terrifying Unionists and plundering pro-Northern stores and settlements. Morgan was also sent as the advance guard for Gen. Braxton Bragg and the regular Confederate army, which hoped to follow up with a full-scale assault on the state.

By July, Morgan had made great strides in Kentucky. He was able to defeat a number of Union outposts and to destroy several Federal rail lines. He held over a thousand prisoners. His movements were so swift and terrifying that the state government nearly collapsed. A sense of great excitement ran through Kentucky with the news that John Morgan was coming. The Union command in Louisville ordered every able-bodied male to fight against the partisans; if not, they were to remain in their houses under the penalty of being shot if they went out.

By December, Morgan's band was three thousand strong. They tore up all the railroads on the way to Louisville in central Kentucky and captured Elizabethtown by firing over a hundred rounds of shells into its center. The garrison of five hundred Federal soldiers surrendered, after which Morgan's men pillaged the entire town, stealing and plundering and even taking medicine and blankets from the local hospital.

In the summer of 1863, Morgan raided across the Ohio River to plunder Indiana and Ohio. This was one of the most audacious partisan movements in American history, a foolish and reckless maneuver that caused Morgan's partisans to surrender and to eventually break up. The object of the raid was to stir up an armed counterrevolution in those two states, where pro-Southern groups, such as the "Sons of Liberty" and the "Knights of the Golden Circle," awaited reinforcements. Morgan's raiders began by burning Lebanon, Kentucky, to the ground on their way north. As they proceeded, they plundered everything in sight and in the process picked up hundreds of recruits, all eager for the "outing" across the Ohio River.

Capturing two steamers, Morgan's men crossed into Indiana in July 1863. They quickly moved north, where they overpowered the town of Corydon, murdering citizens and burning much of the place down. With three hundred stolen horses, they continued their movements, from village to village, in the direction of the Ohio border.

In the meantime, the Indiana government had armed over thirty thousand regulars against these guerrilla intruders. Chased eastward, Morgan moved into Ohio. There he found himself in the same predicament, as thousands of Ohioans had been alerted against him. Union forces were now concentrating on him from all sides, averaging thirty-five miles a day in mounted pursuit, and the soldiers were catching up. The chase took nearly a thousand miles and went on for three weeks. Morgan was finally trapped in northeastern Ohio, near Canton, and was put into an Ohio prison until November 1863, when he made good his escape back into the Confederacy. His partisan raids continued throughout the first part of 1864 in Kentucky and Tennessee, until he was finally laid to rest by a Union bullet in June 1864. By this time, however, there was very little left of his partisan army. Most of them were either killed or captured by the Union in Ohio and in the constant fighting in central Kentucky.

Nathan B. Forrest was another great guerrilla leader of the Kentucky–Tennessee area. Forrest, like John Morgan, was a cavalry officer who took to partisan operations early in the war. Like many other guerrillas in American history, Forrest created an aura of romantic legend around his name; this legend, however, hid a stark reality of death and destruction. Well over six feet tall, with flowing hair and a sweeping mustache, Forrest was as ruthless and impulsive as he was handsome. He was said to have killed thirty-two of the enemy with his own hands by the war's end.

With his own volunteer cavalry, Forrest joined the Civil War attached to General Bragg's army. After the Shiloh defeat, the Confederates were falling back through Alabama. Forrest was sent to harass the flanks of the pursuing Northern army. He found hundreds of sympathizers among the Southern population, and his army grew in size as he moved around the Federal's rear lines. These Deep South partisans burnt ammunition stores used by the Union invader. They tore up railroad lines, ambushed isolated units, and scouted the enemy's position for General Bragg. Forrest's greatest achievement was the capture of a reinforced Union brigade at Murfreesboro, Tennessee. Despite a substantially inferior army, he bluffed the Union command into surrendering, destroying half a million dollars worth of Northern supplies in July 1862.

By 1863 his partisans numbered about four thousand men. They were able to destroy General Grant's lines of communication and supply, lines it took the North several months to rebuild. Forrest interrupted Grant's telegraphic communications northward for a full week. Pushing into Tennessee in December 1863, Forrest set up guerrilla headquarters at Jackson, where even more volunteers joined his men.

He drew supplies from neighboring plantations and sent out raiding parties to gather in cattle and other foodstuffs. But heavy Union columns chased him southward in 1864, when he crossed the border into Mississippi. He would have been destroyed had he not feinted an attack in one direction, only to catch the Union off guard and to escape, by night, in another direction. Forrest had outfoxed the regular Union army and made it back safely to Mississippi.

Restless and impulsive by nature, Forrest refused to sit still. His mobility as a guerrilla raider was helping the South to hold out in the last year of the war. A commentator of the period noted that

> The sphere of General Forrest's duties were at this time enlarged, and their importance increased. He was acknowledged to be one of the most daring and skillful of the Confederate leaders in the West. He seems to have had a sort of roving commission, and the service in which he was engaged partook more of the character of guerrilla than of regular warfare. It being evident that there would be a great struggle between the opposing troops in Northern Georgia, below Chattanooga, Forrest was charged with the special duty of keeping the National forces then on the line of the Mississippi, from Vicksburg to Cairo, employed, and prevent their re-enforcing the army opposed to Johnston.[7]

In March 1864 Forrest was sent out to prevent the Northern army along the Mississippi River area from taking in reinforcements. His mounted raids took him on a wide arc through Tennessee and into Kentucky. Wherever he and his five thousand men rode, plunder followed. Toward the end of the war, Southern guerrillas were becoming professional killers. The war had taken on a personal and vengeful tone. "War means fight, and fight means kill—we want but few prisoners" became Forrest's motto.

His sacking of Fort Pillow, on the Mississippi River near Memphis, was a case in point. Under the cry of "no quarter" the irregulars attacked the garrison, protected by 550 men, in April 1864. Those who tried to escape were shot from behind. The wounded were butchered with everything in sight: clubs, knives, bayonets. Women and children were hacked to death with sabers. The carnage went on until nightfall and was resumed the next day when Forrest's men searched the remaining wounded in order to kill them on the spot. Over three hundred were massacred at Fort Pillow, a body count illustrating the barbarism of total warfare, guerrilla-style. For the remainder of the war, Nathan Forrest and his band of guerrilla horsemen continued interrupting the movements and logistics of the Northern army in Tennessee and Mississippi.

The legacy of unconventional warfare in the American Civil War left the term "guerrilla" in worse repute than before. At most, the Southern irregulars may have prolonged the conflict for an unknown period of time. At worst, guerrillas were responsible for hundreds of small actions that harassed the Union army and caused thousands of extra casualties. They did not appreciably affect the outcome, and at the war's end, the devastation of the South was so overwhelming that there was no serious talk of insurrection. The destruction of the South by Northern regulars, especially in Virginia, Georgia, and South Carolina, showed the power of Northern countermeasures. American culture, especially in the North and East, came to have nothing but contempt for irregular warfare. The idea that the guerrilla was no more than a marauder or bandit was reinforced by the Civil War experience. So, too, was the idea that wholesale destruction and occupation was the only answer to this form of conflict. Northern actions in the Shenandoah Valley were what most Americans thought to be the permanent cure for guerrilla war.

The Union's basic tactic to counter western partisans was to fortify strong points from which troops could fan out through the countryside in the hopes of finding an enemy unit. This was a standard countermeasure for both the American and European armies at the time, particularly in colonial areas. The Union army hoped to launch quick strikes to demoralize rebels, to disrupt their supplies, and to discourage citizens from supporting them. Frequently, the army occupied strategic towns in each county and arrested prominent secessionists. This early U.S. tactic to "drain the swamp" of an elusive irregular enemy rarely worked, and the army eventually went after the guerrilla's base, his farm and territorial refuge. In his annual report of 1863, Gen. Henry W. Halleck defended these methods as "within the recognized laws of war. . . . They were adopted by Wellington in Portugal and by Russian armies in the campaign of 1812."[8] But the protest over these methods back east soon forced Halleck to rescind his orders. Even fighting for their lives, Americans would not condone "uncivilized" irregular war tactics.

The guerrilla threat in the Civil War left an indelible legacy of irregular war implanted in the American strategic culture. According to one historian, the Union soldier held guerrillas in both fear and contempt, worse even than the regular Confederate he faced in battle.

> The enemy that threatened him the most at the time was not the regular Confederate soldier, whom one might encounter on the battlefield, but the irregular, the partisan, the guerrilla— the man who did not abide by the rules of war, the man who pretended to be a civilian—perhaps a Unionist—the figure most indistinguishable from the Southern landscape.[9]

As expressed by one Union soldier, irregulars were "the much de-spised and outlawed Guerrilla—the man who is too mean to enter the Southern army—but goes forth with murder in his heart and a gun in his hand [to] wait to trap a Union Soldier and Shoot him down from ambush—Coward-Assassin." An officer explained the cause and cure against Southern partisans: "The guerrillas have a regular guard estab-lished around our camps. [They] creep up and shoot our pickets in cold blood . . . such men deserve no mercy; hanging is too good for them."[10] The wanton destruction of farmlands down the Mississippi River, for example, was justified by the nature and character of South-ern guerrillas. One officer whose army "was considerably annoyed by Guerrilla parties stationed on the bends and narrow places of the river" removed the source of the discontent:

> All the revenge we could take was to burn the houses, planta-tions and villages near which such depredations had been com-mitted . . . soon the whole river was lined by burning dwell-ings and plantations. . . . The night was a splendid one, and to the splendor of a clear bright sky, was added the horrible gran-deur of hundreds of burning buildings, fired by our troops for resistance they found in landing.[11]

Such emotions had a long and terrible legacy and in some ways were a permanent feature of military attitudes toward guerrillas. This notion of totality as the purpose and direction of warfare, including attacks on civilian populations who "harbor" insurgents, was certainly a key ingredient of the soldier's approach toward Indian warfare.

-5-

Strategic Cultures:
Indians and the Army

Just as the Civil War was more destructive than the War of Independence, the nineteenth century in America was even more violent than the eighteenth. For the American Indian, however, this fact was probably unknown and mattered little. By the time of the American Revolution he had been fighting European settlers for nearly three hundred years in the forests of the East and Northeast and was to continue doing so, in the Deep South and in the plains and mountains of the far West, throughout the nineteenth century. From the soldier's point of view, these were "small" wars against primitive tribes of irregulars. But to the Indians, the ceaseless wars were titanic and challenged not only their way of life, but often their very existence.

Justifications for the advance of white settlement against resident Indian tribes, similar to the larger dimensions of the pursuit of westward expansion through "Manifest Destiny," can isolate a number of rational explanations. The advance of "civilization," however, carried an internal logic and power of its own. Movements that are, by definition, "manifest" will have little trouble for their justifications, either before or after the fact. As initially articulated by the Puritans of New England, and pursued with deterministic logic afterward, the early Americans' expansion over the Indian reflected the will of Providence. John Winthrop of Massachusetts, in *Conclusions for the Plantation in New England*, offered the original justification for taking Indian-held lands:

> The whole earth is the lords garden & he hath given it to the sonnes of men, with a generall condition, increase and multiply, replenish the earth and subdue it . . . the end is double morall and naturall that man might enjoy the fruits of the earth

& god might have his due glory from the creature, why then should we stand here striveing for places of habitation . . . and in ye mean tyme suffer a whole continent, as fruitful & convenient for the use of man to lie waste without any improvement.[1]

Central to the will of Providence thesis is the corollary that the utility of the land—"replenish the earth and subdue it"—was beyond the competence and intentions of the North American Indians and that the pursuit of hunting or the use of the land for mere pleasure cannot fulfill divine, or material, beneficence. Indians, thus, came to be considered in a legal sense as little more than "tenants at will," and the notion that their residence was only a privilege and a temporary occupancy allowed Americans to break treaty after treaty. Invoking the same divine will as expressed by the earlier Puritans, the governor of Georgia in 1830 expressed a similar intention that fairly expressed the will of Manifest Destiny:

Treaties were expedients by which ignorant, intractable, and savage people were induced without bloodshed to yield up what civilized people had a right to possess by virtue of that command of the Creator delivered to man upon his formation— be fruitful, multiply and replenish the earth, and subdue it.[2]

A report of a House committee of the twenty-first Congress came to the same conclusion, that expansion was "sanctioned by the natural superiority allowed to the claims of civilized communities over those of savage tribes."

In 1830 Congress passed the Indian Removal Act, which on paper provided for the legality and administration of displacement but in reality created official justification for the subsequent "Century of Dishonor," described by at least one U.S. secretary of the interior as "in great part a record of broken treaties, of unjust wars, and of cruel spoliation."[3] Many highly placed Americans, among them George Washington, Thomas Jefferson, James Monroe, and John Marshall, had expressed hope for a more benevolent and judicious process, but by the first third of the nineteenth century the trail of broken treaties and Indian concessions had given way to the fierce determination of southern and western Indians to resist and the equal determination of settlers from the East and South to remove them from the path of western expansion.

The ensuing Indian wars lasted through the middle and end of the

nineteenth century. Before that time, going back to colonial days, warfare with Indian tribes was near-continuous but limited in scope and
duration and had no other immediate purpose than settlement protection. For the most part, moreover, these limited wars were fought by
volunteer militia, who frequently enlisted allied Indian tribes. These
wars also took place in an era when the Indians could be placated by
the temporary truce of treaty language, and at a time when the fast and
powerful pace of immigration and expansion was still in the future.

By the mid-nineteenth century, however, all this was beginning to
change. White Americans were multiplying across the western plains,
and the industrial revolution and railroad were fast closing in on the
American Indian. The army was also quickly developing, from a pre-
Civil War frontier force into an outfit of continental proportions, whose
responsibilities involved huge distances and far-flung operations, but
with a very finite human and material resource base. The army had
also inaugurated a definite Indian policy: permanent resettlement into
reservation lands. By mid-century the showdown between two ways
of life on the North American continent was growing near.

To classify the American Indian as a true guerrilla would be misleading. There were simply too many different tribes, fighting over too
long a time period, to make this generalization. Yet, there was at least a
common denominator between all of the tribes and all of the centuries.
The Indians almost always fought in unorthodox, irregular fashion:
their lack of discipline and organization, their stealth and surprise, their
disdain for rules or procedure, their dress, their tactics, their attitudes—
all of these attributes were unorthodox in comparison to either European or U.S. Army training manuals and battle procedures. Some tribes,
moreover, were extremely adept at sustained and disciplined guerrilla
war, as distinguished from irregular battle habits. The Seminoles, the
Sioux, and the Navajo were high on this list. But throughout the long
years of Indian warfare the settler had to cope with the type of adversary he could never understand from textbooks. Indian fighting had to
be learned on the job, with each succeeding generation of Americans
learning it anew.

Taken together, the Indian wars spanned several centuries of American history, from the earliest days of colonial settlement to the massacre at Wounded Knee, South Dakota (1890). But since there was no
singular Indian nation, there was no corresponding Indian national
insurrection against white rule. The scores of different tribes fought
each other as intensively as they did the European intruder. Rather
than having to face a united opposition, the settlers usually fought lo-

cal and tribal contests, regional in scope and limited in content. There was no such thing, therefore, as an American war against the Indians per se. The nature of Indian society dictated, instead, hundreds of separate campaigns against hostile tribes. Having defeated one tribe, the settlers simply pushed farther westward only to face another one. This contest went on century after century, in what was certainly one of the most protracted sets of wars in history. It was a contest the North American Indian could not possibly have won.

Essentially, the Indians lacked the necessary discipline in combat and the requisite social and political institutions to conduct carefully planned and sustained campaigns against settlers. Too often, they were forced into European-style battles, when their natural advantage should have lain in protracted guerrilla operations. Pontiac's Uprising, the most widespread and destructive pan-Indian movement in American history, was quelled during its early stages by British regulars who had lured the rebellious tribes into frontal attacks at Bushy Run, Pennsylvania (1763). Similarly, the resistance to white settlement in the Midwest was broken by regular American militia at Fallen Timbers, Ohio (1794).

The loose structure of Indian society precluded the type of disciplined military units that the Western-trained soldier accepted as logical and necessary. Indian society, in this respect, was remarkably libertarian, exalting the individual rather than the group. In battle, the Indian brave fought for personal glory and survival. The chief customarily had little power of command; after the initial skirmish an Indian force would often lose coherence, with each warrior fighting for himself. Warfare to the Indians, therefore, was more of a "game." Lacking the European's political coherence, numbers, and technology, the Indians fought exceptionally on the individual level but displayed little of the strategic and political coordination that a protracted and enduring campaign requires.

This was generally true of both the forest and Plains Indians. When the Cheyennes, Sioux, and Arapahoes declared a united war to the death against the whites in 1865, for example, they meant something much less than total war or true insurrection as we know it today. The alliance between these tribes resulted in a limited offensive that killed about 60 whites and injured 130. Their revenge satisfied, they then broke up and dispersed in several directions.

Regardless of their tactics, and despite their almost complete neglect of careful strategy, there was really nothing that the American Indians could have done to prevent their eventual defeat. Sheer numbers and technology were the greatest advantages that white America possessed. As the wars dragged on, it came to be precisely these material qualities that eliminated the Indians as an obstacle to the great American push westward.

In the years before the Civil War, the average size of the army and the resultant battles that were fought against Indians were small by any criterion of military strength. During the 1840s and 1850s, for example, the army averaged a strength of about ten thousand men, of whom only about six thousand were stationed on the fifty-four posts of the western command.

By the end of the Civil War, there were only a handful of Indian tribes in the West and Southwest still with the power and will left to contest the westward movement. Totaling less than one hundred thousand individuals, with only a small portion of them adult male braves, they engaged the U.S. Army in the final struggle for territorial supremacy. The army that fought them was a skeleton force of fifty-four thousand in 1866 and faced continued erosion thereafter, with a ceiling of twenty-five thousand in the years after 1874. Even at this figure, actual strength rarely exceeded nineteen thousand, with only a relative handful of these ever having to face Indians in actual combat. A typical engagement against the Plains Indians would number from one hundred to five hundred men. Likewise, the Indians rarely exceeded this total at any given time. The greatest assemblage of warriors for one battle was the estimated 2,500 who slaughtered Custer and his 215 men at Little Big Horn, Montana (1876).

While the Indians rarely fought as allied guerrilla tribes, their military habits were instinctively unconventional. They depended to a great extent on the peculiar advantages that their own terrain afforded. Although they too often engaged in suicidal frontal attacks, many of them also proved extremely adept at the mobile tactics of prolonged retreats, surprise, and ambush that typify the essence of guerrilla war. But the military tragedy of the American Indians is that they were neither true guerrillas nor true soldiers. Falling somewhere in between, they lacked discipline, technology, and numbers and lost campaign after campaign, despite the many local victories they were able to record through ambush attacks or through blunders on the part of the regular army. "Man for man," Robert Utley has written, "the Indian warrior far surpassed his blue-clad adversary in virtually every test of military proficiency."[4]

If the Indians were not defeated by overwhelming numbers of soldiers, neither were they defeated by the army's judicious selection of military strategy. The same poverty in strategic thinking that characterized the American approach to conventional war was reflected also in the military's conception of irregular war against the Indians. Generally, American military authorities seldom altered their own strategy to the ways of their Indian adversaries. Between 1865 and 1898 the U.S. Army fought a total of 943 tactical "actions" against the several Indian tribes of Western America. Throughout this long period of Indian battles, the army generally clung to the methods of warfare and to the organizational features that it had borrowed from European models and that were devised for conflict in the orthodox style. Whatever tactics it eventually adopted to conform more to Indian fighting were the results of the accumulated improvisations and experiences of a handful of individual officers, rather than anything reflective of a consciously developed national strategy. In the decades prior to the Civil War, the main mission of the army was Indian removal, the forced uplifting of whole tribes away from the areas of encroaching white settlement to the designated reservation lands. After the Civil War, with General Sherman in command, the army's duty combined this with a more conclusive strategy that, when confrontations occurred, resembled the wholesale destruction of the opponent that prevailed during Sherman's own devastation of Georgia in the Civil War. In either case, the military seldom budged from its doctrinaire conception of war as a battle-dominated event, with the winning side the one determined by technology and discipline. In each attribute, the army almost always came out first.

After the Mexican War, with the United States now in possession of the entire Southwest and California, the army faced two strategic options in defense of its new possessions. One, advocated by Col. Stephen Watts Kearny, recommended that large, consolidated forces patrol Indian country from a limited number of major bases. These, he felt, would provide Indians a sufficient and necessary reminder of the military might of the American army. But old republican fears of large standing armies forced adoption of the "fort" system, wherein Indian defense came to rest upon scattered, small, but numerous garrisons in outposts near Indian areas. Three major territorial areas, embracing 255 forts, were administered and defended by a post–Civil War cavalry that averaged twenty-five thousand men. However, these forts proved to be too small and insufficiently linked together for the dual missions of protecting whites from Indians and, correspondingly, protecting Indians from marauding settlers. The fort system probably did more to encourage the bloody frontier than it did to discourage or eliminate this chronic problem.

From these bases, roving columns of regular troops would seek out the remaining hostiles that continued to prey upon villages, wagon trains, railroad crews, and other visible forms of advancing settlement. Before the Civil War these columns went out only during the summer, but after the war, under General Sherman's leadership, and subsequently that of his successor, Philip Sheridan, army policy rose to resemble the total-war concept that defeated the Confederacy. The army combined winter campaigns with a total-war philosophy that sanctioned assaults upon the food, shelter, clothing, and stock of the Indians. In a clash of cultures, there was no way American settlers could peacefully coexist with an economy dependent on hunting and raiding. Firepower, technology, and the innate confidence of an advancing population permitted U.S. officials to avoid the type of strategic considerations that a more powerful and disciplined enemy would have compelled. The army was small but acted more like a large police force than a little army. In battle after battle, it emerged as the winner because of its clear superiority in firepower, including artillery. "It [firepower] was without doubt," one authority has testified, "the most important single advantage the soldiers enjoyed over their adversary, and time and again, when test of arms could be engineered, it carried the day."[5]

Throughout the Indian campaigns the army's biggest tactical problem was mobility. In the early years of the nineteenth century, Congress seldom appropriated enough funds for the army to field mounted regiments capable of keeping up with the Indians. Troops had to make do with mule-mounted infantry and, on occasion, the enrollment of frontiersmen as volunteer soldiers for short enlistments. During the Civil War and afterward, the cavalry grew into the preferred arm of the Indian fighter, although the standard offensive still combined columns of heavy infantry with cavalry, linked to slow-moving supply trains, that periodically combed the western hills and plains against an enemy who would scatter and vanish instantaneously. These expeditions recorded many failures, but they also chalked up sufficient successes to discourage any serious questioning of their methods or of possible alternatives.

Most professional soldiers of the time gave little consideration to a full understanding of unconventional war, which still was not considered as a legitimate form of combat and literally went without official "name recognition." Instructive as to how distant orthodox military thinking was from guerrilla war at the time was the international conference held on the subject in 1874, in Brussels. There, state representatives from all of the powers decided the issue within the confines of a strategic vision that, charitably, was totally clueless. To the world at large, this gathering announced that, henceforth, guerrilla armies would have to seek legal recognition, answer to identified commanders, wear distinctive uniforms, carry arms openly, and generally conform to the civilized canons of combat. They did not know it, but all they had done was redefine chivalry. But such quaint notions were natural and entirely in conformity with the dominant strategic culture. In the United States at the same time, the official doctrinal definition of the U.S. Army was prepared by a Sherman protégé, the much-decorated Union veteran Gen. Emory Upton. His advice, officially adopted after the Civil War, urged war through greater numbers, armaments, mass, and firepower, "that the United States adopt a modified form of the German cadre army."[6]

Yet, there were still a number of officers and officials, with years of experience on the frontier, whose shared insights with each other now seem remarkable over one hundred years later. Indian Superintendent J. W. Huntington, for example, employed a mathematical ratio in the 1870s for successful Indian fighting that sounds remarkably similar to that proposed by the modern counterinsurgency specialists of the Vietnam War era. "Ten good soldiers," Huntington wrote, "are required to wage successful war against one Indian."[7] Ezra Hayt was another early American guerrilla specialist. As commissioner of Indian affairs in 1878, Hayt urged Washington to fund a paramilitary force of over three thousand Indian auxiliaries. This idea provoked little interest in the War Department, and Hayt soon found himself out of a job.

The heart of American strategy against the Indians after the Civil War was often revealed by General Sherman, who personally supervised these wars until his retirement as commanding general in 1884. Sherman always believed that time, technology, and the sheer density of white settlement would, in the long run, choke off the Indian "threat" more than any number of cavalry regiments. In this respect, Sherman was a strategic conservative, believing as he did that the onrush of settlers would inevitably engulf the relatively few remaining Indians still willing to resist. Sherman had a deep faith in American technology, especially the railroad, as the ultimate weapon against the scattered and elusive tribes that roamed the western plains and mountains. He viewed the army's mission as an expedient: to protect the rush westward until the vacuum was filled and the Indian tribes smothered into submission. In 1867 he accurately forecast what would happen when the two rail lines under construction were finished:

When these two great thoroughfares reach the base of the
Rocky Mountains, and when the Indian title to roam at will
over the country lying between them is extinguished, then
the solution of this most complicated question of Indian hostilities will be comparatively easy, for this belt of country
will naturally fill up with our own people, who will permanently separate the hostile Indians of the north from those
of the south, and allow us to direct our military forces one or
the other at pleasure if thereafter they continue their acts of
hostility.[8]

Sherman employed force when he felt it was necessary, but he was
remarkably cautious. He would fight only when sufficiently provoked.
As he put it, "time is helping us and killing the Indians fast, so that
every year the task is less."[9] But when finally angered, General Sherman
reacted typically, in a manner not only made famous by himself but, in
a more lasting way, symbolic of the dominant American viewpoint toward war that grew up as the country itself did. In response to the
atrocities of the Cheyennes and Arapahoes in 1868, for example,
Sherman unleashed Philip Sheridan, the conqueror of the Shenandoah
Valley. "I will urge General Sheridan," he ordered,

to push his measure for the utter destruction and subjugation
of all who are outside in a hostile attitude. . . . I propose that
[he] shall prosecute the war with vindictive earnestness against
all hostile Indians, till they are obliterated or beg for mercy;
and therefore all who want peace must get out of the theatre of
war.[10]

Once the military accepted the challenge of war, it pursued that
challenge to its logical and complete termination. "If it results in the
utter annihilation of these Indians," Sherman commanded, "it is but
the result of what they have been warned again and again. . . . I will
say nothing and do nothing to restrain our troops from doing what
they deem proper on the spot, and will allow no more vague charges
of cruelty or inhumanity to tie their hands."[11] Similarly, when the Modoc
tribe rose up in 1873 and assassinated members of a peace parley,
Sherman reacted with characteristic fury. His field officer was told to
make an attack against them "so strong and persistent that their fate
may be commensurate with their crime. You will be fully justified in
their utter extermination."[12]

The American Indian was not outfought, he was overwhelmed. The U.S. government defeated the Indians not because it deeply understood their ways in warfare, nor because it developed efficient and disciplined counter-methods. U.S. officials had no need to convert to classic counterguerrilla war tactics; they could simply rely upon time and the weight of human and material power to accomplish the same task. Whether in conventional or unconventional situations, U.S. military policy was fast assuming a singular and conventional approach to warfare.

While Sherman's total-war philosophy overwhelmed the Indian tribes, it also aroused the consciences of eastern humanitarian groups. The American people have long been known for their impatience with war, an attribute that most recently was displayed during the Vietnam War. In the long wars with the Indians, this same characteristic often surfaced, but most importantly in the era of peace that followed the Civil War. The eastern press frequently became anti-military. Thus, the army was often charged as being the provocateur of the Indian wars and of deliberately conducting campaigns of cruelty and pillage that went far beyond the normal customs of soldiers in battle.

The greatest single massacre of Indian women and children occurred at Sand Creek, Colorado (1864), and was not committed by the regular army. A group of Colorado volunteers, led by John M. Chivington, wantonly butchered a band of Cheyennes. The resultant publicity of this tragedy led to the formation of an assortment of peace groups from the eastern seaboard. They eventually formed a powerful Washington lobby that affected U.S. Indian policy toward a more conciliatory stance. Their basic contention—that U.S. military excesses had provoked most Indian conflicts—was dramatically underlined with every battle in which large casualties resulted or in which Indian women and children were killed. The army obliged them with their own propaganda every time an Indian settlement was attacked or moved.

During the immediate post–Civil War years, there were enough visible aspects of Sherman's tactics to keep the peace groups active. However, the army's ruthlessness was not addressed to the Indian tribes as a whole, but only to those that violated federal policy. After the Indian mutilation of Capt. William Fetterman and all of his forty-nine infantrymen (1866), for example, Sherman telegraphed Grant that "we must act with vindicative earnestness against the Sioux, even to their extermination, men, women and children."[13] Although the Sioux were certainly never exterminated, the severity and determination of army policy stirred the deeply felt emotions of the peace and humanitarian groups. In another instance, General Custer's devastating blow against the Cheyenne at Washita, Oklahoma (1868), where over one hundred warriors, women, and children were slain, brought nationwide denunciations of both him personally and of the army. The Indian agent, Edward Winkoop, resigned in a widely publicized protest. Similarly, when Maj. Eugene Baker and his cavalry nearly destroyed an entire Indian village in Montana (1870), the eastern newspapers became outraged. They accused the army of barbarism and demanded a change in policy. Even President Grant was affected by the increasingly vocal demands for a curtailment of the military's influence in Indian policies. His celebrated "Peace Policy" (dubbed by some "conquest by kindness") brought church and pacifist groups into decision-making roles.

But the continued atrocities committed by the Indians, especially the murder of Gen. Edward Canby during a peace negotiation (1873), ultimately swung public opinion around the other way. The massacre of Custer and his men three years later silenced even the army's most severe critics. Although it eventually ended, the influence of pacifist and anti-military sentiment after the Civil War demonstrated the emotions that can easily surface in reaction to the type of protracted, irregular warfare the army faced against the western Indians. This culture would later return with a vengeance as manifested by major domestic protests against American occupations in overseas expansion.

-6-

Tribal Irregulars vs.
Army Irregulars

Certain tribes of Indians displayed an ability in guerrilla war that sometimes bordered on genius. Similarly, certain American soldiers, notably Gen. George Crook, were able to appreciate the style of war that the Indians used and, in turn, displayed their own version of counterguerrilla tactics that still remain rare classics in American military history. The Seminole Indian tribe of Florida conducted what was certainly the most thoroughly unconventional military campaign in North American history. The army's attempt to remove these Indians from their homes in the Florida swamps and marshes (1835–42) has been labeled by one expert as "the largest, the most costly, and the most frustrating Indian conflict in [the army's] history."[1]

With fewer than one thousand braves, the Seminoles used their own nearly impenetrable terrain, an unusual flair for hit-and-run warfare, plus the relatively clumsy, European-style tactics of American troops to hold out for seven long and, from Washington's viewpoint, exasperating years. This campaign was a true classic in guerrilla war, but characteristically, it has remained a tiny footnote in the sum total of the American military tradition. Before it had run its course, more than fifteen hundred soldiers lost their lives, and the cost of the war reached the then-staggering sum of $40 million. At one time or another, some ten thousand regular troops plus an additional thirty thousand volunteers saw duty in Florida. A procession of eight commanders came and went from this strange and cruel war, and out of them, the only one who emerged with reputation intact was Gen. Zachary Taylor. Fortunately for him, the Seminoles charged his troops frontally on Christmas Day 1837, the only occasion during the whole campaign when they foolishly accepted a major battle with the army. Their resounding defeat made Taylor a hero in a conflict in which heroes were otherwise impossible to find. Yet Taylor's conventional victory, typically, proved illusory and only further convinced the Seminoles against any future suicidal attacks. The insurrection continued while the army's mission remained elusive.

Even the great Winfield Scott was unable to master either the terrain or the tactics of the Florida swamps' elusive guerrillas. Lashing back at the criticism his failing tactics had aroused, the future commanding general ranted against the Florida residents who fled in panic in the face of repeated Indian depredations. "No General, even with extensive means," stormed Scott, "can cure a disease in the public mind, so general and so degrading, without some little effort on the part of the people themselves."[2] One of his earlier critics, and eventual successor as Florida commander, was Gen. Thomas S. Jesup. After Jesup assumed command he became so exasperated by the guerrilla war that he offered a public apology to Scott and to all others who had commanded in Florida. "As an act of justice to all my predecessors in command," he offered with sincere humility,

> I consider it my duty to say, that the difficulties attending military operations in this country can be properly appreciated only by those acquainted with them. . . . If I have at any time, said aught in disparagement of the operations of others in Florida, either verbally or in writing, officially or unofficially, knowing the country as I now know it, I consider myself bound, as a man of honor, solemnly to retract it.[3]

The reason behind these public displays on the part of otherwise deliberate and professional military leaders was simple: for the first time in its history, the United States was fighting an Indian enemy whose methods of warfare were truly guerrilla-insurrectionist. The U.S. Army, tradition-bound in orthodox warfare, was fighting an opponent who profited from every lever of advantage that guerrilla forces have always used in their campaigns against regular troops. Typically, the regular army, led by General Scott, expected to end the war in a single campaign. During the war's initial phases, the army aggressively sought to bring the enemy to battle, succeeding only once in decisive fashion, and even with that, the Indians simply melted away, ghost-like, to launch more raids against a further confused army and citizenry.

The campaign continued to drag on without success. General Jesup reported back to Washington pessimistically, "The campaign will be tedious, but I hope successful in the end. I am not, however, very sanguine; the difficulty is not to fight the enemy, but to find him."[4] Jesup found the Seminoles on sufficient occasions to seemingly end the war in 1837, when the Seminole chiefs signed a capitulation agreement, only to later abruptly break it by reverting to their hostile ways. This was the first in a series of times when the war seemed over, only to have it return full-scale later on. This is characteristic of guerrilla war. Officials in Washington obviously underrated the determination and unity of the Seminole tribe to prevent their expulsion from their historic land. Even the capture of their chief, Osceola, under a flag of truce in October 1837, did not end the conflict, but only served to infuriate the Indians and stiffen their partisan resistance.

As the campaign continued without evident progress, national criticism began to pour down on the heads of U.S. officials. The army's experimental use of bloodhounds in search of random Indians, for example, provoked a rash of dissent from northern humanitarian groups. As the war degenerated into slow-moving search operations against a continually retreating enemy, the lack of visible success in battle grew more embarrassing. Americans had, even then, been long accustomed to judge military affairs purely in terms of victorious battles. The Seminole War offered little in this regard.

There was nothing glamorous or dramatic in the ferreting out, from their vast and wild jungle hiding places, those small groups of Seminoles who persisted in the war. But this was precisely what the army had to do, in an increasingly dragged-out campaign that seemed to promise no end. The mounting cases of deaths from a variety of tropical diseases made Florida duty highly unpopular among volunteers and led to a number of short enlistments and subsequent recruitment difficulties.

In the end, the army won the war by adjusting its strategy. Military leaders learned from experience that the use of orthodox methods, with heavy columns and logistical support, simply could not fight a guerrilla war effectively. During the course of the war the army built or rebuilt over fifty forts, linked together by nearly one thousand miles of new roads. A defensive chain, therefore, was made across northern Florida, and the army hoped to force the recalcitrant irregulars beneath it. But the Indians continued to flee from one swamp to another in defiance of the strategic "line" that was made against them.

General Taylor, then in command, improvised. He divided the area into separate zones each measuring twenty square miles and having a fort placed in the center. Every other day each district commander had to clear his region of Indians. This policy demanded a patience that official Washington did not have. And neither did the citizens of Florida, who grew outwardly hostile to the regular army for its lack of protection. After a temporary truce, the war broke out again with the murder of a detachment of soldiers by Indians who had been able to hide from the periodic military sweeps. General Taylor's request for relief of command was granted.

The end of the war came under the strategy devised by Col. William J. Worth. He refused to continue the six-year-long wild goose chase after an enemy that could seldom be found and, even when found, rarely gave battle. Worth went directly for the jugular of every guerrilla's strategy: his support. Using summer campaigns for the first time (the summer had always been considered too hot), Worth led his men directly against the settlements and crops of the Seminoles, destroying their means of subsistence and preventing them from raising and harvesting further crops. His troops suffered greatly from sickness, but the method worked. Without subsistence, even the fierce resistance of the Indians could not be maintained. Except for a few scattered diehards lost in the interior of the Everglades, the Seminole tribe ended its long opposition to U.S. authority and in 1842 agreed to its transfer to reservation lands west of Arkansas. Still, even years later the spark of resistance arose once more, with a short-lived rebellion among the remaining Florida Seminoles (1856–58). But the bulk of their guerrilla forces had been moved away years before in a classic campaign that undoubtedly left the U.S. Army in no mood to confront guerrilla warfare ever again. More soldiers were killed in Florida than in all the other Indian wars of the nineteenth century combined. This war cost the lives of ten U.S. soldiers and approximately ten thousand dollars for every Seminole either killed or captured.

U.S. military contacts with both the Navajo and Apache tribes of the Southwest saw more examples of Indian guerrilla war strategies. Both of these tribes were more adept at guerrilla action than those of the Midwest plains. Prone to a dispersal-and-retreat method of war, they seldom allowed themselves to be caught in battle. They confronted American troops with the huge distances and uneven terrain of the Southwest, which simply swallowed them up whenever the bluecoats advanced en masse. Between 1854 and 1861, the U.S. southwestern command mounted nearly a dozen offensives against the Navajos, all but two of them inconclusive and exhaustive. The only way in which they could be quieted was by using mobile cavalry units, supplemented by groups of Indian auxiliaries, against the stock herds and crops of the tribe. Led by the famous frontiersman and Indian fighter, Kit Carson, small-unit forces kept the Navajos constantly on the run, while the simultaneous destruction of their sole means of livelihood faced them with the specter of starvation. The Southwest commander, Gen. James S. Carleton, ordered a Sherman-like form of total war against the Navajos. "Go to Bosque Redondo [their reservation]," he ordered, "or we will pursue and destroy you. There can be no other talk on the subject."[5] By late 1864 three-fourths of the tribe (over eight thousand people) had been uprooted from their ancestral homes and forced into the reservation lands.

The Navajos may have been able to prolong their resistance, but neither they nor any other Indian tribe could last forever against the onrushing crush of settlement, nor could they even subsist when the army was systematically looting their property. In addition to the other problems that even the best Indian warriors faced, the lack of a permanent geographic sanctuary meant that they could not expect to hold out forever against the regular army. Tribes that used guerrilla tactics fought continually but lost in the long run. Those that accepted the soldiers' battle terms usually faced permanent defeat. The Pacific Northwest tribes eluded the army for years during the 1850s by their guerrilla-style retreating tactics, but finally met battle defeat so conclusive that they were finished for good. Similarly, the Nez Perce tribe led the cavalry on a masterful fifteen-hundred-mile fighting retreat, only to be stopped just short of sanctuary in Canada (1877). Their chief, Joseph, enshrined an eloquent farewell for the defeated Indians when he addressed his tribe, "Hear me, my chiefs, I am tired; my heart is sick and sad. From where the sun now stands, I will fight no more forever."

While the army was able to eventually defeat Indian irregulars through mass settlement, railroads, and occupation, the more efficient and less brutal methods of counterguerrilla war were experimental to Americans in the late nineteenth century. One American soldier who initiated these experiments was Maj. Gen. George Crook, a Civil War veteran with extensive experience among Indian tribes. Crook began employing native "scouts" in large numbers and initiated swift, small, and mobile paramilitary units for attack. These tactics were also used by European colonial soldiers in Africa and Asia and were models in French colonial war as far back as the Algerian uprisings of the 1840s. Maréchal Thomas-Robert Bugeaud was the author of the French school of counterinsurgency later used by Americans such as Crook. "We must forget those orchestrated and dramatic battles that civilized peoples fight against one another," Bugeaud wrote, "and realize that unconventional tactics are the soul of this war."[6] His successful methods emphasized four principles: mobility, morale, leadership, and firepower. So did Crook's.

No tribe in North America was as militaristic or as wily in guerrilla tactics as the Apache, yet they, too, were eventually subdued. The post–Civil War army that fought this tribe had to learn guerrilla war methods almost from scratch. Evidently, the Seminole experience had been quickly forgotten. The Civil War, on the other hand, reinforced American acceptance of conventional war fought according to orthodox rules. With an army that instinctively relied upon numbers and armament for success, the transition to guerrilla methods, in which deception and mobility were premium, was not an easy task. Only a few commanders mastered it, George Crook being supreme among them. Through years of experience with the western Indians, Crook had become intimate with their culture, their terrain, and the form of warfare that they were best at. The Arizona geography where the Apache lived offered vast and stony mountains clustered between deserts with uncertain and widely separated sources of water. It was an ideal place for the type of mobile, ambush warfare at which the Apaches excelled. But Crook bettered them with his own innovative counterguerrilla methods.

Crook developed rare skill for an American soldier fighting a guerrilla enemy. He understood that Americans were seldom fit for the protracted and erosive type of campaign that Indians knew. Crook applied his experience against the Apaches in uncommon and brilliant examples of the American mastery of irregular warfare. He made extensive use of Indian auxiliaries for intelligence and reconnaissance. Rather than be tied to the lumbering supply columns of the regular army, he used small-unit mule trains, which gave him superb mobility. Crook also knew the habits and mentality of the Indians in a way that was almost unknown in the American army. He had spent years of his life amid their tribes, fighting the Paiutes of Oregon and Idaho, for example, between 1866 and 1868. Already a versatile and experienced Indian fighter by 1872, Crook applied his psychological understanding of the adversary with the skills of a determined antiguerrilla veteran. Between November 1872 and April 1873, Crook's army hounded the Apaches everywhere they went, using the severity of winter and the Apaches' own Indian methods against them. (Implicitly, Crook's methods may have been Hollywood's model in the famous chase scene in *Butch Cassidy and the Sundance Kid,* when Cassidy turns to Sundance and remarks on their pursuers, "Who are those guys anyway?")

Led by Geronimo (far right, bottom), the Apaches fought settlers and U.S. soldiers for years before their surrender and exile to reservation lands. This *Harper's Weekly* illustration from 1886, titled "The Hostile Apaches," depicts the Apaches as armed and dangerous. *Photograph by C. S. Fly, Library of Congress*

By the autumn of 1873 over six thousand Indians had been forced into reservations. One of Crook's lieutenants explained the Indians' dilemma against the army's use of Apache auxiliaries:

They had never been afraid of the Americans alone, but now that their own people were fighting against them, they did not know what to do; they could not go to sleep at night, because they feared to be surrounded before daybreak; they could not hunt—the noise of their guns would attract the troops; they could not cook mescal or anything else; because the flame and smoke would draw down the soldiers; they had retreated to the mountaintops, thinking to hide in the snow until the soldiers followed them.[7]

The test of Crook's antiguerrilla strategy came in 1883 when Geronimo led a band of hostile Apaches away from the reservation lands and down into neighboring Mexico, where they raided both sides of the border at will. Indian forays from across the Mexican border had been a mounting concern for U.S. authorities for some time before Geronimo's flight. Geographic sanctuaries are crucial for irregular forces, and had the U.S. permitted the Apaches the inviolability of their Mexican encampments, no major counterattack would have been feasible. But the United States, with or without official Mexican approval, would not tolerate such restraints. In 1877 President Hayes authorized the following instructions to Gen. Edward Ord, commander of the Department of Texas:

> General Ord will at once notify the Mexican authorities along the Texas border, of the great desire of the President to unite with them in efforts to suppress this long-continued lawlessness. At the same time he will inform those authorities that if the Government of Mexico shall continue to neglect the duty of suppressing these outrages, that duty will devolve upon this government, and will be performed even if its performance should render necessary the occasional crossing of the border by our troops."[8]

With at least the grudging consent of the Mexican government, Crook planned his 1883 offensive into the Sierra Madre mountains against the delinquent Apaches. With him went over two hundred Apache scouts, more than 350 pack mules, plus forty-five troops of Capt. Adna Chafee's Sixth Cavalry. Relentlessly pursuing the Apaches night and day, Crook's select force gave them no rest. Chased even to the top peaks of the towering Sierra Madre mountains, the enemy discovered that there was nowhere they could possibly hide and that their pursuers were coldly determined to follow them to the end. After only one serious fire exchange between the two sides, all of the Apaches— including Geronimo—surrendered and eventually returned to the reservation. Crook's expedition into Mexico took a little over a month and demonstrated well the sociological, geographic, and military requisites for a successful counterguerrilla strategy. Crook defeated the Apache tribe again and again, according to Robert Utley,

> by demonstrating that he could mobilize Apache against Apache in a determined offensive and could penetrate the inner recesses of bastions always thought impregnable. Also, he knew Indian thought patterns well enough to exploit the demoralization this knowledge created once negotiations began. The Sierra Madre campaign of 1883 seemed to validate all the theories of Indian fighting Crook had formulated.[9]

The imagination that George Crook displayed in counterguerrilla warfare was not generalized throughout the U.S. Army, nor was it incorporated into official doctrines. By and large, the United States still fought most of the Indian wars with troops using the regularized tactics that were the natural lessons derived from most American battlefield victories. Even against the Indians, emulations of Crook's policies were infrequent. But there were exceptions. Col. Nelson A. Miles pursued the Sioux and Cheyenne throughout Montana during 1876 and 1877 in an aggressive and mobile campaign that had remarkable Crook-like overtones, even to the point of relying heavily upon Indian auxiliaries for intelligence and reconnaissance. Miles also used Apache auxilaries to subdue Geronimo in 1886 after his band had escaped imprisonment. However important these expeditions may have been, it was, almost always, the clash of battle combined with the spread of the railroad and the settler that wore down the western Indians.

Part II

Foreign Frontiers:

EXPANSION,
INSURRECTION,
AND
COUNTERINSURGENCY

Imperialism

From the earliest days of the founding of America, what came to be called the "expansionist movement" grew, both as a geopolitical raison d'être for the American people in North America and as the ideological rationale for America's unique "strategic culture." Expansion developed both the fundamental purpose of "Americanism" on the continent and, equally, defined the core of the country's societal direction westward throughout most of the nineteenth century, pausing only for the carnage of 1861–65. When the Civil War ended and expansion had reached its natural boundaries on the Rio Grande, the Canadian border, and the Pacific Ocean, the movement went overseas.

The notion of expansion developed from a number of natural and philosophical origins, traceable to the human spirit of the settler and émigré, the enticement to "go west" to the vast and open expanse of the Great Plains, and the encouragement to emigrate in the writings of publicists, politicians, and journalists of nineteenth-century America. The peaceful transfer of the huge Louisiana Purchase from Napoleon Bonaparte to the United States in 1803, and its subsequent exploration by Lewis and Clarke, opened a monumental chapter of westward social and political momentum for the growing millions of American citizen-expanders. To Americans, the movement westward was much more than a "land grab," it was considered to be divinely sponsored and "manifest" by nature, a movement with component parts—"mission," "self-defense," "civilization," etc.—but fundamentally more of a spontaneous human combustion than a series of selective or calculated decisions. Senator Albert J. Beveridge of Indiana, a leading expansionist, embraced expansion as the duty of the American "race":

The Republic could not retreat if it would; whatever its destiny, it must proceed. For the American Republic is a part of the movement of a race—the most powerful race of history—and race movements are not to be stayed by the hand of man. They are mighty answers to divine commands.[1]

Such notions can be traced at least as far back as the 1840s, when the journalist-publicist John O'Sullivan first identified expansion as "Manifest Destiny." That particular term was created to reflect the natural outgrowth of peoples whose goals on the continent were assumed to be authentic and inspired by forces beyond control. To O'Sullivan and the other prophets of American "exceptionalism," the movement was nothing less than divinely inspired. Referring to U.S. claims over the Oregon territory, he proclaimed in the *New York Morning News* on January 5, 1846, that "our claim to Oregon . . . [is] best and strongest. And that claim is by the right of our manifest destiny to overspread and possess the whole of the continent which Providence has given us for the development of the great experiment of liberty and federated self-government entrusted to us."[2]

In this 1872 painting by John Gast, the "angel" of Manifest Destiny guides pioneers and railroads in their westward march. Sent by "Providence," she was unstoppable. *Library of Congress*

Indeed, the apostles of expansion appeared to be inspired from on high, quite different from calculated explorations seeking New World riches or Old World power and glory. Manifest Destiny, in this sense, differed from the imperialisms of the Old World that sought conquest, territory, or colonies. But it was very much in conformity with the other varieties of Old World imperialism insofar as it pursued a civilizing mission, whether it was the "white man's burden" or *la mission civilisatrice*.

From a purely national security viewpoint, expansion often reflected fear and self-defense. Expansion for the sake of national security later was interpreted as an original "preemptive" war doctrine, although it was unknown then by that now-so-familiar nomenclature. From the beginnings of the Republic, as Albert Weinberg has pointed out, "self-defense and expansionism were placed in inevitable association."[3] Even before the Declaration of Independence, the planned invasion of Canada as drawn up by Benedict Arnold cited a "due regard to our own defense." "Preemptive" war is one of America's current strategies for combating terrorism, but it was very much in evidence as early Americans grew concerned about possible aggression from France to the south and west, Spain in the southeast, and Great Britain, still in possession of large portions of the North American continent. As George Washington himself put it, in the U.S. security environment an ounce of prevention was worth a pound of cure: "[O]ffensive operations oftentimes are the surest, if not in some cases the only means of defence."[4] To extend the American frontier westward, by purchase or the movement of settlers, seemed a much better assurance of safety than the armed borders or drawbridges of Old World regimes, the classic "watch on the Rhine" of historic European tensions. Thus, the original definition of an essential U.S. national interest was the security of the frontier, which meant its inevitable expansion.

In its most formal setting, this security interest lay behind the formulation of the Monroe Doctrine, that "we should consider any attempt on their [the Europeans'] part to extend their system to any portion of this hemisphere as dangerous to our peace and safety." As the century progressed, and as American material and human resources multiplied, this defensive conception fed upon itself and expanded the original notion to an offensive doctrine that justified expansion as an early American version of "preemptive" actions. This "worst-case" scenario as a foreign policy was classically expressed by Theodore Roosevelt's secretary of state, Elihu Root, who interpreted the Monroe Doctrine as affirming "the right of every sovereign state to protect itself by preventing a condition in which it will be too late to protect itself." Thus, Root's successor, Robert Lansing, warned Denmark in 1916 that the United States would not hesitate to seize the Danish West Indies should it anticipate future trouble with Germany.

> In the event of an evident intention on the part of Germany to take possession of his country or to compel Denmark to cede the islands to her, the United States would be under the necessity of seizing and annexing them, and, though it would be done with the greatest reluctance, it would be necessary to do it in order to avoid a serious dispute with the German Government over the sovereignty of and title to the islands, as we would never permit the group to become German.[5]

In the case of the Danish West Indies, self-defense and expansion may have been pushed to a reductio ad absurdum: to conceive of self-defense against a potential injury from the potential consequence of a potential action of a potential enemy. This is preemptive action taken to an extreme. But since expansion was, by definition, "manifest," it required no corresponding apologia, not even from a national security perspective. As an assertion of this principle in the war against Spain, the Senate Foreign Relations Committee offered "destiny" as a rationale.[6]

Particularly in the years since the discovery of gold in California in 1848, and developing momentum after the conclusion of the Civil War in 1865, Americans by the millions poured into the western and southwestern frontiers and advanced the tide of white, European civilization. When the railroad joined the parts of the continent and erased obstacles of mountain ranges, prairie wilderness, and torrent rivers, and when the last of the Indian uprisings had been quelled in 1890, the "frontier" in America had come to pass. In 1893 Professor Frederick Jackson Turner of the University of Wisconsin advanced his famous frontier "thesis," announcing the end of one frontier and the beginnings of the next. America was on the verge of its "imperial" era.

Turner explained in his thesis that, unlike European countries with fixed and carefully drawn borders, the American frontier was always considered as the outer margins of settled areas. In life and culture this frontier "mentality" had attracted a unique breed of people, with their own customs, literature, and socio-political values. The Americans had no corresponding equals in the rest of the civilized world, as no other people had equal access to such "free land." Turner believed that continuous contact with this ever-expanding frontier for more than two centuries had defined the American character. He argued that the frontier had molded "a composite nationality for the American people" and that the frontier had been chiefly responsible for the continent-wide movement of democracy, materialism, individualism, practicality, and other related virtues of what became the "white man's burden" when the new frontier followed the navy overseas.

The "expansionists of 1898," as defined by historian J. W. Pratt,[7] can trace their origins to Manifest Destiny at home, and the companion urge to supervise and police alien nations soon developed an equal force in the islands of the Caribbean Sea, the Central American Isthmus, and even more importantly, in the Philippine Islands of the distant western Pacific Ocean.

America's "imperial era" had begun, logically, in the 1890s. With a reconstructed South again an integral part of the Union, and the land frontier also settled, the old energies of Americanism were diverted outward. The United States was bursting with a new sense of power and authority, manufacturing outlets were being aggressively sought in overseas markets, and a sense of "social Darwinism," articulated at the highest levels of the political class, especially by the rising star Theodore Roosevelt, was joined by the outpourings of nationalism as pronounced by "yellow" journalists such as Joseph Pulitzer and William R. Hearst. These sentiments were accompanied by a new strategic purpose led by naval enthusiasts and the great apostle of seapower, Alfred T. Mahan, whose 1890 publication, *The Influence of Seapower Upon History*, still ranks as one of the foremost strategic inspirations in history. The new, two-ocean, battleship-heavy navy, as constructed in the 1890s, had replaced the railroad as the engine of American expansion.

The academic world joined in the effort, and manifestos for imperialism poured forth from the academy's front-rank "hawks." Professor H. H. Powers preached the mission of civilization in the Philippines to his students.

To the question, shall we hold aloof, we have yet to hear the most significant answer. *We cannot hold aloof* [italics original]. . . . The consciousness of power as naturally expresses itself in self-assertion as the consciousness of weakness does in submission. . . . When the slumbering instincts of race, unity, and action are aroused, they brush aside the petty barriers of logic and pseudo-obligation without apology or hesitation.[8]

Professor John Burgess of Columbia, the Ivy League's leading cru-
sader for imperialism, was no less emphatic. In regard to "lesser breeds
without the law," Burgess urged America "not only to answer the call
of the unpolitical populations for aid and direction, but also to force
organization upon them by any means necessary, in their honest judgment, to accomplish this result." The nineteenth-century *Washington
Post* was also an imperial advocate, as this editorial asserts:

A new consciousness seems to have come upon us—the consciousness of strength—and with it a new appetite, the yearn-
ing to show our strength. It might be compared with the effect
upon the animal creation of the taste of blood. Ambition, interest, land hunger, pride, the mere joy of fighting, whatever it
may be, we are animated by a new sensation. We are face to
face with a strange destiny. The taste of empire is in the mouth
of the people even as the taste of blood in the jungle. It means
an imperial policy, the Republic, renascent, taking her place
with the armed nations.[9]

Nor was the literary class immune from the nationalist-jingoist sentiments that were sweeping the country. The poet Walt Whitman offered this moving testimony to the duty of the army in the Philippines:

Have the elder races halted? Do they droop and end their lesson, wearied over there beyond the seas? We take up the task
eternal, and the burden and the lesson, Pioneers, O, Pioneers.[10]

The need to expand was not only considered "liberating," "inevitable," and "necessary" for self-defense, but it was also considered as a
biological manifestation of the unique "social Darwinism" of the period. In referring to the Philippines, Senator Platt of Connecticut, who
inserted the amendment that bears his name into the Cuban constitution, held that annexation of the archipelago would be "in accordance
with the irresistible law of growth."[11] Members of the prestigious American Academy of Political and Social Science held that expansion reflected "the well-known biological principle that growth is a necessary
consequence of life and . . . without it life cannot possibly persist. . . .
[Americans] want the earth—not consciously as a formulated program,
but instinctively."[12]

Congressman Samuel Clark preached an identical breed of determinism derived from national character and manifest destiny: "Ralph

Waldo Emerson said, 'Hitch your wagon to a star.' When the American flag was made we hitched our national wagon to all the stars, and we have got to go their way. We cannot resist them easily; there is not much American desire to resist."[13]

Such sentiments were not only "manifest" to the American political, military, and economic leadership, but they were also accepted by most of the media and a sufficient portion of the population to secure Republican political victories from 1896 to 1908. But, as we shall see, a rising tide of anti-imperialism led by Democrats was to make some of these elections a mandate on U.S. foreign policy and, even more, on the nature of American political culture.

As a logical corollary of the American political founding itself, expansion was considered inevitable—indeed, unstoppable—and opposition to the movement was seen by the national leadership to be both irrational and ignorant. In delivering the Treaty of Paris to Congress in 1898, ending the Spanish-American War, President McKinley stated what had become a de facto principle, that Manifest Destiny was a product of an inevitable expansionist determinism. "[W]ithout any original thought of complete or even partial acquisition, the presence and success of our arms at Manila imposes upon us obligations which we cannot disregard. The march of events rules and overrules human action."[14] McKinley defined the acquisition of Hawaii in identical ways:

> Not only was the union of the Hawaiian territory to the United States no new scheme, but it was considered the inevitable consequence of the relation steadfastly maintained with that mid-Pacific domain for three-quarters of a century. Its accomplishment . . . has been merely a question of time. . . . Under such circumstances annexation is not a change. It is a consummation.[15]

Not surprisingly, President McKinley's war message against Spain in April 1898 was greeted with spontaneous enthusiasm both by Congress and the public. In this burst of excitement, Congress adopted the Teller Amendment to the declaration of war, promising political freedom to the soon-to-be-liberated Cubans. To history's lasting memory, the Teller Amendment was just as quickly supplemented by the Platt Amendment, inserted into Cuba's constitution in 1901. This unwelcome doctrine severely curtailed Cuban independence by reserving for the United States the right to supervise Cuban finances and public order.

The war in Cuba lasted for only 113 days, a reflection more on Spain's decrepit military than any necessary strategic genius on the U.S. side. But to Americans, this conventional conflict par excellence was both splendid and short and gave sufficient testimony to them that their country had finally arrived as a great power. This balloon was soon burst when conquest gave way to consolidation, especially in the Philippines.

Unbeknown to most Americans was the fact that Spain had governed the Philippines for over three centuries, and whomsoever conquered Spain also inherited the Philippines. This was not inevitable; independence was always an option, but the American mood in 1898 had little tolerance for anything less than total control. The United States would govern the Philippines for nearly fifty years, but not until it had overcome an insurrection, which lasted about fifteen times longer and took thousands of times more lives than the "splendid little war" against Spain.

On May 1, 1898, Admiral Dewey blasted the Spanish navy from Manila Bay. Although he confessed that he could not locate the Philippines within two thousand miles on the map, President McKinley sought divine inspiration from his bedside and declared for annexation. In August the American army began arriving on the islands, and in December the Treaty of Paris surrendered authority of the nation to the United States. While the "real" war with Spain was abrupt and short, the "new" and unfamiliar war against the Philippine insurrectos was about to commence. Unwittingly and against its will, the United States had stumbled into another irregular war.

-7-

The Philippine Insurrection: Initial Phase

The Philippine archipelago had been a Spanish province for over four centuries when the Treaty of Paris was signed. After Admiral Dewey's victory over the Spanish fleet in Manila Bay, the United States dispatched twelve thousand soldiers (the Eighth Corps), led by Gen. Wesley Merritt to remove the Spaniards from their stronghold in the city itself. After only token resistance, the Spanish army surrendered, and U.S. troops began occupying Manila and its surroundings. By then, a native independence movement had already been organized around Emilio Aguinaldo, a twenty-nine-year-old revolutionary from Cavite province. Ironically, Aguinaldo had been sent into exile by Spain, only to be returned by U.S. authorities in the naive hope that he would prove useful in the occupation. This was only the first of many mistakes made by the newcomers from North America.

Aguinaldo had been the acknowledged leader of the Philippine nationalist movement against Spanish rule, having won that position through his personal charisma and the military leadership he displayed in the earlier Philippine attacks against Spanish troops. He and his top commander, Gen. Antonio Luna, had already assembled an army of almost eighty thousand and had established a shadow government that included Aguinaldo's own Central Revolutionary Committee and a Filipino congress. But as U.S. actions came more and more to resemble those of an occupying power rather than a liberator, the two sides began preparations for a possible showdown. Aguinaldo's troops were facing the American army in defensive positions in the suburbs around Manila. As the treaty negotiations stretched out through the autumn of 1898, the two armies continued to glare at each other nervously. Filipino hopes for a peaceful transition to independence were dashed when the terms of the treaty were announced. By early 1899 Aguinaldo had already laid plans to forcibly evict the Americans.

The war began as an orthodox combat, but that phase lasted for less than a day. The battle of Manila began on February 4, 1899, when the Filipinos charged the entrenched American positions. When it was over the next day, the Filipinos were scattered into retreat north of the city, having lost nearly three thousand dead, compared to only fifty-nine for the United States. This battle, termed by one historian as "the bloodiest conflict in Philippine history, including World War II,"[1] impressed on Aguinaldo the impossibility of defeating the American army with regular infantry tactics. His conversion to guerrilla war had begun. By the end of March the Filipinos had been pushed away from Manila, and their capital at Malolos, twenty miles to the northwest, had fallen to forces under Gen. Arthur MacArthur.

After the Philippine disaster in Manila, Maj. Gen. Elwell S. Otis, who was in command of the thirty thousand U.S. troops in the Philippines, confidently believed that no more men would be required to quell the nascent rebellion. After the Battle of Manila he reported back that Filipinos were no match for the American army:

> [T]he demoralization of the insurgents which the rough handling they had received from the American mode of conducting warfare hitherto unknown in these islands, and pronounced by them to be new and unsoldiery, continued for two or three days, the leaders confessing that their men were over-matched by our troops, contended that they could overcome by numbers what was lacking in individual characteristics.[2]

Throughout 1899 Otis continued to judge the situation in West Point terms, despite growing evidence that a guerrilla insurrection was brewing. Instead of sending small, mobile columns into the territories vacated by the retreating Filipinos, he sent large columns in two or three directions at once. Rather than occupying territory, he ordered his men back to base, during which time Aguinaldo was permitted to regroup and to reoccupy the areas he had just vacated. The Filipinos were beginning to harass U.S. outposts and to consolidate their growing political support at a time when the American army could have been deployed throughout the archipelago, but wasn't.

General MacArthur, who understood irregular warfare much better than Otis, described Aguinaldo's new battle tactics as a modified Fabian policy, which was based upon the idea of occupying a series of strong defensive positions and therefrom presenting just enough resistance to force the American army to a never-ending repetition of tactical deployments. This policy was carried out with considerable skill and was for a time partially successful, as the native army was thus enabled to hover within easy distance of the American camps and at the same time avoid close combat.[3]

It was not until late in 1899, however, that an American force ventured beyond sixty miles of the capital. During the spring and summer of 1899 Aguinaldo and his force remained just outside the reach of American strength. Beginning in April they launched a series of minor raids against railroads and U.S. installations, killing American troops in the process. Otis sent a division under Maj. Gen. Henry Lawton to destroy them, but after taking twenty-seven days to march through jungle terrain, they had advanced only fifty-eight miles.

Although Lawton had occupied the town of San Isidro, he remained confused as to both his mission and the nature of the enemy. Cabling back to Otis, he wrote,

The delays in my movements disturb me very much. The rice fields are now in places covered with water and twenty-four hours rain will render travel with transportation impossible. The weather is now favorable and every day lost may cost us dearly. I am possibly mistaken, but the enemy has not impressed me as being in very great force or as showing much pertinacity.[4]

At the same time, Americans were beginning to understand the nonmilitary hazards of conducting operations in the tropical denseness of the Philippine jungle canopy. Out of 515 casualties in Lawton's division, only nine killed and thirty-five wounded came from insurgents' bullets; the rest came from dysentery, diarrhea, malaria, heat exhaustion, and other forms of jungle illness. MacArthur's own force, which had been on the move since February, suffered in a similar way. By May, of the 4,800 troops in his division, 2,160 (45 percent) were on sick report, one regiment alone having 70 percent of its troops in the hospital. The great strain imposed on the troops, with the constant patrolling against a nearly invisible enemy, was magnified by these geographic and medical difficulties. Volunteers who had enlisted only for the war with Spain clamored to go home. With the rainy season due for the summer, Otis postponed operations temporarily until weather and fresh troops would permit the destruction of an enemy he had faced only once in battle and which, to his way of thinking, was already defeated.

By the autumn of 1899 the inconclusive war had already surpassed the great victory over Spain in longevity and casualties. Yet against a seemingly ragtag collection of backward and illiterate peasants the American troops found only disease and frustration. General Otis still harbored the orthodox notion that pursuit of the opponent's armed forces was the only strategy to follow in wartime. Yet, his persistent underestimation of the irregulars, plus severe climactic conditions, produced an extremely cautious policy even within his own illusions. The characteristic American impatience with the lack of visible success in battle, however, was beginning to affect viewpoints in Washington. In August, the Office of the Secretary of War (Elihu Root) sent the following telegram to Otis:

> Secretary of War desires to know what, with all the light you now have, you consider an undoubtedly adequate force for complete suppression of insurrection during the coming dry season. In view of the impatience of the public, which may affect legislative provision for conduct of war, rapid and thorough action is important. The Secretary would rather err on the safe side in sending too many troops than too few.[5]

By September 1899 Otis had over forty-five thousand troops, with more promised. He resolved to end the war then and there by sweeping all of the northern province of Luzon with three columns, hoping to capture Aguinaldo in the process. Up to this point, Luzon province had been the theater of war for all the American operations. The United States was basing its military activity on the assumptions that sufficient engagements against the enemy would result in a quick end to the war and that, once the Americans established enough contact with the local populace, mutual good feeling would inevitably result. After that, it was reasoned, whatever threat there might be to U.S. occupation would exist in the form of sporadic "ladronism" (banditry) that had been a historic problem in the more remote regions of the archipelago.

Otis's October offensive was beset with torrential downpours and an irritating lack of supplies. Although Lawton's column was hot on the heels of Aguinaldo, all it was able to do was effect the capture of his mother and sister. The insurgent leader and his main force escaped to the wild mountains of the north, where they began preparations for a more elaborate and systematic adoption of full-scale guerrilla warfare. Although a number of minor engagements occurred, the offensive was simply one of hide and seek. The effect on the American troops, as described by William Sexton, was miserable.

> Many of the men's clothes had not been dry for two weeks. Constant wetness had rotted leather and stitching in shoes, and many of the men were barefoot. The majority were suffering from malarial fever and chills. Many faces were pale and emaciated, the indication of dysentery. Nearly every one had dhobie itch in one form or another. Everyone was hungry.[6]

The fact that the rebels had been forced underground gave the impression to the American commanders that the war was over. U.S. leaders were formally schooled in the art of regular war. When the enemy left the field, conventional war theory taught, the war was over. Nowhere in their schooling and training was the opposite suggested, but in the tradition of guerrilla war the conflict didn't really begin until the rebels had been swept away by the regular troops. This was precisely what was occurring when MacArthur cabled the following wire of November 23, 1899, to Otis: "The so-called Filipino Republic is destroyed. The Congress has dissolved. The President of the so-called Republic is a fugitive as are all his cabinet officers, except one who is in our hands."[7] News like this received a naturally sympathetic hearing from General Otis. Doctrinaire in his understanding of war, he had long since closed his mind to any interpretation beyond the usual one. In a national periodical of the time, *Leslie's Weekly*, he informed the American people that "The war in the Philippines is already over . . . all we have to do now is protect Filipinos against themselves. . . . There will be no more real fighting."[8] During the month of December he cabled Washington to say the war was over on four occasions.

But in a very real sense it had only begun. Aguinaldo's full conversion to guerrilla war took place in November 1899; for nearly three years thereafter his men engaged a total of 125,000 U.S. troops in a protracted political-military campaign that questioned more than just the concept of warfare as it had developed in American society. Before it was over, the Philippine insurrection against American rule brought out issues that touched the very core of American society, particularly issues surrounding the meaning of empires versus republics. Largely forgotten amid the more important conflicts with the world's great powers, this war dragged on intermittently without a visible end in sight—and without any resounding military victories—until President Theodore Roosevelt formally declared it over on July 4, 1902. Like most guerrilla insurrections that fail, this one didn't simply end, it just simmered down to a tolerable level until it faded away. Left in its wake were over 220,000 dead Filipinos, 4,234 American soldiers killed in action (almost an equal number later died of service-connected diseases), and a U.S. war bill of $170 million.

The important military events of the war with Spain occurred in a span of months. It took the United States three and a half years, however, to arrest the rebellion in the Philippines, a time period slightly less than that of the Civil War and about the same length as American participation in World War II. The United States won this war too, less because of its military prowess than because of the political and administrative control it came to exercise over Philippine life. From the beginning, the very nature of this conflict presented to U.S. authorities a challenge to their conception of war—and their corresponding code of operations—that had not been experienced since the army attempted to uproot the Seminole Indians from the Florida swamps two generations before.

The change in the situation—from Fabian tactics to guerrilla insurrection—was only gradually realized by U.S. leaders. With American garrisons occupying all of northern Luzon, the United States took up expeditions through southern Luzon in early 1900. At the same time, the United States began to penetrate the central islands and Mindanao. Little opposition was encountered at first, but military authorities on the ground soon perceived a subtle change in the atmosphere. Only later did this perception reach Manila or, even later, Washington and the American public. When it did, the critical roar at times reached a crescendo. The conflict seemed both unlikely and unreal, and the United States seemed at first, according to one authority, to be "rather blindly waging" it.[9]

By May 1900 virtually every island of consequence in the archipelago had been fortified by American outposts. Military operations were monotonously similar to those of 1899: the insurgents were so wary of American firepower that a U.S. advance served almost as a signal for a rebel retreat. Upon their dispersal, the insurgents would invariably harass the flanks and rear of U.S. columns, occasionally preying upon isolated Americans and, at times, inflicting serious casualties and taking prisoners. But, as U.S. authorities discovered, occupation in guerrilla war was one thing, pacification quite another. During the initial stages of the guerrilla war—in contrast to the last few months of organized resistance by the regular army—U.S. contacts with the enemy doubled, as did casualties. In the last four months of 1899 there were 229 engagements, 69 Americans killed, 302 wounded; for the first four months of 1900—the beginnings of guerrilla war—there were 442 encounters, 130 soldiers killed, 325 wounded. The United States was gradually realizing that guerrilla war was both time-consuming and costly.

Nevertheless, by March 1900 the United States had almost the entire archipelago organized into four separate military districts: northern Luzon under Maj. Gen. Lloyd V. Wheaton, southern Luzon under Maj. Gen. John C. Bates (replacing General Lawton, who was killed in action during December), the Visayas Islands in the center of the archipelago under Brig. Gen. Robert P. Hughes, and the island of Mindanao under Brig. Gen. William A. Kobbe. By November 1, 1899, 53 posts—all in Luzon—were occupied by American troops. By September 1, 1900, the number of posts had increased to 413 and extended throughout the range of the archipelago. By March 1, 1901, there were 503 occupied stations. Correspondingly, the troop strength increased as the war became more serious and prolonged. By December 1900, at the height of the insurrection, the United States had 69,420 officers and men in the Philippines.

Despite this strength, the situation was deteriorating fast. The United States was in occupation of the major towns and had chased the insurrectos from area to area, but there was no end to the war. In May 1900 General Otis was relieved. Nevertheless, he stubbornly repeated a prognosis of the situation that reinforced everything both he and Washington had believed since the conflict began. "I am convinced, " he said, " . . . that the declared guerrilla war will cease in a few months, and that ladrone organizations or robbers in small bands . . . will alone remain to terrorize the people. . . . The ladrone element is large. . . . The American soldier has the inclination and ability to crush it and will be successful."[10] Yet, even as he left, more and more contacts were being made with the increasingly busy irregulars. The army was as far from a cure for the war as it had been a year earlier, and the lack of conclusive operations was beginning to stir comment in official Washington.

General MacArthur succeeded Otis as Philippines commander. Almost immediately, he inaugurated a new amnesty program that brought in 5,000 natives and 140 rifles. As the guerrillas stepped up their attacks, MacArthur sent even more punitive expeditions after them and tightened the interisland blockade that the navy had already started. Nevertheless, the summer and fall of 1900 were worse than anything that had come before. Contacts with the insurgents occurred daily, and on occasion, the U.S. Army experienced legitimate military defeats. On September 17, for example, two companies of soldiers were decimated by an insurgent force, with over twenty Americans killed, including their leader, Capt. David Mitchell. The American force hobbled back to its base in retreat. Again, in the same month, almost an entire company surrendered to insurgents following an ambush attack on the island of Marinduque. This was the first wholesale American surrender to the enemy. Clearly, the campaign was assuming a dimension not yet experienced and certainly never anticipated by most high-ranking U.S. authorities.

Reports from his officers in the field confirmed MacArthur's growing belief that the war was being stepped up by the insurgents. General Bates, in command of southern Luzon, wired,

> I regret that I cannot recommend the reduction of the forces in this Department by so much as a single soldier. The duty of occupation in fact renders necessary a larger number of troops than would be needed in conducting a campaign against armed forces. . . . A single battalion can today march from one end of this Department to the other without encountering enough resistance from the enemy to seriously impede its progress, but small parties of troops cannot leave the garrisoned posts without incurring the danger of attack. The insurrectos, after making an attack, disperse, assume civilian garb and conceal themselves among the peaceable inhabitants by threatening punishment to those who display friendship towards the Americans.[11]

The district commander in Abra province was reporting at the same time that "[t]he insurrection has assumed such proportions in Abra that I do not consider it advisable to send a detachment out with less than 100 rifles,"[12] while General Funston cabled back from Nueva Eiija that

> Everything possible is being done to locate the insurgent bands in this vicinity, but so far without success. Indications are that the greater part of them have hidden their guns and returned to the barrios, though they will no doubt concentrate somewhere again before long.[13]

This 1899 political cartoon from *Judge* magazine shows President McKinley preparing to swat at Emilio Aguinaldo as other insurgent mosquitoes swarm. The caption reads, "Mosquitoes seem to be worse here in the Philippines than they were in Cuba." Both the American military and the political establishments had difficulty appreciating the nature of the Philippine independence movement, led by Aguinaldo but fought by thousands. *Library of Congress*

Despite occupation of all the major islands of the Philippines by U.S. troops, engagements with hostile forces multiplied. Rather than toning down the situation as American officials expected it would, the presence of foreign soldiers had the opposite result. During the first ten months of conflict—the "regular" phase of the war—the United States averaged forty-four contacts per month. Between December 1, 1899, and June 30, 1900—the first seven months of guerrilla insurrec-

tion—the monthly figure more than doubled to 106, despite the extension of U.S. authority over the archipelago and despite the collapse of
any Philippine pretensions to civil or governmental legitimacy. Between
May 1900 and June 1901 the U.S. Army noted 1,026 contacts with guerrillas in a chronological listing that totaled 734 pages.

Nor was the fighting confined to the principal province of Luzon,
where Aguinaldo had his headquarters. The same essential dilemma
was confronting the American army throughout the archipelago: Panay,
Negroes, Leyte, Samar, and to a lesser degree in the islands of Cebu,
Bohol, and in northern Mindanao. After his amnesty decree had failed
to dent the resistance, General MacArthur turned to other conciliatory
measures. He secured $1 million for a project to construct better roads
through the provinces and obtained authority for the organization of a
local constabulary recruited among the natives. This force, named the
"Scouts," received official authorization in February 1901 but never
exceeded more than twelve thousand men during the insurrection. Both
of these projects were intended as long-term solutions, and they reflected a sober reconsideration of the guerrilla problem on the part of
most U.S. officials. The course of the war had finally affected their own
evaluation of its real nature and of the appropriate countermeasures.

General MacArthur had earlier demonstrated an unusual appreciation of the extent of Aguinaldo's support. In 1899 he told an American correspondent, "When I first started against these rebels, I believed
that Aguinaldo's troops represented only a fraction. I did not believe
that the whole population of Luzon was opposed to us; but I have been
reluctantly compelled to believe that the Filipinos are loyal to Aguinaldo
and the government which he represents."[14] In 1900 he further diag-
nosed the same problem as it extended throughout the Philippines.
Noting their "almost complete unity of action," he reported that

> wherever throughout the archipelago there is a group of the
> insurgent army, it is a fact beyond dispute that all the contigu-
> ous towns contribute to its maintenance. . . . Intimidation has
> undoubtedly contributed much to this end; but fear as the only
> motive is hardly sufficient to account for the united and ap-
> parently spontaneous action of several millions of people.[15]

At the same time, General Hughes, commander of the Visayas islands,
revealed a similar belief with regard to his jurisdiction. "These [insur-
gent] commands," he wrote, "live in small barrios in detachments, and
go about in the usual sinimai dress, and as the people of the island are

a unit against us, no case of betrayal has yet occurred. On the question at issue, no Judas has been found in the million of people."[16]

With such a large backing, it became clear to the United States that military measures alone simply could not end the revolution. After almost two years of near-constant fighting it had to be admitted that the situation was much worse than before and that there was no indication of victory in sight. U.S. military officials and administrators were fast gaining an education in the trials and tribulations of irregular warfare. For the first time in their recent memories, military force pushed to its logical conclusion was inappropriate for any meaningful victory. Other measures would have to be found, and in fact, it was precisely the political and administrative course of events—both in the Philippines and at home—that eventually turned the tables on Aguinaldo and the insurrection.

When it became obvious to him that defeating the United States militarily was out of the question, Aguinaldo decided on guerrilla war and, in effect, turned the insurrection from a military to a political affair. Thereafter, the sole rationale for his continued resistance was to exhaust American patience until a Democratic victory in the 1900 U.S. elections would, he hoped, undercut domestic support for the inconclusive war and effect an American withdrawal. The duel between Aguinaldo and MacArthur with their respective forces and strategies came to represent a classic illustration of guerrilla-insurgent versus regular counterinsurgent. Once both contestants understood each other, the conflict was to be settled by a competition between the very fiber and support of their respective societies. In effect, they both waged the war for the other's population. Before it was over, the Philippine insurrection was more than just a war: it was a test of the determination, persistence, and strength of the two peoples.

Aguinaldo's conversion to guerrilla strategy was forced on him by the logic of American military power. He accepted it with equanimity as the only military resource left to him. As Captain Taylor has related the changeover:

The attempt to make war as it was said to be made in civilized countries had utterly failed, and Aguinaldo from now to the end abandoned any attempt to confront the Americans with large masses of men directed by a single leader . . . in making this choice he showed that he knew the nature of his people. He appealed to the hatred of routine, the lust for a wild life which lies deep in the soul of all Malays. . . . The worst passions of the people were to serve him and in arousing them he showed how well he knew the people at whose front he stood.[17]

Apolinario Mabini, the first prime minister of the revolutionary government and the acknowledged intellectual of the movement, once passionately described how a weak people reluctantly decide for guerrilla warfare:

> I am the first to deplore with all my soul the system of guerrillas and ambuscades which the Filipinos have adopted . . . but for this we have [the justification] that the laws of war which authorize for the great nations the employment of their powerful resources for waging combat with weak people lacking such resources are the same laws which counsel the weak people to resort to the said system, above all, when endeavoring to defend its home and liberties from an invasion.[18]

In organizing the archipelago against the Americans, Aguinaldo had a ready-made network—the *Katipunan*—that had served the revolutionaries in their raids against Spanish rule in 1896–97. The Katipunan ("patriots' league") had about a quarter of a million members even before the first American had set foot on Philippine soil. It was a clandestine, revolutionary organization that had its own propaganda outlets and its own political and military agencies. It attracted mostly middle-to-lower-class Filipinos and based its appeal upon the human rights concepts of the French Revolution, combined with an unwavering dedication to national independence. The Katipunan was much more than a political party, it was a military revolutionary-nationalist movement that bound its members together with fanatical oaths and blood pacts and declared a total war for independence against first Spain and then the United States. In the process, it also waged a near-civil war of terrorism against those Filipinos who showed even the least hesitation or inclination toward collaboration.

The insurrection against American rule was organized on lines broadly similar to those structured against Spain, even though the character of military operations had changed considerably. In 1898 the Katipunan had developed an internal split that threatened the bonds that so far had carried the revolution against Spain. For the sake of national unity, Aguinaldo formally dissolved the society, declaring the entire Philippines as the "new" Katipunan and vowing "swift penalty to any one who would bring about trouble or dissension."[19] Throughout the archipelago, the fight against the Americans was continued through a variety of secret organizations that displayed all the characteristic features of the Katipunan, whether they retained the name or not.

In a de facto sense, therefore, the Katipunan spread throughout most of the islands during 1899–1900, even though the organization proper no longer existed and even though there was no hierarchical superstructure united under a common direction. The insurgent organization became very pluralistic: as soon as the U.S. Army occupied new territory, the local guerrilla chief acted as though on cue, usually with the same individuals and a similar organization as against the Spanish. The towns acted as depots of supply for men, money, and food, with the local municipal president normally under the jurisdiction of the guerrilla commander. Information on the whereabouts of American troops was expected from all residents; those refusing were subject to death, torture, or some other method of coercion.

The Katipunan also enforced internal order and often was even more harsh on reluctant Filipinos than on the Americans. This is typical of insurgent units, as the infighting is another form of civil war. Intimidation, impressment, the forced collection of taxes, assassination, and sheer brutality were common tools against recalcitrants or others who simply wavered in their espousal of the insurgent's cause. The coercive and terrorist campaign against other Filipinos was so widespread and effective that it made a mockery of any serious attempts to gauge the specific degree of support that Aguinaldo had. With the means at his disposal, he waged a total war against both his own population and against the Americans who were there to control the political destiny of the Philippines.

Even though almost all the towns were held by American detachments, the guerrillas were able to collect tax contributions and to exact penalties against traitors. As Gen. Adna Chaffee testified, a notorious double-agent system

> existed everywhere, in strongly garrisoned towns like Manila and in the smallest barrio alike; all were doubtless oath-bound in the great Katipunan league. . . . In all lawful matters they served with due appearance of loyalty the American government, while at the same time they labored secretly and diligently in the interest of the insurrection. In gross violation of the laws of war, they secretly levied and collected taxes and

exacted contributions from the people, who, with universal accord, submitted silently thereto. They held communications with the enemy, and in all ways open to them gave the guerrilla bands aid and comfort.[20]

Not only was the town expected to furnish supplies to the guerrillas, but it had also to afford them secure places of refuge and information on the movements of U.S. troops. It became axiomatic of Filipino guerrilla tactics to use nearby towns as sanctuaries if they were too hard-pressed by the Americans. They would simply dissolve into the general population, immersing themselves therein, almost always escaping the attention of U.S. Army patrols. The U.S. soldiers, being alien to the culture and unaccustomed to ferreting out guerrillas, could not possibly have discovered the transformation. It grew into such a quick and instinctive, chameleon-like procedure that U.S. military officials became convinced of the absolute unity of the Philippine population against them. As Captain Taylor has written, the changeover "was quickly done by reason of the assistance of the people and the ease with which the Filipino soldier was transferred into the appearance of a peaceful native."[21] This was guerrilla war in its classic sense.

The number of deaths that resulted directly from insurgent reprisals has never even been approximated. The total, however, was assuredly very high. U.S. military records often reported the more flagrant cases—such as mass burials, the burning of towns, mutilation of large numbers of persons, etc.—but a systematic counting was never attempted. Occasional accounts were sent back, however, reporting, in one instance, that in Luzon alone during December 1900, 340 people were assassinated, of whom 63 were municipal officials, and 439 were either assaulted or kidnapped, 52 of these being local officials. Brig. Gen. F. D. Grant, in early 1901, told the *Chicago Tribune*, "In the province of Pampanga they killed over a thousand people because they would not swear allegiance to the insurrection. In one narrow district, over three hundred people were buried alive."[22] Even allowing for the exaggeration that might naturally be inherent in estimates of this type, the kind of civil war that invariably accompanies guerrilla insurrections was obviously a central part of the campaign waged by Aguinaldo and the Philippine revolutionaries.

Aguinaldo and his lieutenants were also masters in the techniques of political and psychological warfare. While fear and terrorism certainly played an important role, the nationalistic basis that underpinned the whole movement undeniably made the difference. Even General MacArthur was forced to concede that "the adhesive principle comes from ethnological homogeneity which induces men to respond for a time to the appeals of consanguinous leadership."[23] Not only were the Filipino leaders tenacious and dedicated in purpose, but they knew how to communicate their cause to the great mass of the people. Their propaganda depicted the Americans as ponderous and awkward agents of empire, intent on robbing the archipelago of its natural right of independence. The twin themes of courage in the face of U.S. strength and political liberty for Filipinos were time and again used against the occupying power. The following excerpt from the newspaper *La Independencia* was typical of how the Filipino insurgents propagandized irregular warfare:

> Our enemies will be able—why should they not?—to wheel their heavy wagons of war over our fields. They will leave the imprints of their vandal heels in our villages. But at every turning in their path, behind every bush, at every corner, they will meet resistance—a handful of men, who will check their course, who will disturb their triumphant passage, who will be the little rock to spring the wheel of their vehicle off its axle, the boghole in which their gun-carriage will mire, and who will make them see most clearly that in vain do they juggle with the rights of a people that desires to be united, free, and sovereign.[24]

Although the United States was able to control the surface aspects of the war, the guerrillas were the real masters of the country in spite of the fact that they held very little real estate. Aguinaldo was a supreme manipulator of the psychology of the Philippine nation; he was their spokesman and hero, and personified their aspirations. He was also just as personally ruthless against his own rivals inside the system as he was against those who violated its mandates. He connived in the murder of his best general, Antonio Luna, and helped remove his chief political rival, Apolinario Mabini, from office. His Achilles' heel, however, lay in the fact that he depended too much on his ability to influence political events inside the United States. He probably could have continued the insurrection indefinitely, but he realized the futility of a system that offered no hope whatever of military victory. His only chance lay in the exhaustion of the American electorate's patience against an inconclusive and politically divisive war.

He pinned his hopes, therefore, on the electoral victory of William Jennings Bryan and the Democrats who, at the time, were riding the crest of an increasingly vitriolic "anti-imperialist" crusade against the McKinley administration's occupation of the Philippines.

-8-

The Philippine Insurrection: Protest and Victory

The Philippine insurrection became the focal point in a well-executed, highly organized, and vocal campaign against American political domination of foreign nationalities. The anti-imperialist movement began in New England, particularly Massachusetts, as a reaction to the growth of expansionist and jingoist foreign policies that were increasingly advocated by prominent industrialists, militarists, and politicians of the late nineteenth century. As a group, the anti-imperialists were a liberal, reformist, well-educated, and fairly established sample of upper- and middle-class easterners. At the core of its leadership were the Boston "Brahmins" who represented the city's old wealth and its ministerial and professional adjuncts. Most of the members of the Anti-Imperialist League were lawyers, educators, businessmen, Protestant preachers, and newspaper editors. Many recalled the abolition crusades of the slavery days and, from that time forward, had opposed the imposition of American rule upon alien people whenever the idea came forward.

With the American takeover of Puerto Rico, Hawaii, Samoa, Guam, and the Philippines an already established fact, the anti-imperialists set their sights on the 1900 presidential election as the great contest to decide the future direction of American foreign policy. In a deeper sense the debate of 1899–1900 involved more than just policy issues. In the way in which it was presented, especially by the anti-imperialists, the issue concerned the very fiber and substance of American society: was the United States a republic or an empire? Between the two extremes there was no compromise; to the anti-imperialists there was a fundamental incompatibility between a democracy and imperialism.

Although the anti-imperialists had nearly defeated the Treaty of
Paris, the continued guerrilla war in the Philippines focused the debate
in even sharper detail. The treaty itself carried the Senate with only one
vote to spare, with almost all Republicans in favor and twenty-four of
the twenty-nine opposing votes coming from Democrats. Still, the issue
was not exclusively divided along party lines. The leading opponent of
the treaty was the influential Republican from Massachusetts, George F.
Hoar, while eleven crucial votes from Democratic senators helped save
the day for the McKinley administration. But as the inconclusive war
dragged on, the opposition gathered momentum and, under the leadership of the New England anti-imperialists, it captured popular support
throughout the country and in Congress. Having lost the first battle
against the treaty, it hastened to the second, a battle that decided the fate
of both the movement itself and the very cause that Aguinaldo was espousing from his mountain hideout seven thousand miles away.

During 1899 and 1900, antiwar sentiment spread from New England
and crossed the country, according to one analyst, "at floodtide."[1] Scores
of anti-imperialist organizations, clubs, and societies were formed, pamphlets and atrocity stories were circulated, and a host of prominent individuals publicly supported the cause. The national split was reflected in
both political parties and in Congress. In general, the Democrats, assisted by Anti-Imperialist League officers such as Senators Caffery (Louisiana) and Tillman (South Carolina), attacked the Republicans, whose
leadership in the Senate came to rest in the persons of Senators Lodge
(Massachusetts) and Beveridge (Indiana). While there were a number of
defections from both sides, party leadership was generally able to hold
ranks during the campaign. The Republicans came to be identified as
the expansionists, the Democrats as the anti-imperialists. In the Democratic platform of 1900 the issue of imperialism came first, even ahead of
the "free silver" question that had long been the one popularly associated with the Democratic candidate, William Jennings Bryan.

In their attacks against the war, the anti-imperialists marshalled a
spectrum of arguments that revealed sentiments much different than
the traditional pacifism usually associated with groups such as the
Quakers. In addition to their ideological antipathy to expansion, certain of the anti-imperialists saw in the continued fighting much deeper
contradictions within American political culture. The war was attacked
along constitutional lines as an unauthorized conflict waged without
the consent of Congress. The villains, in this respect, were the small
number of administration decision makers who were pictured as thrust-
ing an unwanted war upon the American public.

Another argument involved the implication of a few large corporations lurking in the background, prodding the Republican leaders, and anxiously awaiting the financial spoils of victory. This point emerged as the central thesis of Bryan's electoral campaign. In his acceptance speech, he specified this viewpoint:

> Imperialism would be profitable to the army contractors; it would be profitable to the shipowners, who would carry live soldiers to the Philippines and bring dead soldiers back; it would be profitable to those who would seize upon the franchise, and it would be profitable to the officials whose salaries would be fixed and paid there; but to the farmer and the laboring man, and to the vast majority of those engaged in other occupations, it would bring expenditures without returns and risk without reward.[2]

An additional argument of the anti-imperialists held that the millions spent on the war burdened the nation with oppressive sums on behalf of militarism when the domestic needs of American society cried out for attention. Bryan blasted the Republicans for funding the military instead of the nation's schools, roads, and irrigation projects. The administration, he said, "would rather waste blood than save water."[3]

Racism as an issue also crept into the national debate. Southerners were not the only ones reluctant to welcome nonwhites into the American system, albeit as colonial subjects. Other anti-imperialists from the North understood how America's already profound racial problems would only be increased by imperial absorption. But the race issue had another side to it. Many of the anti-imperialists had a long history of espousing the cause of minorities, including blacks and Indians. They identified the pursuit of Philippine annexation as a form of racial exploitation of the "white man's burden" variety. The habitual reference by some U.S. soldiers to the Filipino as "nigger" gained wide attention back home. This simply fanned the flames of an already-burning issue and characterized the war as an Anglo-Saxon hunting expedition. Both liberals and racists found themselves uncomfortable bedfellows in their opposition to U.S. policy in the Philippines.

For the most part, the antiwar activists were content to marshall their arguments and await the election results. By 1900 there were about forty thousand members of the Anti-Imperialist League, with approximately forty nationwide branches. Its Boston headquarters, from which over half a million antiwar pamphlets were mailed out in six months' time, was described by the pro-Republican *Boston Globe* as "the storm center of a discussion sweeping from sea to sea."[4]

Seldom did the anti-imperialists venture so far as to publicly adopt the Philippine cause; their arguments were largely domestic. Yet there were exceptions. Gamaliel Bradford, the initiator of the movement, drew wide attention in 1899 when he called for an American military defeat and "a moral alliance with the Filipinos."[5] Edward Atkinson, another important figure, became a thorn in the side of the administration with his steady publication of antiwar pamphlets, such as *The Cost of a National Crime, Criminal Aggression,* and others. He then became even more obnoxious to U.S. officials when he announced his intention to distribute these among the armed forces in the theater. Over 135,000 of his pamphlets were distributed, some of which, like the following, advocated avoiding military duty: "The way has already become plain for the youth of the land to avoid disease and death in the tropics by refusing to volunteer or to enlist in the army or navy of the United States."[6] Other Atkinson pamphlets pilloried the United States for conducting an unnecessary, costly, and barbarous war. They were usually full of tales of atrocities, widespread disease, and the needless destruction of livestock, crops, and Filipino homes.

The McKinley administration reacted against Atkinson by seizing his literature from mail sacks in San Francisco and by accusing him of treason. The public furor over the government's heavy-handed and obviously agitated reaction only made Atkinson a cause célèbre and increased the appeal of his activities. But the administration and its supporters were not amused. Theodore Roosevelt claimed that the anti-imperialists were responsible for prolonging the war, while General Lawton summarized the military's view with this comment:

> If the so-called anti-imperialists . . . would honestly ascertain the truth on the ground and not in distant America, they would be convinced of the error of their statements and conclusions, and of the unfortunate effect of their publications here. If I am shot by a Filipino bullet it might just as well come from one of my own men, because I know from observations confirmed by captured prisoners that the continuance of fighting is chiefly due to reports that are sent out from America.[7]

Lawton was killed by an insurrecto bullet shortly after sending this message.

In addition to the other charges against it, the administration was also vulnerable to what was termed during the Vietnam War as a "credibility gap." The well-publicized and overly optimistic statements by General Otis and other leaders did not sit well against a military expedition that was nearly into its third year without evident progress, despite more than double the original number of U.S. soldiers in the islands.

The military's censorship of news from Manila, furthermore, ran against the grain of the strong American tradition of freedom of the press. From the beginning, the official U.S. view of the war was challenged by many American journalists. Their view, based upon personal observation, detected a massive political revolt, and not simply the marauding bands of robbers that were often alluded to by General Otis as the primary source of the fighting. The journalists stressed the small number of rifles that the United States had been able to take from the enemy, plus the fact that most of the insurgent leaders were still at large, as evidence of a continuing war rather than a sporadic series of flare-ups. Furthermore, they wrote back home, there existed a paramilitary underground organization, headed by Aguinaldo, that had united almost the entire archipelago against the United States. Otis slapped a heavy censorship on news dispatches, but many got through. To a man, the journalists bitterly protested the censorship and continued to mail dispatches that described the seriousness of the conflict.

We believe that, owing to official dispatches from Manila made public in Washington, the people in the United States have not received a correct impression of the situation in the Philippines, but that these dispatches have presented an ultra-optimistic view that is not shared by the general officers in the field. We believe the dispatches err in the declaration that the "situation is well in hand," and in the assumption that the insurrection can be speedily ended without a greatly increased force. We think the tenacity of the Filipino purpose has been underestimated, and that the statements are unfounded that volunteers are willing to engage in further service.[8]

Despite the antiwar movement, McKinley was reelected by a plurality of 7,104,779 votes to Bryan's 6,502,925. While this defeat crippled the anti-imperialist movement, it did not end it. In the Philippines, however, the Republican victory shattered the insurrection more than all the previous military defeats combined. Since his initial adoption of guerrilla war, Aguinaldo had determined that his only hope lay in the protracted erosion of the American willpower to remain in the archipelago. The insurgents were inspired by the split in U.S. domestic ranks and, in retrospect, naively came to believe in their own propaganda. Without any real appreciation of the U.S. political system, the Philippine insurgents looked forward to November 1900 when, as Aguinaldo put it, "the great Democratic party of the United States will win the next fall election . . . [and] imperialism will fail in its mad attempts to subjugate us by force of arms."[9]

With McKinley back in the White House, and particularly with the pugnacious Theodore Roosevelt as vice president, the insurrecto cause rapidly disintegrated. Almost immediately after the results were in, the administration, released from the pressures of having to defend its policy for an election, adopted much harsher methods against the guerrillas. With over seventy thousand fresh troops, MacArthur inaugurated martial law over the entire archipelago. Mass arrests and imprisonments followed, and thirty-two Filipino leaders were rounded up and deported to Guam. Seventy-nine important captives were convicted of war crimes, and all were executed. The press was muzzled, and those Filipino papers that refused to publish U.S. handouts were immediately suppressed. In his December 1900 announcement of martial law, MacArthur stated that, henceforth, any insurgent captured was guilty of violating the recognized "laws of war" and would be subject, therefore, to either death or imprisonment. At the same time, the institution of the Federal Party, composed of wealthy and conservative Filipinos favorable to American rule, offered the country an alternative to Aguinaldo's lingering movement.

The results of MacArthur's more systematic and militant policy showed in the battle statistics. During September and October 1900, at the height of the election campaign, there were 241 clashes, 52 of these labeled "aggressive" on the part of the insurgents. During November and December, however, the clashes were reduced to 198, and only 27 of these were classified as aggressive. During September and October only 54 guerrillas surrendered; in the months of November and December 2,534 came in. In February 1901, moreover, the enlistment of natives from the Maccabee tribe (the same tribe that had earlier helped the Spanish) began the auxiliary "scout" troops that aided the United States considerably in intelligence and reconnaissance functions.

It was a troop of scouts, in fact, that a month later abetted the United States in what undoubtedly was its greatest single "maneuver" of the entire war: the capture of Aguinaldo. More than any other event, this ruse de guerre broke the guerrilla resistance and, coming as it did in

This 1899 photograph of homes burning in the Philippines illustrates the consequences of an insurgent war on the general population, who often suffer from the brutal tactics of both the guerrillas, who force support when it does not come willingly, and the foreign soldiers, who attempt to eliminate that source of support. *Library of Congress*

the wake of McKinley's victory and General MacArthur's new toughness, sealed for good the fate of Philippine independence. Gen. Frederick Funston discovered through a captured insurgent that Aguinaldo, still directing the war from his hideout in northeastern Luzon, needed four hundred more guerrillas immediately. Exploiting this rare piece of intelligence, Funston sent eighty-one Maccabee scouts as guerrilla replacements, with himself and four other American officers disguised as prisoners. After a strenuous march of over one hundred miles this extraordinary group penetrated Aguinaldo's heretofore unknown retreat, took him prisoner, and returned triumphant to American territory. Soon afterward, the ex-rebel chieftain swore allegiance to the American flag and delivered an appeal for surrender. Funston emerged as probably the only legitimate hero from this nasty and increasingly vicious guerrilla war. He was subsequently given a commission in the regular array as brigadier general, in addition to the Congressional Medal of Honor. With plaudits coming from all corners of the nation, there was even talk of him running for the presidency in 1904.

With the leader of the insurrection out of the picture, the fighting in the main area of Luzon subsided considerably. In the rest of the islands, ambushes, raids, and covert resistance to U.S. authority went on, but increasingly, the rebellion began to resemble the writhing death throes of a headless body. Between June and September 1901, scores of officers and over four thousand formerly active insurgents surrendered. By June of the same year the number of U.S. troops in the Philippines had been reduced to forty-two thousand, and over twenty-three thousand insurgent rifles had already been collected.

The insurgents were fast running out of time, men, and equipment, while the United States was at the same time assuming political dominance over the Philippines with the satisfaction of only one conventional battle victory. Since the very beginnings of the conflict the army had had to assume an inordinate amount of the administrative and civil duties of an occupying power. Army officers had to organize the important functions of the police, tax collection, sanitation, education, and the essential municipal activities of local government. If experience was lacking, the army improvised. In the main, it was a very creditable achievement of on-the-job training. In the meantime, the administration in Washington, preparing for the day when the war would be over, sent an investigative committee headed by Judge Gould Schurman to report on the civil administration of the Philippines. The commission's final report, dated January 31, 1900, discussed existing conditions at length and detailed the organizational and administrative problems of eventual takeover. Claiming that the Filipinos were "wholly unprepared for independence," the report concluded that "the United States cannot withdraw from the Philippines. We are there and duty binds us to remain. There is no escape from our responsibility."[10]

Washington then gradually began transferring administrative authority from military officers to civil authorities. In 1900 a second Philippine Commission, headed by William Howard Taft, was dispatched to the Philippines with authority to supervise all phases of the intervention, including eventually even the military. Beginning in September all legislative power of the government was to be exercised by this commission. During the first few months in which it exercised legislative powers, Taft's group passed 157 acts dealing with almost every conceivable phase of administrative life: civil service, education, war relief, sanitation, mining, forestry, the administration of justice, tax collection, the regulation of commerce, etc. In effect, the Taft commission supervised all the essential, nonmilitary policies of the Philippine islands.

In the provinces that were not deemed sufficiently pacified for the full inauguration of civilian rule, the military still exercised authority. As fast as pacified provinces could be organized, and civilian rule established in them, they were removed from military jurisdiction and placed under Taft's supervision. By the middle of 1901 civil government had begun in twenty-two of the archipelago's seventy-seven provinces, but these constituted about half the full population of the country (approximately seven million people out of fourteen million). In the remaining provinces in which military rule still prevailed, resistance to U.S. authority continued but was not as intense or as systematic as before. These areas were relatively wild and sparsely settled, and some of them had not even been occupied by the Spanish. By September 1901 thirteen more provinces had been placed under civil authorities, as the insurrection seemed clearly on the wane.

Then, in the same month, an incident occurred that almost overnight rekindled the fires of antiwar sentiment back home that had seemingly been extinguished the previous November. At Balangiga, on the island of Samar, hundreds of insurrectos surprised a company of American infantry at dawn. In the ensuing massacre, of the seventy-four men present, forty-four were killed outright, four were never seen again, and twenty-two were severely wounded. Of the few survivors that managed to stagger back to the nearest U.S. post, only one was still able to coherently talk. The tale of butchery and bloodletting that he revealed was confirmed the next day when an infantry company led by Capt. Edwin Bookmiller returned to the scene. After driving the insurgents away, they saw the horrible evidence of guerrilla brutality: the U.S. barracks was still on fire, consuming the bodies of American soldiers who had been surprised at their breakfast mess, some of them still holding knives and forks, with their heads severed and laying on the table before them. The late company's lieutenant was found outside, his body mutilated and his face smeared with jam to attract ants. The bodies of the soldiers were found scattered throughout the town, horribly mutilated beyond recognition. Others, who had tried to escape by boat, were found cut to pieces on the river's edge.

The American retaliation for the massacre at Samar would provide antiwar critics their biggest issue yet. The job of pacifying Samar was given to Brig. Gen. Jacob "Howling Jake" Smith. As soon as he arrived at headquarters, he ordered all civilians in Samar out of the jungle and into the coastal towns; those remaining in the interior were considered insurgents and thereby guilty of murder. With a zeal common to soldiers who have witnessed the realities of irregular violence, Smith waged a campaign of death and destruction unique in the annals of American warfare. Promising to make Samar "a howling wilderness," he instructed Marine Corps major Littleton Waller, "I want no prisoners. I wish you to burn and kill; the more you burn and kill the better it will please me."[11] Waller carried out his orders to the letter, destroying the villages he came across and killing all those over ten years of age (Smith's explicit orders), men, women, and children. Within six months time Samar "was as quiet as a cemetery."[12] In the resultant furor over these methods, both officers were court-martialed (although Waller was acquitted on a technicality).

Yet the Philippine insurrection, even at this late stage, was by no means over. More cruelty and loss of life was still ahead, as the Americans were rapidly discovering that attempting to end a guerrilla war was akin to bailing out a leaky boat. No sooner had Samar been pacified than it became necessary to calm down the provinces immediately south of Manila—Batangas, Cavite, and Tabayas—where over five thousand insurgents led by Miguel Malvar had reestablished their authority. Coming as close to Manila as it did, and in an area believed to have been pacified, this renewed effort revealed to U.S. authorities the intricate duplicity of which the Filipinos under them were still capable. In a campaign led by Brig. Gen. J. Franklin Bell, the United States this time moved into southern Luzon for good.

Using methods similar to Smith's at Samar—early twentieth-century examples of the later "strategic hamlet" concept—Bell discarded any notion of a policy of "attraction," believing that fear as a motive was now the only method to end resistance. He instituted a policy of reconcentration of all natives residing inside the designated areas. No neutrals were tolerated—all Filipinos were defined as either friends or enemies. All enemies, of whatever sex or age, were to be killed or captured. All friendly citizens had to move into the zones established by the military; those found outside these zones could be shot on sight. The local police were disarmed, and inside the military zones a strict 8 p.m. curfew was enforced. Whenever an American soldier was killed, a Filipino prisoner was chosen by lot and executed. Whenever army property or telegraph lines were destroyed, Filipino houses were also destroyed.

Outside the concentration areas, Bell went after Malvar with a ruthless determination that reminded many of the policies that England was simultaneously pursuing against the Boers in South Africa. Troops scoured the countryside, systematically confiscating all food and military supplies uncovered. Thousands of Filipinos flocked into the military zones, many of them on the verge of starvation. Epidemics broke out, and the shortage of food became widespread. In Batangas alone fifty-four thousand civilians perished. The captain of a Kansas regiment wrote home about his experience in "pacifying" a Filipino town: "Caloocan was supposed to contain 17,000 inhabitants. The Twentieth Kansas swept through it, and now Caloocan contains not one living native. Of the buildings, the battered walls of the great church and the dismal prison alone remain."[13] In the last campaign of the Philippine insurrection, Bell's men pursued the retreating guerrillas relentlessly, giving them not a second to relax. As Bell himself testified,

> We continued to pursue them with relentless persistence. Not waiting for them to come out of hiding we penetrated into the heart of every mountain range, searching every ravine and mountain top. We continually found their barracks and hidden food in the most unexpected and remote hiding places. We burned hundreds of small barracks and shelters as fast as they could construct them. We destroyed their clothing and supplies and pursued them so persistently that they finally ceased to stay more than twenty-four hours in one place.[14]

Bell's methods were harsh and difficult for those back home to accept. Although he was thoroughly condemned by anti-imperialists, he was never court-martialed like Smith and Waller were. In reality, the punitive expedition that he led in early 1902 was a classic of its kind. Stripped of any access to either material or native support, Malvar surrendered on April 16. The American soldiers who captured the last of the Filipino insurgents had conducted a devastating—but eminently successful—counterguerrilla operation. The effect on them, however, was at times as harmful as it was to those they were hunting. James H. Blount, then a lieutenant of volunteers and later a judge in the Philippines, wrote, "The American soldier in officially sanctioned wrath is a thing so ugly and dangerous that it would take a Kipling to describe him."[15]

With the end of organized resistance in Luzon, the insurrection effectively was over. On July 4, 1902, Theodore Roosevelt, who became president following McKinley's assassination, announced its termination. Except for the Muslim uprisings on the island of Mindanao, pacification of the archipelago was complete. In spite of the domestic criticism that the intervention brought out, the army had accomplished its task. But credit must go equally to the administrative takeover executed by the Taft commission. The policy of suppression had to be accompanied by one of attraction if the intervention was to be complete and permanent. Taft intuitively recognized the need to win popular support from the insurgents. He established a vast civil affairs program that went on for years afterward. He systematically de-emphasized the military in the enforcement of order against bandits and other groups that occasionally disturbed the public order. Gradually, government was transferred to the local inhabitants. By the end of formal resistance Taft had given most of the population a strong incentive to accept U.S. sovereignty and to preserve intact a future in which they could share. The great success of this policy during subsequent decades is a lasting testimony to both the American and Filipino people and their respective leaders.

The end of the insurrection came as a tremendous relief to the American people, leaving in its wake, however, a legacy of bitterness that disturbed some Americans for years thereafter. In the Senate, George F. Hoar—the most outspoken opponent of the affair right from the beginning—expressed the indignation of all anti-imperialists with these words:

> What has been the practical statesmanship which comes from your ideals and sentimentalities? You have wasted six hundred millions of treasure. You have sacrificed nearly ten thousand American lives, the flower of our youth. You have devastated provinces. You have slain uncounted thousands of the people you desire to benefit. You have established concentration camps. Your generals are coming home from their harvest, bringing their sheaves with them, in the shape of other thousands of sick and wounded and insane. . . . Your practical statesmanship has succeeded in converting a [grateful] people into sullen and irreconcilable enemies, possessed of a hatred which centuries cannot eradicate.[16]

The senator, however, was wrong in his predictions. The official use of torture and military sweeps against civilians by American soldiers may have been barbarous to the people back home, but to the soldier's mind these were necessary measures. Cruel as they were, they certainly helped end the Philippine insurrection, while Taft's reforms promised a solid bond of U.S.–Philippine friendship.

When the Philippine insurrection finally ended, American forces had to contend with an altogether new guerrilla conflict centered in the

Muslim provinces of Mindanao, Sulu, Basilan, and Palawan in the far southern end of the archipelago. The American campaign against the Filipino Muslims ("Moros") was distinct from the Philippine insurrection in several ways. The geographic isolation of the Mindanao area from Manila was matched by a religious animosity that had kept both Muslim and Christian Filipinos in a virtual apartheid existence for centuries. Not only were the Moros distant from the insurrection, but they also opposed it actively in the same manner in which they had fought both the Spanish conquistadors and the Manila government throughout history.

The Moros were famous for their fanaticism and brutality; theirs was a "society based on war." Slavery and piracy were key features of their life as much as their religious devotion to Islam. U.S. authorities ignored Mindanao and the other Muslim areas until the Aguinaldo revolt had been pacified, but when Gen. Leonard Wood established an American presence there in 1903, hostilities immediately commenced. Although the Moros had cooperated with the United States against the insurrectos, they resented Wood's efforts to "civilize" their habits. By 1904 the Muslim areas were in full revolt against the new conquistadors from North America.

U.S. authorities made encampments throughout Moro tribal lands. These bases were normally occupation zones carved out of the dense forest, and American soldiers would protect against Moro assaults by clearing a fifty- to seventy-five yard perimeter from camp. Often the Moro raiders, inspired by a ceremony known as *juramentado*, would simply brave the empty space and race into the base, waving swords and small arms in reckless pursuit of the Americans. During the more than two years of Wood's authority, U.S. troops and Moro warriors fought hundreds of small engagements, usually guerrilla combat but occasionally larger battles. To combat the Moros' ferocious charges, the U.S. Army replaced the .38-caliber pistol with the .45 revolver.

The juramentado practice, described by U.S. soldiers as "running amuk," originated from the Spanish word for oath-taking and involved an elaborate Islamic ceremony in which warriors swore vengeance against all Christians. Under juramentado, the fighter received absolution from a Muslim priest, shaved his body of hair, and bound himself tightly with cloth, so that, if wounded, he would not bleed to death before killing a Christian. He then donned a white robe and turban, attached a charm to his waist, and went forth to kill. Moros were famous for this practice and for killing indiscriminately without warning. A Moro warrior believed that Muslim paradise would follow the death of a Christian, and the idea that he might be killed was regarded as his reward; he had died for the faith and Allah gave him a martyr's crown. American troops had to be continuously armed and ventured into "no-man's-land" only with the greatest trepidation and terror. "He cares no more what Christian he kills," remarked the American governor of Sulu, "than you care which one of a bunch of railway tickets you receive, any one of which will take you to your destination."[17]

After being appointed governor of the Moro provinces, Gen. John J. Pershing insisted upon a total disarmament of Moro soldiers, which had previously been considered impossible. With an editorial in the government newspaper, *Sulu News*, Pershing appealed to the Moros to view their disarmament as appealing:

> You do not know when some misguided person will run amuk (juramentado), or who he will be. He may be your own father, or brother or son, and in his madness, he may kill you or some member of your family. What, then, could be a better protection against amuks than to forbid everyone to carry arms? If the amuk, when the murder-madness comes under him, has no arms at hand, the search for weapons will cause delay and may permit of his capture, or even recovery from the obsession, before he actually commits any crime.

Pershing and his staff applied military and disarmament policies with a political warfare campaign, which included a divide-and-rule policy combined with local civic action, to eventually erode resistance. Divide and rule kept the Moros from uniting while economic development projects, local "trade fairs," and other civic improvements attracted them to the occupation. This was new to Mindanao and other Muslim areas, quite the opposite to the centuries of Spanish repression, and proved important in quelling much of the extreme behavior.

Pershing's view of the Moro situation reflected an unusual ability to see beyond the purely military and to get to the heart of the reasons for the Moro rebellion in the first place. After taking political control he reflected upon the distance that separated American rule from Moro reality:

> It does not seem that we have made much impression on the native mind. I do not believe that we get out among these people enough. We have been sticking too close to the coast and to the

military posts. We must branch out and let the people of the Moro Province know that there is a government which is looking after them and which proposes and intends to encourage and protect them.

Pershing inaugurated a political policy in which Philippine Scouts led by American officers were stationed in key Moro locales to provide a visible and protecting governmental presence. This was a tall order, in a jungle and mountainous terrain, dotted with hundreds of inland lakes and streams. Mindanao alone comprised sixty-three thousand square miles, the size of Wisconsin, in which about four hundred thousand Muslims lived. Pershing also reformed the abusive plantation culture in which Moro workers received slave wages for ten- to twelve-hour days. Abuses conducted by both the Philippine and American armies were also punished. Pershing made personal visits to all the districts in the Moro provinces, listening to complaints and issuing reform instructions to local chiefs and his own staff. In one such visit Pershing appealed to the Moro sense of nationalism and the American wish to respect that:

I wish to impress upon the Moros here that this country is the country of the Moros; that they are a strong race of people, in fact, the strongest race that I have seen in the island. . . . Again I wish to state that this is not the country of the Americans, but is the country of you Moros, and we are not going to bring here Americans to push you out.

Pershing's political reforms affected almost every facet of Moro life and led to an eventual Moro acceptance of the aims and objectives of the Americans. Instead of seeing the newcomers as Spanish replacements, Moros gradually saw them as benefactors and partners. Pershing made great pains to respect Islam. "I believe that the Moros should live according to the teachings of the Koran," he proclaimed, "because I think that the Koran is the best book that they can follow." Thereafter, Moros came to understand that the Americans were not there to persecute them or to convert them to Christianity. Prison reforms, judicial streamlining of the court system, new labor laws, huge investment and trade increases, giant improvements in roads and telephone lines, schools, bridges, wharves, all followed in order as General Pershing discovered the administrative talents of a military commander. He also moved to eventually eliminate the military presence in Moro administration. When he arrived as provincial governor in 1909 every district governor and district secretary was military. By the time he left in 1913 only one was military—himself—and his replacement was Frank Carpenter, his own carefully recommended civilian.

But Pershing combined a policy of attraction with one of force, if it was required. While his initial disarmament campaign met with success, certain Moro tribes refused to cooperate. Moros on the island of Jolo, in particular, continued their attacks on American outposts, prompting U.S. authorities to evacuate all military dependants. Pershing resolved to end this problem once and for all, but he was fully aware of the degree of fanaticism that was imbedded in the Moro mentality. "No one who is familiar with Moro character," he wrote, "is at all surprised at any turn affairs may take. The more foolish and asinine the thing is, the more likely the Moro is to do it. They make a sudden resolve to die and try to get as many people to die with them as they can." By mid-June 1913, a group of over fifteen hundred Moros, using women and children as shields, had retreated into a series of mountainous fortresses in the deep interior of Jolo. Pershing's force of about twelve hundred soldiers and native scouts were armed with mountain artillery loaded with canister shot. The first advance began on June 13 and forced the warriors deeper and higher into the mountains. During the night the Moros beat tom-toms and made a great deal of noise shouting. Maj. George C. Shaw, an experienced soldier, described the ordeal the men went through during the night: "It was a very dangerous place, as there were Moros all around us and we did not know when they might take a notion to rush us. . . . There were alarms during the night, probably from animals, but while there was some firing, nothing happened, and we were very glad when daylight came."

At 9:30 a.m. they poured out of their hideouts with blood-curdling yells and screams, waving their spears and daggers at the soldiers, coming straight at Shaw's men. Soldiers in the ranks shouted out, "They're going to charge. They've gotten themselves all dressed up to die." As the mountain guns belched out flame and shrapnel not a single Moro reached the U.S. lines. All were slaughtered. "This rush," Shaw said later, "was a most exciting and spectacular affair and is an illustration of the fanatical bravery of the Moro."

On June 15, another attack occurred at the peak of Jolo's highest mountain, "Bud Bagsak," a great volcanic cone rising twenty-two hundred feet above sea level and topped by a sheer perpendicular rise. Bagsak had been considered impregnable. When ten Philippine Scouts attempted a rush toward the top all were either killed or wounded. At

9 a.m. on June 15 an infantry charge commenced, led by American officers but composed of scout troops. After initial success the scouts fell back. Pershing then released his American infantry against the fences and trenches of the defending Moro holdouts. "The effect was electric," one officer later reflected. As Pershing himself described this last stand, "They were given a thrashing which I think they will not soon forget. The backbone of outlawry and resistance in Jolo is broken."

By combining a political policy of socioeconomic attraction with a policy of judicious and overwhelming force Pershing and his men had succeeded in ending the savage and protracted guerrilla rebellion of the Moro fanatics of the Philippines, a remarkable achievement that ought not to be lost to history.

-9-

Mexico:
Texas Rangers to Pancho Villa

In contrast to the relatively stable U.S.–Canadian border, the U.S.–Mexican boundary, especially with Texas, has been one of the most volatile frontiers on earth. From the beginnings of Mexican independence from Spain (1821), this area, which includes the Arizona and New Mexico borders, has been the scene of a chronic and violent political anarchy and warfare, both regular and guerrilla, which still plagues the citizens of both sides in the terrorist atmosphere of the early twenty-first century. Although the border now hosts disorder of a much different kind, including drug running and illegal immigration, the scene still recalls a long and unsavory tradition, which often saw opponents from both sides take the law into their own hands.

The lawlessness that prevailed in the border area encouraged a great variety of American and Mexican outlaws, Indians, and settlers to encroach upon each other, and upon the civilian population, with reckless and repetitive abandon. The geographic centerpiece at the beginning was the uncertain political future of Texas. By 1835 over thirty thousand U.S. citizens had immigrated into Texas (the beginnings of the "illegal" problem, but in reverse) and were openly challenging the sovereignty of Mexico. The massacre of nearly two hundred Texans, including Davy Crockett and Jim Bowie, by Mexican dictator Santa Anna at the Alamo in March 1836 was actually exceeded shortly afterward when nearly four hundred Texans were surrounded and systematically shot at Goliad. Nevertheless, "Remember the Alamo!" became the cry that inspired other Texans, led by Sam Houston, to capture and defeat Santa Anna in April 1836, thus granting the "Lone Star" state independence, down to the Rio Grande.

Santa Anna subsequently repudiated the treaty, and the political status of Texas remained open and uncertain, caught between Mexican revanche, British and French intrigues, and southern U.S. political ambitions for admission to the union as a slave state. Adding fuel to these high-stakes fires was what historian Walter Prescott Webb called "a three-cornered racial and cultural conflict" between the Indians of Texas, Mexicans to the south, and the "Anglo-Americans" (Texans) who were immigrating every year by the thousands. The Comanche Indians, Mexican *vaqueros,* and the Texas Rangers offer excellent examples of frontier Americans in their roles as paramilitary guerrilla units.

To give order to the anarchy of early Texas, the Rangers were formed in 1835. Born amid revolution, they copied many of the politico-military features of the original American war against Great Britain. Reminiscent of the revolutionary Whigs, rebellious Texans formed local committees of safety and correspondence to promote political cohesion against Mexico. Their fighting style was unconventional: they were individualistic, without uniforms, and often made their own ammunition. At first equipped with long rifles and shotguns, they originally fought on foot, but later adoption of the Colt revolver allowed their platoons to fire from the saddle, a tactic that made them the match of even the best Indian warriors. The unconventional nature of the Texas Rangers came from the improvisations necessary to hunt down hostile Indians and Mexican outlaws and from economics. From the outset, the Texas government found it impossible to finance regular armies, which cost millions of dollars. Instead, Texas legislated the formation of companies of rangers, to be raised for three to six months (at all times) at little expense.

The Texas Rangers were deliberately set apart from regular militia and local police forces. Their organization was simple and small and, until much later, was not even considered permanent. The very quality of the individual ranger, furthermore, precluded regular discipline. He was the characteristically rugged frontiersman and cowboy who had migrated into Texas and who resented the intrusions of a disciplined routine and government. He lived strictly off the land and learned his riding and shooting skills as a youth. He fought in the winter and in the summer and was as familiar with the local terrain, rivers, mountains, and plains as were the Indian opponents who preceded him by centuries. Webb's account of the irregular profile of the Texas Rangers gives testimony to these early American irregulars:

They were entirely distinct from the soldiers of the regular army, from the militia, and from the local police. The organization was simple, almost primitive, something like the band of Comanche braves who followed their chief, or the *posse comitatus* of the early Germans. The term of service was short, either three or six months. At first there was nothing like a *permanent force*.... Another characteristic of these early organizations, and this applies to every force that has borne the name, was the absence of formal discipline. The simplicity of the organization and the small size of the force and the character of the work made military rule of the formal sort impossible. Furthermore, the very qualities necessary for a Texas Ranger made him impatient of discipline. The natural turbulence and independence of the frontiersman made obedience distasteful to him.[1]

During most of the nineteenth century, the Rangers' main preoccupation was to defend the state's frontiers against irregular outlaws and defiant Indians. Seldom over a thousand strong, they systematically defeated Cherokees, Comanches, Wacos, Apaches, and other tribes that threatened the onrush of white civilization. Like General Crook of the Union army, the Texas Rangers used mobile and small-war tactics to defeat the Indian tribes at their own game. Sam Houston gave this personal testimony to Ranger resourcefulness as local partisans:

It is evident to my mind that Texas Rangers stand pre-eminent on the score of economy and usefulness.... They are excellent horsemen, accustomed to hardships, and the horses of Texas, having been raised on grass, can perform service without requiring grain to subsist them.... The Texans are acquainted with Indian habits, and also their mode of warfare. They are woodsmen and marksmen. They know how to find the haunts of the savages, and how to trail and make successful pursuit after them. They, too, have their families, their kindred, and their neighbors to protect. They have the recollections of a thousand outrages committed upon those dear to them by the savage, to impel them onward; and if, in pursuit of the foe, they get out of rations, they can subsist on game, being dexterous hunters. What are privations, suffering and danger to them, in comparison with the plaudits of their fellow citizens.... They are accustomed to the heat of the prairies, and the severe northers to which we are subject. They need no tents to shelter their hardy frames from the night winds, but are content with the earth for a bed and a blanket for a covering. Such a force as this, continually on the alert, will be a terror to the savage.[2]

The warfare between Rangers and Indians wound down shortly before the Civil War when the last of the tribes was driven from the state. Henceforth it was illegal for Indians to reside in Texas, and all were considered to be outlaws. Subsequently, as related by Webb,

No Indian had any business in Texas. If he came now, it was at his own peril, and it was the duty of any Texan to kill him and then inquire as to his intentions. The Indians continued to come in despite of the danger, but they walked more circumspectly than ever along the borders where Texas Rangers stood to greet them.[3]

"Terror to the savage," in Sam Houston's phrase, fairly described the border wars and included defense against outlaws who crossed the border from Mexico to rustle cattle, plunder towns, and rob banks and stores. Indeed, a constant irregular warfare involving both Mexican rebels and American outlaws prevailed on or near the border throughout the nineteenth century until the early 1920s. Little-known contests, such as "Cortina's War" against the Mexican political-irregular Juan N. Cortinas (1859–60) and the "Red Raid" of the 1870s, offer typical samples of the problems the Rangers had in policing the Mexican–American border. Ranger Capt. L. H. McNelly reported back to headquarters his own assessment of the problem as it existed in June 1875:

I find that the killing of those parties has developed a most alarming state of things on this frontier. The Mexicans on the other side of the river are very much infuriated and threaten to kill ten Americans for each of their Bravos. And then on this side the Mexican residents of Brownsville . . . are pubic in their denunciation of the killing and the attention given my dead soldier seems to have exasperated them beyond measure. I really consider the place in danger as Cortinas is known to have twelve or fifteen hundred men that he can muster in three or four days. The U.S. forces here only amount to about two hundred and fifty all told, officers, soldiers and servants.[4]

Lawlessness in Texas was not confined to the border but reigned supreme throughout the state, aided by the return of armed and embittered Confederate veterans, the arrival of carpetbaggers from the North, the rule of reconstruction, the presence of Union armies in occupation, and the growth of the Ku Klux Klan as a major homegrown terrorist outfit. To police what Webb has called "a lawless land,"[5] Texas Rangers formed what came to be known as the Frontier Battalion, initially led by a Maj. John B. Jones, whose task, as he related it, was both unconventional and multifaceted.

> Besides the scouting for Indians, the battalion has rendered much service to the frontier people by breaking up bands of desperadoes who had established themselves in those thirty settled counties, where they could depredate upon the property of good citizens, secure from arrest by the ordinary processes of law, and by turning over to the civil authorities many cattle and horse thieves, and other fugitives from justice in the older counties.[6]

Such a condition was fairly typical for Texas and the border during the remainder of the nineteenth century. Texas Rangers maintained a diligence in the region throughout this time period, as hundreds of skirmishes within the triangle—Indians, Mexicans, and Texans—persisted into the twentieth century. The conflicts among these antagonists have long since been erased from the collective memory, but disputes such as the Mason County War (between ethnic Germans and Texans), the Kimble County Clean-Up (of thieves and armed gangs), the El Paso Salt War (Mexican riots against U.S.-owned salt preserves), and the Las Cuevas War (border raids against Mexican soldiers and guerrillas) kept the Texas Rangers busy against banditry and irregular violence both in Texas and, at times, across the frontier inside Mexico.

In the twentieth century the Texas Rangers continued their patrols against bandits at home but saw increased service on the border, particularly during the 1910 Mexican revolution, which gave rise to dramatic cross-border forays by Pancho Villa and other politically driven "banditos." As a finale to nearly a century of existence as independent, American paramilitary units, a group of six Texas Rangers, led by Capt. Frank Hamer, ambushed and killed the notorious bank robbers and murderers Bonnie Parker and Clyde Barrow on May 23, 1934. Today, the Rangers use modern technology and information-war tactics to hunt illegal aliens and terrorists in the post-9/11 atmosphere, true descendants of their original namesakes. Their stubborn tenacity over nearly two centuries attests to the lasting American capacity for self-defense either within or outside official authority.

The origins of the Mexican War (1846–48) are still today a topic of controversy among those few Americans who have bothered to study it. Yet, this long forgotten conflict may have experienced an unwelcome and troubling renaissance, especially within the increasing Latino immigrant population of California, where the war serves as a convenient political platform for a resurgent Hispanic nationalistic revanche. This goes far beyond the boundaries of this book, but it is important to remember that, like many other conflicts in U.S. history—the War of 1812, certain of the Indian campaigns, the Vietnam War, and the present war in Iraq—many of America's great conventional contests developed domestic political controversy that never really ended. The evolution of these conflicts into counterterrorist and guerrilla operations has prompted even further division and protest that never really ended. In some U.S. quarters, the Mexican War remains a live and valid issue today, just as the Vietnam War dominated much of the 2004 presidential race.

The capture of the U.S. presidency in 1844 by the expansionist Democrat, James K. Polk of Tennessee, probably made war with Mexico inevitable. Embracing the doctrine of Manifest Destiny, the Democrat platform called for an immediate "reannexation of Texas." Polk was also intensely interested in acquiring California from Mexico, and early in his term he offered $25 million to the Mexican government. Mexico not only refused to entertain the gesture but severed diplomatic relations and threatened war when the United States finally annexed Texas on July 4, 1845.

Polk was prepared to force a showdown, and on January 3, 1846, he dispatched fifteen hundred men under Gen. Zachary Taylor to march south to the Rio Grande in direct proximity to the Mexican army, encamped on the other side. The Mexicans obliged him and attacked Taylor on April 24. In his war message, Polk made much of the idea that the United States was attacked on its own territory, justifying passage of a declaration of war by Congress. While a patriotic Congress overwhelmingly approved war, a certain Whig congressman, Abraham Lincoln of Illinois, offered a number of resolutions that requested evidence of the exact "spot" on American soil where the attack took place. Since Mexico's claim to the land on the northern side of the Rio Grande had a certain historic and legal validity, Lincoln's point was not lost on others. So persistent was Lincoln in his "spot" resolutions that he came to be known as "Spotty" Lincoln. As the war went on, more antislavery northern agitators, most of them Whigs, labeled Polk a liar, with the nickname "Polk the Mendacious."

Ironically, one person ardently opposed to the war with Mexico was, arguably, America's greatest—and most grimly violent—prosecutor of war, Ulysses S. Grant. As a lieutenant fresh out of West Point in 1847, Grant helped wage the war against Mexico despite the misgivings he privately entertained. In his *Memoirs*, published shortly before his death in 1885, Grant's passion against the Mexican War was emphatic. He labeled the conflict as "the most unjust war ever waged by a stronger against a weaker nation . . . an instance of a republic following the bad example of European monarchies."[7]

Although subsequent historians, notably Justin Smith in his thoroughly researched two-volume book *The War With Mexico*, have disagreed with Grant, it is true, as John Eisenhower has written, that "without a doubt, the preponderance of American opinion has agreed with Grant that the United States treated Mexico unjustly."[8]

While the beginnings of the Mexican War saw widespread support both in Congress and in the general population, some of this support began to wear thin as casualties mounted and as the contest went into its second year without result. The cost in American lives, especially measured in pre–Civil War terms, was staggering. Of the more than one hundred thousand volunteers who eventually served, 13,768 died (most from disease), a figure that, Eisenhower writes, remains "the highest death rate of any war in our history."

The conduct of the conventional war campaign, however, is still a classic in American military history, especially by the infantry, logistical, and artillery tactics. It is still not fully appreciated how difficult the logistics of operating a volunteer army inside Mexico's vast interior was, especially for an army that had never operated beyond the confines of American soil. Nor has it been fully appreciated how far outnumbered U.S. forces actually were, considering that the commanding general, Winfield Scott, had only six thousand soldiers in 1847 amid a hostile population of seven million. Even after this figure was augmented to twenty-four thousand, the Americans were outnumbered in every single action of consequence. On February 22–23, 1847, for example, General Taylor's lumbering but weakened columns had crossed the Rio Grande with five thousand men, only to be met at Buena Vista by Santa Anna with over twenty thousand. After a bloody engagement, the Mexicans were beaten back by the vast American superiority in firepower. Similarly, Scott's campaign inland from Veracruz on the Gulf Coast depended upon artillery firepower, since he also was outnumbered in each engagement. With limited resources, the U.S. Army did not really *conquer* Mexico, but rather it was able to keep supply lines open and to capture vital areas such as Mexico City, Veracruz, Tampico, Cuernavaca, Pachuca, and Toluca through the use of superior technology. John Eisenhower has also noted this critical feature of the Mexican campaign, which would subsequently define the essential quality of the American way of war.

> Logistical factors, then, restricted the amount of force that the United States could deliver to any given point inland. With the size of the armies so limited, American troops were outnumbered in every inland battle fought. Taylor's and Scott's men were much better organized, disciplined, and motivated than their Mexican counterparts; but in some instances, as at Buena Vista, Mexican numerical superiority was so great that decimation of the American force would have been inevitable save for one factor: superior weaponry and the ability to use it.[9]

In the course of the war, as Mexican defeats multiplied and the occupation of major cities became a reality, remnants of the Mexican army, in league with the citizenry, adopted guerrilla tactics. There was a precedent for this, as guerrillas had helped defeat the Spanish army in the path toward independence in 1821. Most of this action began in March 1847, when Scott landed at Veracruz and began his march westward to Mexico City, a distance of about two hundred miles. The scene was the broken and mountainous country—the so-called "Veracruz line"—that consisted of a succession of peaks and gorges, narrow mountain passages, and forested thickets; ideal country for the type of guerrilla action the Mexican irregulars had resorted to after the defeat of their main army.

The Mexican guerrillas carried out successful attacks on the American army. They ambushed Scott's line and killed isolated units whenever they roamed too far away from the main body of the army. In April the guerrilla leader J. C. Robelledo captured ten supply wagons. In June Colonel McIntosh lost one-quarter of his wagon trains and a number of men in passing westward along the Veracruz line. In July General Pierce lost one hundred out of his force of one thousand to a guerrilla raid; Captain Wells then lost forty out of his two hundred men. The situation was approaching major proportions, but the regular command floundered in its initial tactics, as related by J. J. Oswandel in his review of a soldier's diary:

> On Thursday several parties went out after *pollitos* and *carne*, [they] "fell in with some rancheros or guerrillas . . . the result was . . . that several of our men were killed." On Friday the Illinois company went out after *carne* and guerrillas; they came back without dead guerrillas but with two dead soldiers. Saturday two men belong to the Illinois regiment and one from the New York regiment were killed by guerrillas. Sunday morning more Illinois men went out to avenge the death of their companions. Later in the afternoon they returned. Two of their men had been lassoed, dragged on the ground at full speed, and speared to death.[10]

The transformation to guerrilla war was endorsed by the Mexican government, including Gen. Santa Anna. "Guerrillas of vengeance" were instructed to make "war without pity. Let the echo of the mountains repeat the cry of war and liberty" proclaimed the Congress of Veracruz.[11]

Another guerrilla leader, Antonio Canales, claimed responsibility for the murder of 161 Americans in one month alone. To avenge these deaths, Scott sent Texas Rangers under Capt. Samuel A. Walker against the mountain partisans of Mexico. Walker struck them a dose of their own medicine. On June 20 his men caught a group of guerrillas by surprise and killed the entire lot. Walker's cry was "no quarter," and— true to his word—he took no prisoners. Walker and his Rangers remained on the Veracruz line throughout the summer of 1847, scouting the roads and chasing the partisans away. He often brought in captured supplies and horses, but he rarely brought a Mexican back. An observer of the time has described how this nineteenth-century counterinsurgency soldier behaved:

> Should Capt. Walker come across the guerrillas God help them, for he seldom brings in prisoners. The Captain and most all of his men are very prejudiced and embittered against every guerrilla in the country.[12]

Justin Smith, in his landmark 1919 study, has given us reasons why American soldiers came to hate guerrillas just as so many of their predecessors had:

The dagger, said the official newspaper, was the favorite weapon of the people. Unarmed men could burn wagons and intercept communications, it was pointed out. Even women and children could help. A thorough knowledge of the country, its mountains and its by-paths, would evidently constitute an enormous advantage. Light corps of the abstemious rancheros, embarrassed with no baggage, could travel quickly day and night, concentrate in large numbers against an American detachment, strike, vanish, and then, when least expected, reappear, making the most of all neglects, all mistakes, nullifying superior strength by avoiding it, and nullifying discipline by fighting in a style that had no need of discipline. Situated even more favorably than Spain for such warfare, the Mexicans were to outdo her example.[13]

The U.S. infantry had very little success in ferreting out the armed guerrillas of Mexico, but mobile and light units, such as Walker's, were able to pursue the Mexican partisans without rest. When Walker was killed in October 1847, President Polk himself instructed another Texas Ranger, Col. Jack Hays, to finish the job. Hays's men each carried a rifle and four pistols. They wore outlandish clothing: long-tailed blue coats and bobtailed black ones, felt hats, panama hats, and black leather caps. Most of them sported long and bushy beards. But they knew how to do the job. Hays was as merciless as was Walker before him. No quarter was given, and the Mexican insurgents were hounded day and night.

By the end of 1847 the U.S. command was pursuing the conclusion of the Mexican War in earnest. In December an order was given that all guerrillas caught should be executed on sight. The Americans were now eager to control the guerrilla problem. As described by Justin Smith, this endeavor involved an energetic counterguerrilla war deep inside Mexico.

Infuriated by their treacheries and cruelties, the Americans were persistent and unsparing in severity. Patrols who seemed never to sleep hunted out their nests in the mountains. On the march, flanking parties would force their way through the woods five miles or more from the road to catch them between two fires. The torch was applied with much liberality on suspicion, and sometimes on general principles, to huts and villages; and in the end a black swath of devastation, leagues in width, marked the route.[14]

True to form, and in search of much-needed supplies, the Mexican guerrillas began to prey upon their own people. They plundered their own society, and frantic complaints started to come in for the Americans to protect the Mexican population against the insurgents. The guerrillas robbed women and children and killed those civilians who refused cooperation. They pillaged churches and stores, seized bank funds, and attacked haciendas.

In the states of Puebla, Mexico, and Oaxaca, guerrillas were organized by the Mexican general Jose Rea. His officers adopted a set of insurgency "rules," but here, too, the guerrillas wantonly attacked unarmed civilians as well as American soldiers. Forces under Gen. Joseph Lane cornered Rea's irregulars at the city of Puebla, where a short firefight drove them away. Lane followed the remainder some twenty miles southwest, where his artillery destroyed their hideouts in the town of Atlixo. Aided by Texas Rangers, Lane then went after other guerrilla forces on the roads beyond Mexico City, where he routed them time and again. Inside the capital itself, the Texas Rangers quickly restored order their own way. As the memoirs of one observer recalled,

> When Adam Allsens of Robert's company was murdered in a part of the city called "Cutthroat," the Rangers took a bloody vengeance. The Mexicans carried in their dead on a wooden litter. At breakfast time they had brought in fifty-three corpses. . . . In the evening the Captain reported more than eighty bodies lying in the morgue. . . . They had been shot in the streets and left lying.[15]

By February 1848 Rea was finished as a partisan leader and a peace treaty was signed by the two governments. But for months thereafter the Veracruz line continued to witness lawless ambush attacks and robberies by Mexican irregulars who refused to acknowledge the war's end.

Justin Smith has related the savagery of the Mexican guerrillas against their own kind, a savagery almost unmatched in history.

> By taking bribes for letting merchandise pass up to the interior and sometimes even guarding it, they violated the laws on which their existence rested. Mostly they were brave only where they felt safe. When laden with booty they would scatter to their homes, no matter how important the business in hand.

Rivalries and even hostilities between parties operating in the same district arose. Cooperation could seldom be reckoned upon, and hardly any would face the climate far above Jalapa. Soon learning that it was more wholesome to waylay Mexicans than Americans, they plundered their fellow-countrymen without ceremony; and they would rob even old women or young children of their needful clothing. Sheafs of complaints against them piled up in the state and national archives. People organized to fight them, and sometimes appealed to the Americans against the very men who were to have been their champions. "The Mexicans have sown to the storm, they are now reaping the whirlwind," said an American officer.[16]

The generous terms of the 1848 Treaty of Guadalupe Hidalgo, which confirmed Texas as a U.S. state and ceded all of New Mexico and California to the United States, by no means ended the expansionist drive of the American nation. The fact that few Mexicans became American as a result of the war mattered little either, for the relatively swift victory only nurtured expansionism and raised the idea of Manifest Destiny to a higher level of sophistication. The Mexican War established a greater trend toward power and expansion that subsequently led to further interventions in the Caribbean and, when the time came, back into Mexico again. Behind this movement was the notion that American political ideals are available for a near-universal transfer, whether the recipient is ready and willing or not. In the twentieth century this idea was espoused by President Woodrow Wilson and has since been termed by foreign policy analysts as "Wilsonianism." As Albert Weinberg described it nearly seventy-five years ago,

> Expansionist ideology changed during the strange tutelage of a war from an almost Nietzschean self-realization to a quasi-altruism. The moral inspiration of the expansionists during the [Mexican] war was derived from the conception of a religious duty to regenerate the unfortunate people of the enemy country by bringing them into the life-giving shrine of American democracy.[17]

The spirit of expansionist embrace through annexation began as early as the spring of 1847 and grew into a national ideology by the end of the war. By 1848 nearly every avenue of the American media, including almost every newspaper, was calling for the absorption of defeated Mexico into the nation. The expressions of the *New York Herald* were typical of the sentiment behind the newly found spirit of democratic expansionism: "The universal Yankee nation can regenerate and disenthrall the people of Mexico in a few years; and we believe it is a part of our destiny to civilize that beautiful country and enable its inhabitants to appreciate some of the many advantages and blessings they enjoy."[18]

The groundswell of American opinion toward an overlordship of Mexico, and in some cases the remainder of Latin America, has been described as nothing less than an imperialist ideology, which, in Weinberg's words, "presented the mission of regeneration as a ground for an effort or a willingness to acquire all Mexico, a large part of it, or at least a virtual protectorate involving indefinitely a military occupation."[19] During the 1848 Democratic National Convention, the new American mission abroad received official party endorsement. The words of Senator H. V. Johnson were fairly typical, an early version of that same ideological embrace that most Americans assume to be original to Woodrow Wilson. Not so, as Johnson's ringing endorsement of a war to make "the world safe for democracy" (or at least Mexico) should demonstrate:

> I would not force the adoption of our form of government upon any people by the sword. But if war is forced upon us, as this has been, and the increase of our territory, and consequently the extension of the area of human liberty and happiness, shall be one of the incidents of such a contest, I believe we should be recreant to our noble mission, if we refused acquiescence in the high purposes of a wise Providence. War has its evils. In all ages it has been the minister of wholesale death and appalling desolation; but however inscrutable to us, it has also been made, by the Allwise Dispenser of events, the instrumentality of accomplishing the great end of human elevation and human happiness. . . . It is in this view, that I subscribe to the doctrine of "manifest destiny."[20]

The poet, Carl Schurz, in a popular essay on Manifest Destiny, inspired the American people in the belief that "this republic, being charged with the mission of bearing the banner of freedom over the whole civilized world, could transform any country, inhabited by any kind of population, into something like itself simply by extending over it the magic charm of its institutions."[21]

Nevertheless, the arrival of the treaty that ended the war presented the American people with a largess of territorial gain and a fait accompli that satisfied most of the country and led to a general war-weariness against further projects of intervention. Yet, the aspiration to extend and project the American shadow over Mexico never entirely disappeared and was often accompanied by the felt need to intervene against potential European intrusions. For this reason, Polk urged an occupation of Yucatan in 1848, and ten years later President James Buchanan offered a similar proposal that the U.S. occupy northern Mexico. French armed intervention into Mexico during the Civil War, with the installation of the Archduke Maximilian as emperor, led to strong U.S. protests once the war ended. But war with France was averted when the Mexicans themselves overthrew and executed this pretender in 1867. The great exhaustions of the Civil War arrested any further American imperial expansion against Mexico. The latent urge to expand American ideals and symbols of democracy, however, never fell very far from the surface of the American ideology and would resume in the Caribbean in the early twentieth century.

When Mexico collapsed into another period of chaos in 1910 Americans reacted with another sense of mission. In this case, the thirty-five-year dictatorship of Mexican president Porfirio Diaz had finally ended, and after it came political anarchy. For the next ten years Mexico experienced eleven presidents, all of whom assumed office through either murder or revolution. Nine of these served between 1911 and 1915, one for a term that lasted exactly twenty-eight minutes. The repercussions of these disorders were not seriously felt on the U.S.–Mexico border until 1912, when skirmishes occurred in Juarez, opposite El Paso. In 1914 violence erupted at the seaport of Tampico, and a party of Americans was arrested and detained. President Wilson refused to recognize the administration of President (Gen.) Victoriano Huerta, and announcing that he was "going to teach the South American republics to elect good men," sent troops to occupy Veracruz in April. Nineteen Americans and 126 Mexicans died in the operation, but Wilson defiantly upheld the morality of the new renaissance of the American "mission": "We are the friends of constitutional government in America; we are more than its friends, we are its champions; because in no other way can our neighbors, to whom we would wish in every way to make proof of our friendship, work out their own development in peace and liberty."[22]

Two years later, in early 1916, the same type of political and social anarchy on the border led Wilson on still another expedition into Mexico.

This was preceded by two audacious military strikes by the northern guerrilla jefe, Pancho Villa. The first of these occurred in January, when Villa's band murdered sixteen American engineers in a train robbery near Sonora. Villa's army, which at one time numbered about eight thousand partisans or "Villistas," then crossed the border on March 9, 1916, and destroyed the town of Columbus, New Mexico, killing eight U.S. soldiers and ten civilians. At the time, Villa was already forty-five years old and had an outlaw and insurgent past stretching back to his teens. But his appetite for terror and war was combined with a political savvy that understood the attraction of policies of force combined with a façade of socialist-populism. He appreciated the peasant's demand for land reform, and his guerrilla bands were deliberately generous in civic works—repairing buildings and streets and engaging in widely publicized demonstrations of land distribution. At the same time, he led an army of terrorists/killers, with captains such as Fausto Borunda, known to never give quarter, and Rodolfo Fierro, alleged to have killed three hundred federal prisoners on one spot.

Villa never specifically revealed the motivation for his cross-border raid in 1916. It may have come as revenge against a U.S. arms embargo. Some have speculated that he was retaliating against an earlier American murder of several Mexican nationals in El Paso; others believe that his purpose was to spark another U.S.–Mexican war, a conflict that could have propelled him to the presidency. There is also the theory that Villa's ego had promoted his raids, since years of insurgency had failed to win power for the Villistas and, indeed, his forces were dwindling. He needed, according to this hypothesis, another attention-grabber. This, after all, was a guerrilla movement that was the first in history to use film and "spin" in pursuit of its aims. Villa was a masterful propagandist and sought the aid of Hollywood movie studios to advertise his methods and efforts to overthrow the Mexican government. Silent film crews, in fact, had crossed the border to enhance Villa's image as a modern Mexican Robin Hood. Although most of the battle scenes in these first-edition silent films were staged, some were also authentic, giving the U.S. public a glimpse of history's first documentaries of actual war.

Villa's image as a defender of the poor and downtrodden, however, masked a fierce and cruel political personality. Relentless in his pursuit of power, he cut a wide swath through northern Mexico and ruled as a virtual dictator. His weapons were, as was typical for guerrillas, stolen from the Mexican government, smuggled from the United States, or exacted by force and terror from the towns of Chihuahua province. Villa was an early twentieth-century terrorist, both against the inhabitants in the areas where he reigned and against the American population where his murderous raids took place. While certainly not as powerful as the modern terrorist network of 9/11 fame, Villa's destruction of an American town was equally effective in its own time in arousing the indignation and vengeance of the American people.

Whatever his motive for the raid against Columbus, Villa caught the U.S. public off guard. Soldiers of the Thirteenth U.S. Cavalry, stationed at Camp Furlong near Columbus on that morning, were awakened to the sound of blistering rifle fire and the shouts of more than five hundred Villista horsemen trampling the streets of Columbus and setting fire to public buildings. When the cavalry regrouped and began returning heavy fire to the Villistas, the Mexicans retreated back across the border, but left the town virtually demolished.

President Wilson acted immediately. He ordered Gen. John J. Pershing, a veteran of both the Indian and Philippine campaigns, into Mexico with five thousand cavalry to catch and punish the Villista guerrillas. Pershing's official objective was to break up the Villista army that had been plaguing the border area for several years. He also wanted to capture Villa and eliminate entirely the guerrilla forces under the Mexican leader's command. While he was very successful in the first objective, the second—and the most publicized one—was never accomplished, even though an American bullet at one point seriously wounded Villa. Failing to capture the guerrilla leader stigmatized the "Punitive Expedition" (as it was called). But Pershing was able to force the retreat of the Villistas into seclusion, silencing them for the short duration of U.S. occupation. Even after the American withdrawal in early 1917, when Villa once again began his military activity, the guerrilla was careful never again to raid across the U.S. border.

The Punitive Expedition lasted less than a year (March 1916 to January 1917). From the outset it was complicated by the serious diplomatic and military problems between the U.S. and Mexican governments. Mexico was sliding dangerously close to the German side in World War I. Hovering over the entire episode, therefore, was the impending U.S. war with Germany, and as the European situation became more tense, U.S. officials began seeking ways to bring the army back from Mexico. The imminence of U.S. involvement in the European war, in fact, was a major consideration in the final withdrawal. Despite its brevity, however, the intervention into Mexico contained classic features of unconventional war in the United States, features that the military had faced many times before and that, reluctantly, they were to face again in the future.

Initially, U.S. authorities were forced to rediscover and improvise against the natural handicaps involved in military expeditions in foreign territory where their very presence, especially under the conditions of political revolution, strengthened the civilian loyalty of the populace to the guerrillas. In comparison to the invading Americans, with their long and winding columns, stretching miles in the hot Mexican sun, the native Villista partisans appeared as patriots and political saviors. Accompanying Pershing's cavalry was a string of Dodge motor vehicles for mobility and a nascent air force of six scout planes, all of which crashed within a month. This orthodox use of force had little success in the early months of the campaign and clearly hindered the overall effort. As one specialist on the Punitive Expedition has written, "Going into Chihuahua to lay hands on Villa was like the Sheriff of Nottingham entering Sherwood Forest expecting the peasants to help him land Robin Hood. Pershing could not count on idolaters to help him catch the idol."[23]

The U.S. military sent long columns of troops, burdened with heavy equipment and a hot sun, into unfamiliar Mexican terrain to search for Pancho Villa, whose forces were more mobile and knowledgeable of the land. This confrontation between regular and irregular troops produced a great deal of frustration for the army, and Villa was never captured. *Photograph by William Fox, Library of Congress*

But this was not due to any undue benevolence on the part of Villa toward the inhabitants of Chihuahua. Like most other guerrilla leaders, he seldom winced at repressive measures, including torture and murder, deemed necessary to corral the population to his side. Even the residents of Chihuahua who were not in sympathy with the Villa faction of the Mexican civil war were afraid to render assistance to the Americans. But their fear was also derived from contempt against an outside army encamped within their own borders and was independent of their fear of Villa. Few people enjoy foreign domination. "Probably most anti-Villa Mexicans," Clarence Clendenen has concluded, "hated the Americans more than they hated Villa."[24]

The frustrations inherent in conducting antiguerrilla operations in hostile country played a significant role in the eventual decision to curtail Pershing's operations. The quest to capture Pancho Villa was also the last campaign waged by the American horse soldier. The technology of the future—tanks, mechanization, machine guns, and barbed wire—would make the Punitive Expedition the "last hurrah" for this most romanticized of the military branches. The terrain where Pershing crossed with horses, trucks, and biplanes was formidable to strangers but offered magnificent sanctuary to the native partisans of Villa's army. The twelve-thousand-foot peaks of the towering Sierra Madre mountains, with their deep and winding canyons shaded in the daytime sun, protected the fleeing Villistas as much as they confounded the pursuing Americans. Villa, as usual, was fighting in his own backyard, which was mostly unmapped wilderness.

While General Pershing set up camp in the town of Colonia Dublan, his men crisscrossed the rugged terrain as if searching for ghosts, which they rarely found. About the only notable tactical episode of the entire intervention launched the career of the legendary George S. Patton. It was there where the young Lieutenant Patton, fresh out of West Point, piled with ten other soldiers plus guides into three Dodge touring convertibles in search of retreating Villistas. After a brief firefight they killed three. Patton roped the bodies unceremoniously to the hood of his truck, as hunters do deer, and drove back to camp, where their photographs finally gave the public back home something to cheer about. The incident, of course, did little to improve relations with the Mexican people and had no significant effect on the outcome of the conflict. For the American soldier and public, however, this was about as much PR as they could expect.

Toward the end of the expedition, the U.S. force of sixty-six thousand "Doughboys" (so named because of the white chalk dust that collected on their uniforms) was restricted to within 150 miles of the border. Not only were Mexicans united in opposing the soldiers, but the forces of the Carranza government hampered their movements whenever they could, even to the point of armed resistance. The U.S. Army fought the Mexican army in several bloody clashes. "If this campaign should eventually prove successful," Pershing commented, "it will be without the real assistance of any natives this side of [the] line."[25]

The expedition enjoyed a small degree of success because of Pershing's swift pursuit of the Villistas. Here was a military leader who had a good measure of experience against irregular forces, including five years against American Indians and an equal time against the Moro insurgents in the Philippines. Pershing was a soldier's soldier. He maintained a strict and traditional discipline in the ranks but lived the life of a noncommissioned officer in his personal association with the men. He refused to even use an officer's tent, slept in the field with the ordinary enlistee, and traveled freely throughout the war zone with only one or two orderlies accompanying him, often directly in the line of fire.

At first, Pershing's army, understandably, was completely unprepared for the type of mobile operations that chasing Villa would entail. The expedition not only caught U.S. authorities by surprise, but all contingent plans for war in Mexico were, as Donald Smythe has written, dependent upon the traditional use of force that Americans had been accustomed to. "Plans on file made no provision for chasing a single guerrilla. All plans were based on the assumption of a full-scale war, with seaborne operations at Vera Cruz and Guaymas. Any expedition hunting Villa would have to 'play it by ear.'"[26] Improvisation, as usual, guided strategy.

Not only did the expedition operate in unfamiliar terrain, but the army did not even have accurate maps of Chihuahua. Villa knew every corner of the area, lived off the country, and roamed at will among the barren and arid wastelands of north-central Mexico. After less than a month in the country, Pershing understood anew the implications of counterguerrilla war. Cabling his superiors, he stated, "Now evident capture Villa will require many months' difficult work by small columns and well organized secret service."[27]

Pershing confronted the Villistas with the type of "flying columns" that were made famous by the French colonial army. Combining four such small and mobile groups with three forward columns of the regular type, the Punitive Expedition resembled at times the highly maneuverable operations that General Crook used against hostile Apaches many years before. While more often than not they combed the vicinity without finding a trace of the enemy, the encounters they did have all succeeded in routing the Villistas, forcing them further away from the settled areas of the state. With the guerrillas either hiding or in retreat, Pershing organized the area of operations into five military districts, each occupied by a regiment.

In the meantime, relations between the United States and Mexico had so deteriorated that Washington had mobilized fifteen thousand national guardsmen on the border, with war an imminent possibility. Under these circumstances, both sides stepped back from the brink, and the pursuit of Villa by the American army ceased altogether. In the month of August 1917, Villa took full advantage of this respite and exploded from hiding, still full of fury against both the U.S. Army and Carranza's Mexican forces. By October he had stormed several cities and was in full control of central Chihuahua. Pershing, straining at the leash, wrote his superiors that "A swift blow delivered by this command should be made at once. . . . Our own prestige in Mexico should receive consideration at this time. . . . [F]urther inactivity of this command does not seem desirable."[28]

The sensitive nature of Mexican–American relations plus the upcoming war in Europe, however, prevailed against further action. In January 1917 President Wilson ordered the army back home. The Punitive Expedition was over; it was a success in that Mexicans no longer raided U.S. territory. While it was active, it had succeeded in containing Villa's guerrillas, although they were never eliminated. After the withdrawal, with the United States fully committed to Europe, Pancho Villa almost succeeded in reestablishing his authority in Chihuahua, but this time at the expense of the Mexican government only, and not that of the United States.

Villa's active military career, ironically, ended at the hands of the United States when, in June 1919, his advance to the border town of Juarez provoked an American counterattack so devastating that his army was finished as a serious factor in Mexican politics thereafter. Characteristically enough, the famous guerrilla of northern Mexico saw his career come to ruins on the only occasion when he chose to match his army's strength with that of American regulars. After 1919 Villa finally made peace with the government and was given a pension and large hacienda, which he enjoyed until he was also done in by "the sword," ambushed and killed by a political rival on July 20, 1923.

The Punitive Expedition into Mexico was the responsibility of the army, coming as it did fourteen years after the formal end of the army's war in the Philippines. The remaining counterguerrilla wars from 1916 on were all confined to the Caribbean area and Central America and became the responsibility of the navy, with the Marine Corps assuming primary duty on the ground.

-10-

The Caribbean:
The Dominican Republic and Haiti

During the early part of the twentieth century, the United States experienced a number of problems in the preservation of internal order in the small countries of the Caribbean and Central America that had become American dependents in the power politics of the Western Hemisphere. The situation in the two states that shared the island of Hispaniola, just a few miles across the windward passage southeast of Cuba, offered the worst-case scenarios. During its long occupations of both Haiti and the Dominican Republic, the United States encountered combat against irregulars of a kind that directly challenged the orthodox interpretations of warfare U.S. officers and soldiers were taught in formal training.

The relative ease with which American forces had crushed Spain in Cuba in 1898 and the easy intervention in Nicaragua in 1909 were deceptive and gave no warning of the potential for guerrilla warfare in the region. Especially with the swift "taking" of Panama in 1903 and the ongoing construction of an interoceanic canal, the United States appeared justified in viewing the Caribbean and Central America as a special preserve. But the protracted campaigns to eliminate disorder, "banditry," and irregular opposition in that same area would eventually end this complacency, at least for the generation that had to supervise the political wreckage left behind.

In the period between 1898 and 1933, between the Spanish–American War and the New Deal, the United States sent its military forces into Latin American countries on more than twenty-five separate occasions, several of these involving long and difficult occupations. During these expeditions the United States found itself deeply involved in counterguerrilla military (or paramilitary) operations, for which the

161

forces had to rediscover tactics originally improvised in the nineteenth century. On these occasions, as well, the United States had to relearn how unpopular such conflicts could become with the American public and how difficult it was to explain why military interventions in backward, impoverished countries against irregulars failed to produce results, year after year.

U.S. decision makers also rediscovered the ancient truth that while occupation may bring benefits to occupied peoples, it can also produce resentments that invariably lead to political backlash and, ultimately, to revolt. The long American experience in Latin America, from 1898 to the declaration of the Good Neighbor policy by Franklin D. Roosevelt in 1933, is largely the story of this evolution in political realities. It is also a story of the difficulties and frustrations of what is now termed "nation building."

The idea of Manifest Destiny formed the background here as it did also with the Philippines, Mexico, and continental expansion. After the quick military success against Spain, the United States had turned the Monroe Doctrine around, from a defensive shield against European intrusions to an offensive sword with the capacity for "preemptive" intervention against the *potential* of intrusions. Thus, the notion of "preemptive" war, central to contemporary American strategic doctrine, actually predates George W. Bush by centuries.

The most compelling expression of this "doctrine" came in 1904, when President Theodore Roosevelt proclaimed that American "police power" in the Western Hemisphere was necessary:

> Chronic wrongdoing, or an impotence which results in a general loosening of the ties of civilized society, may in America, as elsewhere, ultimately require intervention by some civilized nation, and in the Western Hemisphere the adherence of the United States to the Monroe Doctrine may force the United States, however reluctantly, in flagrant cases of such wrongdoing or impotence, to the exercise of an international police power.[1]

While it is true that Roosevelt's interpretation of the Monroe Doctrine led to little more than American supervision of the Dominican Republic's finances and a brief intervention into Cuba, his "corollary" laid the basis for the more ambitious actions of future administrations. The notion of a U.S. dominion inside the entire region soon became an article of faith of American foreign policy. The political motives for

"Dollar Diplomacy" as practiced by the Taft administration were articulated by Secretary of State Philander C. Knox:

> The logic of political geography and of strategy, and now our tremendous national interest created by the Panama Canal, make the safety, the peace, and the prosperity of Central America and the zone of the Caribbean of paramount interest to the Government of the United States. Thus the malady of revolutions and financial collapse is most acute precisely in the region where it is most dangerous to us. It is here that we seek to apply a remedy.[2]

This belief would be put to its severest test in the midst of world war, but in the Caribbean, not in the trenches of France. American intervention into the Dominican Republic first occurred in May 1916, in response to a civil war between two political factions that threatened to upset the existing order that Washington depended upon. The United States has had concrete interests in the Dominican Republic since at least 1904, when President Theodore Roosevelt first began American supervision over the country's finances. A number of European creditors were threatening intervention of their own; Roosevelt's action not only stopped short this threat but it also led to his famous corollary, while pledging a U.S. guarantee of Dominican stability thereafter. This was a large order, even for the powerful United States.

Dominican history was replete with political and economic instability. Between 1844 and 1916 the country saw a succession of forty-three presidents, most of them military dictators, who came and went in an endless procession of revolutions and coups. Even during its receivership over the country's finances, the United States was forced more than once to dispatch Marines to quell the generic disorders that seemed always to accompany local politics. In 1916 the situation was worse than before, with rebel bands led by Desiderio Arias in control of the capital city of Santo Domingo.

American occupation of the capital was deceptively easy. Learning that the Marines intended to occupy the city, Arias and his band of one thousand irregulars fled to Santiago, in the interior, where they proclaimed a rebel government. In order to end this pretension, it was necessary for the United States to extend its control to the central and northern reaches of the country. With little resistance, the Marines landed in the northern ports of Puerto Plata and Monte Cristi, thus effectively squeezing the rebels into the mountainous central regions.

With rebel political strength gaining momentum, the United States increased the number of Marines on shore and began a drive toward Santiago to crush the revolution in one gigantic military push. This, too, was deceptively simple. While the Marine offensive succeeded in the usual manner against forces that had yet to learn the ways of insurrection, the initial victories opened a chapter of military operations that were to engage U.S. forces in a seemingly endless guerrilla war. During its worst phase in 1920–21, the situation from Washington appeared insoluble.

With nearly eighteen hundred officers and men in the country by June 1916, Col. J. H. Pendleton inaugurated his drive against the rebel stronghold at Las Trencheras, a ridge near Santiago where the insurgents had built a defensive network of trenches. The campaign was a conventional operation, as Col. Clyde Metcalf, USMC, has related:

> The enemy retired to a second line of trenches higher up the ridge from which the Marines easily drove them with their rifle fire. The attack was the first experience of Marines advancing with the support of modern artillery and machine guns. Las Trencheras had been for many years considered impregnable. On it the Dominicans had successfully defied the Spaniards in the 1860s. Its capture was a great moral victory for Pendleton. In this rather extensive engagement the Marines lost but one killed and four wounded.[3]

With a similar victory at Guayacanas, Pendleton's force linked with another Marine column and took the rebel city of Santiago without opposition. The insurgents, decimated by Marine firepower and totally demoralized, appeared finished. After only two serious, but lopsided, battles, the United States began its occupation of the countryside in the routine manner that it was accustomed to in other Caribbean areas. Yet, consistent with the history of guerrilla war, the real conflict had just begun.

In the Dominican Republic, political conditions had been so turbulent that the State Department concluded that an American military government was the only short-run solution. Consequently, the United States immediately put into effect a series of enforcements, such as strict censorship and an absolute prohibition of firearms, to keep peace in the country. Another motive also figured in the U.S. decision for total military control. From the very beginnings of the intervention, an endemic hostility against the American presence on the part of *all* classes of Dominican citizens, whether rebel or pro-government, was manifest everywhere the Marines went. The intervention had obviously touched a sensitive chord of nationalism that transcended even the normal hatreds of local politics. "Since anti-American sentiment remained general during most of 1916 and 1917," Robert Heinl has related, "few responsible Dominicans would assist the military government, and Marine and naval officers thus had to assume political duties far afield from any taught at Annapolis or the School of Application."[4]

The Marines were even more unprepared for the guerrilla insurrection that would confront them in the Dominican Republic for the next six years. Devious and clever in their tactics, the Dominican insurgents had great popular appeal in the countryside, and led the Marines on a wild goose chase for such a long time that their revolt seemed endless. The resistance that began in early 1917 was, typically, viewed by Washington as another in a series of "bandit" depredations that a few sharp repulses would quell. To counter such resistance the United States established a local national guard. With an authorized force of 1,234 men, the Guardia Nacional Dominicana faced immediate morale problems. Confronted with a massive indifference, if not hostility, on the part of the natives, the half-trained Guardia was prematurely rushed into service against the guerrillas in 1917 and 1918. Neither by leadership nor by training was it ready for this task. "In almost every case," one specialist has written, "the native officers failed to weld their men into cohesive, disciplined bodies, and the recruits tended to impose upon the civilian population."[5] Whatever instruction they had, furthermore, had little to do with the task at hand, i.e., counterguerrilla war. (It was not until 1921 that the Haina Military Academy was founded for the Guardia. Here, future Dominican officers were schooled in the traditional military tactics of a regular army, in addition to such instruction as engineering and administration.)

During 1917 the remaining U.S. forces in the country collected whatever weapons were surrendered, while the two specified military districts—northern and southern—were each garrisoned by a regiment of Marines. Meanwhile, the center of trouble in the eastern half of the country was being visited by the likes of revolutionists Dios Olivario and Vincentico Evangelista and their respective guerrilla bands. During the first half of the year, over one hundred separate Marine patrols fought more than a score of engagements with them. Although the insurgents were usually able to elude the fast-paced American patrols, the few pitched battles that did occur overwhelmingly resulted in Marine victories. On one occasion, for example, Vincentico launched a daringly premature attack on a large Marine detachment, losing in the process at least fifteen men. The guerrilla leader then retreated into a mountain stronghold, where the Marines found him and forced the entire band into surrender. A short time later Vincentico was killed while attempting to escape.

By the end of 1917, with the country apparently returning to normal, the United States was led to believe that the war was over. In his annual report, the commandant of the Marine Corps stated that "all the bandit leaders have been captured or killed and their followers dispersed."[6] In reality, this was still another example of the historic lulls in irregular operations that have so often deceived the leaders of conventional armies. While the United States was settling into the routines of occupation, the remaining guerrillas and their leaders were preparing themselves for extended operations in the eastern half of the country. According to the historian of the Dominican Republic (and future U.S. secretary of state) Sumner Welles,

> Over a great portion of the uncultivated part of Seybo Province there spreads a thick growth of forest and brush in which the *gavilleros*, as the bandits were colloquially termed, found it easy to take refuge, with the constantly increasing numbers of their followers, after their raiding forays, and thus to elude the detachments of Marines sent in their pursuit. The Marines and their commanding officers, unfamiliar with the country, unable to speak Spanish, unable to elicit from the inhabitants of the Province any information which would make it possible for them to learn the whereabouts of the marauders, confronted a condition of affairs with which it was difficult for them to cope. As time went on and conditions deteriorated rather than improved, the tempers of both officers and men became exacerbated.[7]

With two thousand officers and men divided into numerous small patrols, and aided by the auxiliary Guardia, the Marines took off after the insurgents during 1918. Although they were able to overrun the main camp of Olivario, he had long since departed and, characteristically, remained well ahead of his pursuers. The year went badly for the Marine Corps. Despite numerous contacts with the guerrillas, the Marines were unable to bring them to any decisive engagement. Olivario was waging a brilliant guerrilla war. On occasion, he was even able to defeat the small patrols sent after him. One ambush, for example, nearly resulted in the extinction of a combined Marine-Guardia patrol. The frustrations of the Marines, who were used to having their way in the Caribbean area, have been described by Colonel Metcalf:

> The hardships involved in carrying on such campaigns in infested tropical countries, especially during the rainy season, are difficult for the uninitiated to imagine. Malaria and dengue, especially, wore down the effective strength of the Marines. The patrolling which took place almost continuously, was nearly all on foot, as mounts were only available for about one-fifth of the men. The danger to patrols was increased by the fact that each patrol sent out was usually quite small. At times several groups operated in conjunction, at varying distances apart, in order to gain contact with bandit groups. This practice was carried on, even at the risk of having small patrols completely wiped out by greatly superior groups of bandits.[8]

During early 1919 U.S. forces were augmented by over one thousand men plus a squadron of aviation. With still very little assistance from the Guardia, the Marines made over two hundred contacts with the enemy during 1919, but at year's end, absolutely no material progress had been made. The population was more hostile than ever, and the insurgents seemed to be able to control the war's tempo at will. The U.S. command, spinning its wheels against a nigh-invisible enemy, grew edgy and frustrated. The men, too, became bitter against both the people they were supposed to be helping and against the enemy they could not quite bring to battle. As has happened so often in counterguerrilla campaigns, the situation produced intolerance and repression. "It is a fact," Mr. Welles reported, "that a policy of repression was carried out by the Forces of occupation over a protracted period in the eastern provinces of the Dominican Republic, which was inherently unwise, which reacted primarily upon peaceful civilians, and as the result of which many atrocities were undoubtedly committed."[9]

Despite the evident success of their military methods, Olivario and other irregular leaders were unable to succeed in major offensives against the Americans, although this didn't stop them from trying. On several occasions during 1919 they united their forces and attacked the Marines openly. One such force, for example, struck a Marine patrol in May but was driven off by superior firepower, including bombing and strafing from the aviation squadron. Nevertheless, the guerrillas were exhausting both the Marines in the field and the political willpower of official Washington.

During 1919, the strength of the brigade was gradually allowed to run down. Most of those serving in the Dominican Republic had enlisted during World War I and expected, therefore, to fight a "real" war; instead they remained on a tropical island amid a hostile people chasing guerrillas. This condition, along with the hardships of the campaign, had a serious effect on the morale of the command. U.S. intervention, in addition, had provoked a rash of protest from Latin America. Both the Brazilian and Uruguayan governments advised an end to the occupation, while most of the press of Latin and Central America began a determined campaign against U.S. policy in the Dominican Republic. Inside the country itself a vitriolic newspaper attack against the U.S. presence only intensified Washington's frustration with the whole affair. Toward the end of 1920, with the guerrillas still at large and more active than ever, the United States decided to terminate its military intervention as soon as possible.

During 1920 opposition to U.S. rule was so widespread that Brig. Gen. Logan Feland, the brigade commander, asked for more Marines to combat the internal political situation that amounted to revolution. Although the Dominican guerrillas did not enjoy the advantages of a true monolithic political organization, the public opposition to the American presence aided them wherever they went. When the United States announced a postponement of its military withdrawal, for example, a widespread public protest arose from every quarter of the Dominican Republic. Not even the good deeds of the U.S. military, in such areas as public works, education, and sanitation, seemed to have been appreciated by the Dominican people.

As a last resort, in a more than five-year effort to eliminate resistance, the United States decided, in 1921, on a system of "cordons" to rid the eastern part of the country of active partisans. Although this system was instrumental in the final pacification, it aroused more civilian opposition than any other measure to date. In effect, the cordon system was a form of American total war against the population of the affected areas. According to this early twentieth-century conceptual "strategic hamlet," large numbers of U.S. troops blocked off an area of the country and rounded up virtually every adult male, for a series of mass lineups in which concealed informers would identify known insurgents. These were usually conducted at night, with the informers hidden in a darkened tent and the suspects under a spotlight in front. After five months of this, with nine roundups having been made, the

United States convicted more than six hundred guerrillas. The protests of innocent civilians who became involved in this form of counterguerrilla lineup became so violent, however, that the system had to be ended. After that, the military governor, Brig. Gen. Harry Lee, offered a two-month period of amnesty in order to encourage the remaining guerrillas to come in.

With the country finally on its way to pacification, the United States undertook to train a number of the Guardia (shortly later renamed the "Policia," to distinguish it from a traditional national army) in true antiguerrilla tactics. This was a rare innovation in American training. Guardia members were carefully chosen, using only those who had previously suffered at the hands of the insurgents. They were organized into special, elite antiguerrilla outfits and were then sent out in small patrols. The nascent Dominican "special forces" had six contacts with insurgents, all of them highly successful. This success combined with the stepped-up patrolling of Marine forces wiped out the guerrillas as a factor in Dominican politics by May 1922, when the final amnesty period ended. The guerrillas' demise was undoubtedly hastened by a gradual change in attitude on the part of many Dominicans after definite plans for an American withdrawal had been made. This announcement, coupled with the more benevolent policy toward the citizenry, went a long way toward soothing the feelings of a population that had nursed grievances against the army of occupation since its first landing in 1916.

The United States succeeded in ending the guerrilla war in the Dominican Republic only after it announced an end to its own military government and only after it had systematically rounded up most of the population of the guerrilla areas. Unlike other wars against native partisans, such as in the Philippines, this one did not produce a storm of domestic criticism, although it was a minor factor in the 1920 election. With some exceptions, the American public didn't denounce military methods in the Dominican Republic because they simply didn't know about them. During most of the occupation the State Department, preoccupied with European events, left the Dominican situation entirely up to the military. As Sumner Welles has written, the result was that

> beyond a nominal supervision, the Military Governor of the Dominican Republic, with his Cabinet, constituted a dictatorship whose actions there was none to criticize. The censorship of the press in the Dominican Republic had become so rigid

that the slightest criticism of measures adopted by the Military
Government was stringently punished, and comparative freedom of speech had long since become a thing of the past.[10]

Nevertheless, even without the backlash of an aroused public opinion at home, the United States was more than eager to leave the Dominican Republic to its own devices. The campaign was arduous, brutal, and
unrewarding. In 1924 the last Marine left the Dominican Republic.

Marine frustrations in the 1920s were repeated at the same time by
similar experiences in Haiti, the country which shares the island of
Hispaniola with the Dominican Republic. At the time of American intervention, Haiti was practically ungoverned. Between 1908 and 1915,
seven Haitian presidents were elected and then deposed by violence.
The economy was dependent on the exertions of small farmers—mostly
engaged in subsistence cultivation. There were few passable roads in
an area about the size of New York state and the country had three
automobiles.

The word "Haiti" means mountainous, and the geographic isolation of the country left ultimate political power in the hands of the cacos,
a large band of independent warriors who had established their own
brand of native authority in the rugged and mountainous interior. Like
the bird of prey with its red plume wherefrom they derived their name,
the cacos lived off the peasants, and were recognized by a patch of red
cloth worn on their sleeves.

A definition of the romantic-sounding rebels was given at the time
by Gen. L. W. T. Waller, USMC (the same man who, as a major, helped
lead the U.S. attack on the Philippine island of Samar in 1902):

It must be explained that the cacos have been the controlling
element in all revolutions; they were purchased by first one
candidate and then another. Finishing a contract with one man,
they, having put him in power, would immediately sell their
services to the next aspirant to unseat the first.[11]

The cacos had no military organization, no uniforms, no modern arms or supplies of their own, yet they fought the Marines in a
guerrilla war from the first day of the intervention in 1915. They
eventually lost, but not until 1920, not until they had succeeded in
challenging the right of the United States to govern Haiti itself, and
not until their stubborn resistance had voiced its protests right up to
the halls of the U.S. Congress and to the White House itself.

U.S. intervention began in the summer of 1915 after a bloody revolution had torn apart the fabric of Haitian society and posed the possibility of foreign (including German) military intervention to collect
overdue debts. World War I was already into its second year and Washington was extremely sensitive about possible European intrusions into
the Caribbean. British, French, and German warships had, in fact,
already landed their forces in 1914. By July 1915, with Haiti again in a
condition of anarchy, the United States decided on full armed intervention with the intention of restoring law and order and of protecting
American and foreign interests against mob rule. During August a force
of two thousand officers and men occupied Port au Prince and lesser
towns of the country.

With the exception of the resistance they began to encounter in the
caco areas, the Marines were able to occupy Haiti without serious
trouble. Since they knew little of caco history, the Marine command
expected little trouble from the north. But the fierce cacos refused to
give up. Brave to the point of foolishness, they feared no outside army,
not even the Marine Corps with its artillery and machine guns. They
nearly surrounded a Marine force in Cap Haitien on the northern coast,
and were it not for reinforcements that arrived at the last minute, they
would probably have driven the Marines out. Beaten back by the beefed-
up Americans, the cacos left behind forty dead.

But these Haitian warriors had a problem that becomes insurmountable when fighting a superior army: they had no place to go. With the
seacoast to their back, and with the Dominican border sealed off by U.S.
forces, the cacos found themselves captive on their own island. After a
six-day reconnaissance trip that covered 120 miles, the Marines began a
determined offensive against the caco stronghold, an eighteenth-century brick and stone bastion named Fort Reviere. In their retreat to Fort
Reviere, the cacos eluded Marine patrols as much as possible, preferring
to ambush their adversary if they could. Nevertheless, they could not
run forever. Trapped in their stronghold, they had no choice but to fight
it out, usually a disaster for even the best-equipped guerrillas. The result was predictable. The Marines stormed the fort, believed impregnable by the superstitious cacos, and killed fifty of them, including several of their leaders. A ton of dynamite demolished the fort, and for the
time being, the caco resistance against American rule was broken.

This initial reaction to foreign occupation in Haiti offers a classic
reminder of the vital requirement of a geographic sanctuary for guerrilla war. Even if the cacos had fully understood the tactics of guerrilla
war—which they clearly did not—the geographic handicaps of Haiti

probably would have strangled their rebellion anyway. They knew only how to fight their enemies head on. They neither understood the subtleties of protracted action nor did they develop even a vaguely constructive program of social and political resistance. Consequently, the Marines were able to lull them into the type of trap that usually spells the end of irregular forces. In 1918, however, under different leadership and with the memories of 1915 still in their minds, the cacos rose once more, this time in a more planned and widespread action against U.S. authority.

In the meantime, the United States formed a national guard, the Gendarmerie d'Haiti, which rapidly assumed police duties for the entire country. Led by 115 Marine and naval officers, the Gendarmerie came to have 2,533 Haitian troops. In discipline, training, and gear, it became a near-replica of the Marine Corps. Training was completely standard in both theory and practice, the gendarmes using the orthodox infantry drill regulations right until the eventual end of American occupation in 1934.

The very serious caco revolt in 1918 was triggered by the American enforcement of the corvée—an obligation for every Haitian to perform unpaid labor in the construction of public roads. As the country's almost complete lack of passable highways attested, this system had been practically ignored in the past. But the U.S. insistence on its enforcement, however reasonable this may have been, opened a second caco revolt that, before it was over, involved the whole country in an insurrection against American rule. Initial fighting occurred in June 1918 when a gendarme force, sent out to enforce the edict, was severely beaten by a group of cacos. During the summer and fall of 1918, the cacos developed a military force of three thousand men, with the active assistance of about one-fifth of the entire Haitian people. Led by the charismatic Charlemagne Peralte, they organized a fairly sophisticated system of intelligence and security, forcing peasants to join up while terrorizing those who refused.

The cacos took the offensive to the Gendarmerie, burning their barracks and, on occasion, administering severe defeats on the newly formed outfit. The movement began to assume the proportions of a full-scale revolution, led by Charlemagne's cry to "drive the invaders into the sea and free Haiti." With the Gendarmerie clearly on the defensive, the country tottered on the brink of disaster. In March 1919 the government of Haiti made a belated call for another Marine intervention.

In the campaign that followed, the combined Marine-gendarme force faced a much superior enemy than the one the Marines had so easily destroyed in 1915. Charlemagne and an equally formidable caco chieftain, Benoit Batraville, succeeded in organizing over one-quarter of the country in a formidable and sustained irregular military operation against the Marine presence. Although the United States always insisted that the war was only against outlawed "bandits," the essentially political character of the revolt was manifest in both caco propaganda against the United States as well as in the traditional political aims of caco history. The racial implications of the intervention were used to the fullest by the cacos: it became a war against white invaders.

Militarily, the cacos were careful to stay away from the main body of Marine strength, although they still occasionally evidenced an overzealous taste for battle. Their successful ambush of a large Marine patrol in April 1919 amounted to a tactical victory of sorts, and stimulated their hopes for eventual success. Nevertheless, between April and September the two sides engaged each other on over one hundred occasions, sometimes in pitched battles but more often in small skirmishes, usually ending with the retreat of the insurgents into the bush. Although the Marines were able to find the cacos and rout them from their encampments, they were unable to eliminate the rebellion that was still in high gear after six months of hard campaigning. Growing bolder as a result of their swift evasions of Marine patrols, both Charlemagne and Benoit, in October 1919, "rode higher than ever."[12]

With a force of three hundred men, Charlemagne launched an attack on Port au Prince itself on October 7, probably one of the more premature military moves in the annals of irregular war. Although this force was joined by clandestine insurgents inside the capital, both the Marines and the gendarmerie were ready. The raid turned into a full-scale retreat. The next day the Gendarmerie followed the fleeing rebels into the bush, killing thirty and capturing most of their weapons.

The attack on Port au Prince set the rebellion back considerably but in no way ended it. Charlemagne's defeat in the capitol was typical of his lack of caution against the militarily superior Marines. But the very idea of the scheme itself, and the fact that it was even allowed to materialize awakened U.S. authorities to the extent of the problem in Haiti. The United States was ill prepared to wage a protracted counterinsurgency, and the close call inside the capital city caused the Marines to take matters into their own hands. Before that, the combination of Marine-gendarme activity had been poorly handled, and the United States did not fully appreciate the political depths of the revolution. As a Marine Corps historian has written,

In the operations in general there appears to have been considerable confusion and lack of coordination between the Marines and the gendarmes. Through lack of knowledge of each other's activities, gendarmerie patrols fired upon each other on more than one occasion; this resulted in the death of a number of Marines and gendarmes. Apparently there had been a tendency to discount the seriousness of the caco revolt and to suppress information about it. . . . The fact remains that there was serious blame somewhere for the turn of events in Haiti. A great deal of criticism resulted.[13]

At this point, the United States tried to end the rebellion by capturing Charlemagne, dead or alive. The Marine commander of the Gendarmerie, Col. F. M. Wise, has related the problem as it was viewed in 1919:

It was a pretty big order. It meant running down one Haitian out of several millions of Haitians in a country as big as the state of New York. And that one Haitian was surrounded by his friends, operating in a country which was almost entirely sympathetic to him, was protected by a fanatical body guard, never slept two nights in the same place, and must be run down in a tangled maze of mountains and valleys and jungles, of which there were no accurate maps.[14]

As the weary campaign dragged on, the assassination of Charlemagne was accomplished by Sgt. H. H. Hanneken, USMC, in an adventure that must rank as one of the greatest deceptions in the history of guerrilla war. In a planned series of moves that, eighty-five years later, still seems incredulous, Hanneken succeeded in planting a Haitian spy into Charlemagne's ranks. Jean Conze, a wealthy Haitian who fooled the entire populace into believing that he was converted to the revolutionary cause, conspired to kill Charlemagne.

Hanneken and Conze went so far as to simulate a mock battle between gendarmes and Conze's men and a planned "defeat" of the gendarmes, which further convinced all of Haiti that Conze was a committed rebel. Sergeant Hanneken, feigning a wounded arm supposedly injured in the "battle," publicly traveled through Haiti for the next several weeks with a sling deliberately stained by red ink taken from a field desk. On the night of October 30 Conze provided Hanneken with details on Charlemagne's whereabouts. With sixteen handpicked gendarmes, Hanneken and his second in command, Cpl. William R. Button, USMC, went through six caco outposts undetected. They were inspected by flashlight at each point, but incredibly enough, they were able to disguise their skin by the use of burnt cork to make blackface. They made it through each outpost undetected, white men "dressed" in caco skin.

When they arrived at the main rebel base, their guide pointed out Charlemagne hovering near the light of a small campfire. The American sergeant pumped two .45-caliber slugs into the betrayed leader, killing him instantly. The bodyguard was also instantly felled by automatic rifle fire. The next morning the Marines returned with the body of Charlemagne slung over one of his own mules, done in by both the stupidity and treachery of his own men.

The American attempt to restore law and order to an unstable Haiti devolved into tedious Marine expeditions to capture elusive "bandits," as shown in this photo from 1919. After nineteen years, the U.S. forces withdrew, having failed to achieve political or social stability. *Department of Defense photo, National Archives at College Park*

After the loss of Charlemagne, insurgency in northern Haiti was hurt, but not defeated. Leadership of the cacos fell to Benoit Batraville, who still controlled about twenty-five hundred irregulars in central Haiti.

In the meantime, the Marine command revised its estimate of the black enemy, which had lost its leader but was still at large. "It was clear," a Marine historian has written, "that, despite the windfall of Hanneken's enormous success, the existing organization, strength, and efficiency of both the Brigade and the Gendarmerie had not been adequate to deal with the cacos uprising."[15]

Under a new brigade commander, Col. John H. Russell, the United States took steps to improve gendarme-Marine coordination and inaugurated an improved intelligence network. Russell divided the caco areas into squares of responsibility, wherein each Marine patrol was instructed to systematically search out hostile cacos until the vicinity was rid of further resistance.

With over thirteen hundred officers and men, aided by twenty-seven hundred gendarmes, the United States opened the year 1920 with a concerted effort to rid Haiti of the insurgent war that had torn it apart for nearly two years. For the next six months, the improved force of Marines and gendarmes relentlessly drove the cacos back whenever they met. The Marines were assisted by the innovation of coordinated air-ground attacks through the use of airplanes, including six Curtiss "Jennies." In nearly two hundred engagements, most of the remaining irregulars were killed, were captured, or surrendered themselves under protection of the government's new amnesty program. Another attempt on Port au Prince failed even more dramatically than the previous one.

By March over three thousand cacos had turned themselves in. In June the war was effectively ended with the death of Benoit in a surprise attack on his main camp. The final tally was revealing: about 2,000 cacos had been killed since the renewed fighting in 1918, compared to only 250 in the 1915 campaign. The Marines lost only seven killed and ten wounded, and the Gendarmerie lost twenty-seven with forty-five wounded, despite the fact that the Marines did most of the fighting.

The Haitian war was plagued from the start with political and racial problems, most of which were not anticipated by Washington. Most educated Haitians were opposed to the presence of American troops. The peasants in the countryside actively aided the cacos, willingly or not. The fact that the U.S. presence had deprived a number of prominent Haitians of their historic opportunities for power and profit was undoubtedly a factor in this general hostility. But the instinctive magnet of patriotism was a formidable barrier between occupier and occupied. "Disorganization and slowness of American action," one expert on the intervention has maintained, "continuance of military rule and of domination of the United States, fear of exploitation and of loss of independence—these were either causes of hostility or provoked subject matter for propaganda."[16]

Haitian newspapers often attacked the United States openly in their editorials. In response, the United States slammed a tight censorship over these offenders, under conditions of martial law, that effectively ended the public disclosures of internal political opposition. U.S. censorship, for a time, was also extended to include telegram and postal correspondence. Very few Americans were aware of what was happening in Haiti during the war.

Back in the United States, criticism of the intervention still managed to surface among liberal and black opponents of "imperialism" Many newspapers joined in the attack, and by 1920 U.S. officials "were subjected to widespread criticism, and occasional vigorous opposition in the form of persistent agitation and systematic propaganda."[17] The newly born NAACP raised its own protest against the intervention, as did a growing chorus of anti-U.S. voices from Latin America. During the 1920 presidential election in the United States, Republican candidate Warren G. Harding adopted a curiously anti-imperialist stance of his own, telling one audience, for example, "I will not empower an Assistant Secretary of the Navy to draft a constitution for helpless neighbors in the West Indies and jam it down their throats at the points of bayonets borne by United States Marines."[18]

While Haitian delegates to Washington brought public protests against U.S. occupation policies, a group of twenty-four American lawyers were presenting to the secretary of state a booklet, *The Seizure of Haiti by the United States*, which demanded an end to the intervention.

The protests against alleged tactics like torture and the shooting of prisoners reached such proportions that the U.S. Senate Committee of Inquiry held a series of hearings on the matter from August to December 1921. While the Senate report admitted that a number of such incidents had occurred in Haiti, the Marine Corps was officially exonerated, while overall U.S. occupation policies were instructed to become more efficient and coordinated and more "sensitive" to the needs of the Haitian society.

Despite the efforts of successive U.S. administrations to bring democracy and modernity to Haiti, the resentment of the population remained just below the surface. In 1929 it broke through. A student revolt led to a national strike against the U.S. presence. Riots sprung up in major cities. In Aux Cayes, a group of Marines became surrounded by a crowd of fifteen hundred hostile peasants. The frightened Americans opened fire, killing twelve and wounding many more. Washington soon decided for an "exit strategy," with the Marines being withdrawn expeditiously until their final departure in 1934. For Haiti's part, it continued its long tradition of tyrannical rule, including the bloody dictatorships of the Duvalier family.

The American occupation of Haiti was a classic case in failed nation-building, despite vast improvements made by U.S. administration. American control over health, agriculture, public works, and police made the country at least stable and reasonably prosperous. During the course of the nineteen years of occupation, including the five years spent fighting cacos, Americans (especially Assistant Secretary of the Navy Franklin D. Roosevelt) wrote and imposed a new constitution. Americans supervised every election; 1,600 miles of roads were built, plus 15 steel, 68 concrete, and 127 wooden bridges. In 1915 Haiti had three cars; in 1929 there were three thousand. The United States installed a new telephone system, built new wharves and lighthouses, school buildings, courthouses, and a new national college. Clean water was supplied to ten cities and sixty-four villages. The new Gendarmerie of natives was expected to carry on after the Marines left, although the terms of the occupation were open-ended.

Just one year prior to this the United States had also evacuated Nicaragua, ending a long and inconclusive irregular war against one of history's craftiest guerrillas: Augusto C. Sandino.

-11-

Nicaragua:
Optimism Turns Into Frustration

With construction of the Panama Canal under way after 1903, the United States grew increasingly sensitive to disturbances in the political order of the region in and around Panama. The civil wars, coups, and revolutions that, seemingly, were endemic to the region had become much more important to the United States by this time. Not only were they a challenge to the coherence of U.S. foreign policy but they also invited various forms of foreign intrigue and interest. Nicaragua was considered a major troublemaker for the United States, with a history of instability going back decades. Beginning in 1909, a series of uprisings and attempted coups kept the country in a continuous state of disorder. When a revolution threatened full-scale civil war in 1912, the Nicaraguan government requested American intervention. For the next two decades, the United States governed Nicaragua, according to one commentator, "more completely than the American Federal Government rules any state in the Union."[1] U.S. bankers ran the economy and American officials supervised elections. A Legation Guard of Marines, stationed in the capital city of Managua, kept internal peace. In 1925, with the country apparently pacified, the United States withdrew the Marines. Almost immediately, political violence flared up again.

Warring factions of "liberals" and "conservatives" (simply political conveniences with little relevance to policy or philosophy) fought it out in organized combat that, by late 1926, had turned the entire country into a battleground. In order to end this turmoil, Washington reluctantly decided on another troop intervention. In addition, intrigues by the Mexican government were increasingly viewed as a potential threat to American hegemony in Central America, which had existed since the turn of the century.

Relations between the United States and Mexico had already been strained when the Nicaraguan fighting began. Mexico was still influenced by its 1910 nationalist revolution, and during the mid-1920s its government grew more aggressive in foreign policy. On several occasions this produced friction with the United States. The anticlerical provisions of the Mexican constitution aroused a storm of American Catholic opposition, and there was a widely held belief that the Mexican government was dominated by some form of "Bolshevism." By 1926 Washington became convinced that Mexico was materially aiding the Nicaraguan rebels. On January 10, 1927, referring to Mexico, President Coolidge told Congress,

> I have the most conclusive evidence that arms and munitions in large quantities have been, on several occasions since August 1926, shipped to the revolutionists in Nicaragua. . . . The United States cannot fail to view with deep concern any serious threat to stability and constitutional government in Nicaragua tending toward anarchy and jeopardizing American interests, especially if such a state of affairs is contributed to or brought about by outside influence or by a foreign power.[2]

A State Department memorandum of January 1927 provided a confidential assessment of how the United States viewed the potential of Mexican displacement of American influence in the area:

> At this moment a deliberate attempt to undermine our position and set aside our special relationship to Central America is being made. The action of Mexico in the Nicaraguan crisis is a direct challenge to the United States. . . . To all intents and purposes we are practically at war with Mexico now. . . . If this Mexican maneuver succeeds it will take many years to recover the ground we shall have lost. . . . For the moment we stand face to face with the possibility of a Mexicanized Nicaragua.

A "Mexicanized" Nicaragua may have been the initial motivation for the dispatch of U.S. troops, but as in so many other cases of intervention, the allegations of a national security threat soon became lost in the atmospherics of occupation, and like the "quagmire" it became, the occupation of Nicaragua soon took on a life of its own. Although the Mexican "threat" almost immediately evaporated, the reaction of U.S. authorities, in retrospect, can be seen as a final stage in a long history of Manifest Destiny implemented via Marines. In one last gesture of justification of our final occupation of the period, Assistant Secretary of State Robert Olds wrote a policy paper summarizing the vision that had occupied American foreign policy for over three decades:

> Geographical facts cannot be ignored. The Central American area down to and including the Isthmus of Panama constitutes a legitimate sphere of influence for the United States; if we are to have due regard for our own safety and protection. Call it a sphere of influence, or what you will, we do control the destinies of Central America, and we do it for the simple reason that the national interest absolutely dictates such a course.

Olds, in fact, was only repeating what had developed into America's "canal" or "isthmian" policy, which had guided successive administrations since the first shovel had unearthed dirt from the Isthmus of Panama in 1904. Secretary of State Charles Evans Hughes expressed this dogmatic tenet as follows:

> [W]e have a definite policy of protecting the Panama Canal. We deem it to be essential to our national policy to hold the control of the Canal and we could not yield to any foreign power the maintaining of any position which could interfere with our right adequately to protect the Canal or would menace its approaches or the freedom of our communications. This applies just as well to American powers as to non-American powers.[3]

Under the spell of such a course of geopolitical determinism, the Coolidge administration began landing more than two thousand Marines in Nicaragua and was openly selling arms and supplies to the government army. No further mention of Mexican influence ever surfaced, but the civil war in Nicaragua, with or without Mexican influence, continued to tear the country apart.

President Coolidge then sent Henry L. Stimson, a prominent Republican lawyer and former secretary of war, to negotiate with rebel leaders for an end to the insurgency. The Stimson mission ended in May 1927 with an American promise to supervise subsequent elections and to organize and train a constabulary capable of maintaining order. Pending the establishment of this constabulary (later renamed the Guardia Nacional), the United States would retain a Marine presence in Nicaragua.

During the month of May, a force of Marines sufficient "to reduce the country to ruins overnight if it so desired"[4] began to arrive. By late June the total reached thirty-four hundred. The Marines were placed at strategic points within the country and also began to disarm remaining revolutionary groups unwilling to submit to U.S. or Nicaraguan authority.

Stimson ended his mission on an optimistic note. While reconciled to token resistance by small and scattered bands of rebels, he felt that "there will be no organized resistance to our action," and "there also seems to be less danger of banditry and guerrilla warfare than I at first feared." (This delusion would not be confined to the Stimson mission, since similar presumptions have seemed always to attend the initial stage of invasion—up to and including Iraq.)

Still, Stimson had obligated the armed forces to remain in Nicaragua for as long as necessary in order to conduct the same kind of civilizing mission that had accompanied earlier interventions throughout Latin America. This task was soon to engage the United States in what a Marine Corps historian later termed the "long drawn out and almost futile effort to stamp out banditry and restore order": the campaign against Sandino.[5] This war continued until late 1932 and produced one of the most frustrating cases of counterguerrilla operations in American history.

Augusto C. Sandino, a revolutionary "general" during the civil war, had until then been a comparatively little-known Nicaraguan who had spent at least a portion of his life rallying native workers against U.S.-owned commercial enterprises. After Stimson's truce, he rejected the implications of U.S. authority and defiantly retired into the mountains with approximately three hundred armed men. His outfit was a "splinter" rebel group. Most of the revolutionaries accepted the truce peacefully, and when their military hero, Gen. Jose Moncada, became president of Nicaragua in 1928 he worked closely—but not always harmoniously—with U.S. authorities to eliminate Sandino.

Since Sandino and his growing body of men refused to disarm peacefully, a Marine Corps ultimatum was issued to them in late June. Sandino rejected the ultimatum and concentrated his forces near the city of Ocotal in northwest Nicaragua. In mid-July hundreds of "Sandinistas"—as they came to be called—stormed Ocotal, then defended by a unit of thirty-nine Marines plus Guardia. The battle lasted for almost a day, until the introduction of Marine airpower flushed the Sandinistas from cover and swept them away from the city. As they fled with the planes in pursuit, they were cut down repeatedly with small bombs and machine-gun fire. This was the first known dive-bombing attack ever organized in support of American ground troops, and it resulted in at least fifty enemy dead. Marine losses were extremely light—one killed and four wounded—but by the time the planes arrived the men had run short of ammunition and could not have held out much longer. According to one Marine's testimony to a House committee in 1928, "if the planes had not brought immediate assistance, there is no question but the whole band would have been slaughtered."

The Battle of Ocotal, more than any other single event, determined the nature of Sandino's subsequent campaign against U.S. occupation. After such a staggering loss, he understood the futility of meeting the Marines in battle and resorted, instead, to the classic methods of guerrilla war. Although he had no formal military schooling, the terrain of northern Nicaragua plus the sympathy of the residents instinctively dictated his course. Like guerrilla leaders throughout history, Sandino discovered that his most reliable allies existed in his own backyard. During most of the next five and a half years, Sandino would confine his warfare to the northern and eastern sections of the country, conveniently located next to the Honduran border. These parts of Nicaragua, as testified to by one Marine,

furnish ideal terrain for guerrilla warfare. Vast in extent, they consist of almost unbroken chains of mountains, whose rugged peaks afford ideal lookouts and whose densely forested slopes and secluded valleys furnish numerous hiding places secure from observation and attack from airplanes and inaccessible to all but the most lightly equipped of ground troops.[6]

The Battle of Ocotal also marked the emergence of Sandino as an international figure. Reports of the extensive loss of Nicaraguan lives, reaching both the U.S. and the Latin American press, accelerated in the United States the revival of the "anti-imperialist" movement against interventions and in Latin America turned Sandino into a hero who openly defied the "Colossus of the North." Sandinista propaganda, thus introduced as a result of Ocotal, would soon mushroom to worldwide proportions and would provide a major problem for American foreign policy.

For the remainder of 1927 Sandino and his men made sporadic raids on neighboring towns and ranches and occasionally attacked Marine columns. Sandino was in the process of organizing, according to the secretary of the navy, "the population of the northern part of western Nicaragua into a complex system of intelligence and supply." His frequent use of Honduras as a sanctuary further complicated U.S. policy. "It will be very difficult," U.S. Charge Dana Munro wrote, "to improve conditions in Nueva Segovia [the border province] so long as these bandits are permitted to cross the frontier at will and subsequently take refuge in Honduranean territory."

As conditions in northern Nicaragua grew into a state of insurrection, the United States began to take the Sandino movement more seriously. In December a column of Marines sent after Sandino was ambushed by about 450 insurgents. Superior firepower finally drove the guerrillas off, but when the mauled column reached headquarters in early January, it was badly disorganized.

The situation was by then deteriorating rapidly. Charge Munro concluded that "it was utterly impossible with the forces now available to control the whole area of Nueva Segovia," while Adm. David F. Sellers, commander of the Special Service Squadron, noted the "fact that the bandits are apparently better organized and equipped than the Brigade Commander had reason to believe."

Indeed, it was not until late in the year that the United States, belatedly, began to revise its estimate of the enemy it was facing in northern Nicaragua. After the battle of Ocotal, the Marine force in Nicaragua was quickly reduced, while Sandino, permanently silenced according to the dictates of conventional war doctrine, retired to a mountain fortress—"El Chipote," located near the Honduran border. At one point in 1927, the United States could have taken this base, but missed the opportunity. Maj. Oliver Floyd, patrolling his men near the area, had a chance to surprise the Sandinistas but passed it by, declaring classic strategic doctrine: "I will never divide my force in the presence of the enemy."[7]

Like Floyd, few Marines strayed very far from the type of orthodoxy reflected in these tactics. "Sandino's power is broken," Marine intelligence noted in August, "there should be no further trouble of any nature in the entire republic."[8] Clearly, the Marines still didn't appreciate guerrilla war. The brigade commander told the American press that Sandino was through, he has "failed with his inferior forces." This "credibility gap" would haunt both the Coolidge and Hoover administrations, just as it did President Johnson during the Vietnam War.

On September 19 the Sandinistas struck again. An attack was made near Telpaneca by forces under Carlos Salgado, one of Sandino's field lieutenants. It resulted in the death of two Marines and twenty-five guerrillas and rocked the complacency of the U.S. command. The following three months witnessed a major rise in guerrilla activity against a reduced Marine unit, which, despite token reinforcements in the north, was forced onto the strategic defensive. Marine patrols that ventured deeply enough into the Segovia mountains were subjected to harassing ambushes and sniping attacks by the well-hidden enemy. The Sandinistas had no uniforms but wore black and red kerchiefs as symbols of rebellion.

Marine aviators began reconnaissance of the north, and their efforts provided the best available intelligence on the constantly moving Sandino. But the aviators were often fooled by Sandino's guerrilla tactics. On several occasions their bombing runs hit innocent towns that the Sandinistas had evacuated. Murra and other hamlets were bombed into near ruin, without any military results.

On numerous occasions these planes received ground fire from hidden bands of Sandinistas, but without losses. On October 8 their luck ran out. After a brief engagement with guerrillas, a two-seater manned by Lt. E. A. Thomas and Sgt. F. E. Dowdell was downed near Quilali. The two pilots were caught and macheted to death. A photograph of Lieutenant Thomas's body hanging from a tree was found later, but a rescue patrol was ambushed near Jicaro by about four hundred guerrillas and had to turn back. The bodies of the fliers were never found.

The situation in the north was fast approaching the intolerable. Marines and small Guardia units were holding the larger towns, but numerous groups of guerrillas roamed almost at will through the country, committing murders and terrorizing the area. Although skirmishes were numerous, the Marines had been unable to successfully pursue the insurgents, mostly because of the tremendous difficulties of transportation during the rainy season and partly because of a lack of adequate forces.

Official Washington was by now more aware of the nature of the situation. Secretary of State Kellogg could now write that the problem in Nicaragua "is a species of guerrilla warfare which takes place in rather wild, unsettled regions of the country." The State Department, however, was still optimistic, with Kellogg expecting "that within a short time the entire burden can be assumed by the constabulary, permitting the withdrawal of the Marines." Exactly the opposite, in fact, was about to happen.

The Marines and Guardia continued to have frequent contacts with small groups of Sandinistas, with little result. In late November, however, Marine pilots finally located Sandino's headquarters on El Chipote

Mountain. This fortress had been the subject of much earlier speculation and mystery, and some authorities had even doubted that it existed. But the Marines quickly realized the importance of the discovery. If they could corner Sandino in one place, they could get rid of him
once and for all. Repeated air attacks, however, failed to dislodge the
guerrillas.

On December 18 Capt. Richard Livingston left Matagalpa for Nueva
Segovia with six officers and 108 men. His contingent was soon en-
larged by sixty others when it was joined at Quilali by a column led by
Lt. M. A. Richal. Both groups then began the march to wipe out
Sandino's strength in the Jicaro-Chipote region. Simultaneously, small
Marine units began converging northward to meet with the others near
Chipote.

As the patrols moved, they were constantly ambushed along the
route by the mobile and well-informed Sandinistas. On one occasion,
two hundred well-armed guerrillas, some wearing Honduran army uniforms, surprised a small Marine unit, killing one. On December 30
Sandino suddenly moved against Livingston in an apparently well-
planned and concerted action. In an ambush involving about four to
five hundred enemy, the Marines suffered five killed and six wounded,
while the Guardia reserve lost one, with two wounded. On the same
day, Richal's column was attacked by about fifty Sandinistas but had
only one minor casualty.

As the year 1927 closed, the Marine Command began to take serious note of Sandino's obviously improved efficiency, numbers, weapons, and discipline. They also became more suspicious that he was
receiving large quantities of material aid from Honduras. In the meantime the plodding Richal column was again ambushed, this time six
miles outside of Quilali by a force of about 450 guerrillas. The Marines
were caught in single file on a narrow trail while the insurgents struck
simultaneously from several angles. The Marine first sergeant, Thomas C. Bruce, was killed, and Richal himself was wounded in the head.
Superior firepower finally drove the guerrillas off, but the mauled column reached Quilali on January 3 in disrepair.

For the United States, the war was an exercise in frustration. The
Marines and Guardia sent after Sandino had not only failed to locate
him but had been seriously sidetracked along the way. U.S. Marines
were the world's greatest amphibious and naval-auxiliary combat soldiers, but they found the Nicaraguan mountains totally alien to their
own style. The guerrilla war was becoming an embarrassment and a
complex nuisance.

Nor had U.S. authorities yet understood Sandino's political profile as a rebel-nationalist. The frequent reference to him as the leader of "bandits" revealed an absolute ignorance of his native ideological convictions as a leader protesting the U.S. presence. This appreciation by Washington would have to wait until the final stage of the occupation. Militarily, the United States also did not fully appreciate the terrain and weather problems as well as the nature of small-war tactics. Sandino's power was growing despite American occupation. "They still had a lot to learn about our methods," he wrote.[9] It would take a dramatic and substantial increase in U.S. forces to calm the country. These extra forces began arriving in early January 1928.

As the year turned, the situation was becoming grim. The December 1927 fiasco in Quilali shook the United States out of its earlier complacency. The month of January witnessed the first in a series of Marine escalations, which proceeded throughout the year until the November election. The United States was now more than ever aware of the seriousness of Sandino's threat and the capabilities of his irregular army. Sandino's enhanced position would, according to Charge Munro, "make very much more difficult the destruction of his army which now seems to have been definitely undertaken."

A much stronger and determined Marine force resumed operations against El Chipote in January. While the columns headed north, Marine air patrols scouted ahead and reported the mountain to be a beehive of guerrilla activity. On January 14 wave after wave of airplanes bombed the wooded fortress, destroying vast quantities of equipment and supplies and leaving about forty-five dead. Sandino's force quickly broke up into small groups and evacuated the mountain.

By January 26 the arriving Marine ground units found the fortress empty with no trace of Sandino. All they found were burning campfire embers and straw dummies with black and red kerchiefs (intended to draw away Marine firepower). Continued patrolling failed to come up with anything substantial, and the second mission against El Chipote had still not pinned down Sandino, although it had chased him away. The Sandinistas then moved southward, where they plundered ranches and small towns in the departments of Esteli and Jinotega.

The U.S. charge in Managua then requested permission from the State Department to declare a state of war in Nueva Segovia. Washington, however, refused the request, with the official rationale that such a move would convert "Sandino's status from that of a mere bandit into that of a leader of an organized rebellion, with possibilities of recognition of his belligerency by an outside power." Clearly, the State Department wished to quickly eliminate the Sandinista movement without the attendant publicity and difficulty that the term "war" would give. Nevertheless, the *New York Times* noted that "not since the World War has the United States encountered such a fight as Sandino is carrying on in the mountains and jungles of Nicaragua."[10] In a last effort to induce Sandino to surrender, Admiral Sellers penned a letter to Sandino demanding his acceptance of the Stimson agreement. "It is equally superfluous," Sellers concluded, "for me to point out that the energetic and intensive campaign that our forces are shortly to undertake can have but one final result."

Like past efforts to cause Sandino's surrender, this too failed. The rebel leader's reply stated his immediate demands: "The only way to put an end to this struggle is the immediate withdrawal of the invading forces from our territory" and "supervising the coming elections by representatives of Latin America instead of by American Marines."

So the war went on. Sandino had been chased but not defeated. Rumors concerning his position circulated around the country, but as Admiral Sellers noted, "these reports often placed Sandino in widely separated places at the same time." Sandino was becoming a legend in his own time, and with each day that his elusive defiance went on, the legend grew.

The enlarged Marine brigade, although not positive of Sandino's exact location, kept on the offensive, pressing the insurgents away from settlements. The Marines themselves, however, did not believe that he would soon be captured. The initial optimism of 1927 had slowly given away to a sober reality.

Sandino's tactics—attacking unexpectedly and then fleeing before the Marines could strike back—his unwillingness to give battle except in ambush, and the extreme mobility of his forces, as compared to organized troops, had by early 1928 forced a reappraisal by the U.S. Command. The commanding general now admitted that the capture of Sandino would probably be "a matter of months or even years," while Admiral Sellers noted that the restoration of order "will be a slow process." But the country had to be pacified before the November 1928 election, and despite the new difficulties involved, Marine Commandant Lejeune expressed confidence that "we think we will be able to do it."

In early 1928 a comprehensive account of the Sandino problem as viewed by U.S. officials was cabled to Washington by Gen. Frank R. McCoy, chief of the U.S. Electoral Mission. Its essence distills the nature of the Sandinista guerrilla war and is worth quoting at length.

I have been seriously concerned over the military situation here. I have so expressed myself to the Marine Commandant with whom I have had daily conferences and have discussed with Admiral Sellers means for bringing about more effective prosecution of the operations. . . . The operations are generally of a type somewhat different from those for which the normal Marine corps training and equipment are well adapted. Sandino's forces have the advantage of the local language, thorough familiarity with the terrain, of the assistance, particularly as regards information, of elements some of which are in sympathy with Sandino while others either consider the continuance of his operations favorable to their immediate political purposes or else do not dare to incur the hostility of the outlaws by giving information or assistance to our forces. . . . Sandino has cleverly taken advantage of the factors favoring his operations including his superior mobility. Such encounters as have occurred have been largely at times and places of his own selection and such checks as he has suffered have usually been followed by loss of contact with his forces. . . . As regards the plan of the campaign, the necessity of the elimination of Sandino by determined and unrelenting pressure and pursuit has been constantly emphasized in my interviews with General Feland. Admiral Sellers representing the Navy Department and in command of both sea and land forces is a strong man, fully conscious of his mission and of the necessity for vigorous effort.

By this stage in the campaign the military command had no illusions regarding the nature of the war in which political leaders had placed them. A decisive defeat of the Sandinistas was no longer a practical objective. "The outlaw situation here will end," wrote General Feland, "by a collapse of their organization and a practical cessation of their activities only when their spirit is broken by constant pressure of the Marines. Such has ever been the end of Guerrilla Warfare." In early June he realized that "to insure the early elimination of Sandino a force would be required that would be so large that it would be impossible to supply it in the country where it would have to operate." The Marines realized that they were in a guerrilla war of attrition.

With the coming of the rainy season, active patrolling ended, with one exception. A river expedition of Marines was sent north in the hope that it could catch Sandino off guard and eliminate him quickly. The expedition was led by Capt. Merritt A. Edson and headed north for

Poteca on July 26. Although Poteca lay four hundred miles upstream, Edson and his ninety-man unit volunteered to make the trip up the rain-swollen Coco River in dugout canoes manned by native boatmen. As they proceeded along the hazardous river, boats capsized (intentionally, with the help of native boatmen, Edson soon realized), supplies were lost in the swift jungle river, men faltered with malaria, food ran short, and the patrol would have starved to death if it hadn't been for airdrops.

But the Coco River Patrol forged on, undaunted. On August 7 they reached Wamblan, Sandino's main outpost in the north. The engagement that followed left one Marine and ten guerrillas dead. Pursuing this advantage, Edson continued up the river toward Poteca, where the Sandinistas had fled. General Feland held out the hope that Edson would "virtually dispose of what is now the main body of them." Sandino's force was now in retreat, with Marine planes strafing them as they moved. On August 17 the Edson column finally reached Poteca, but as had happened so often in the past, they found it abandoned. Edson then sent out smaller patrols to catch the fleeing enemy but to no avail—they had already melted away into the dense countryside.

A lull in military activity followed this chase up the river. Sandino's forces were well scattered, with roving bands moving in several directions at once. Captured prisoners told Marines that Sandino himself had crossed into Honduras. The United States, however, was now fully committed to a fair and safe election in Nicaragua. By November over five thousand Marines and sailors were in occupation of all major polling districts.

Meanwhile, Sandino and his lieutenants had moved back into Nueva Segovia and Jinotega. The rebel leader Salgado, for example, had ninety men in the Segovia mountains, but constant Marine patrolling kept him moving. The biggest objective of the Sandinistas was to disrupt the American-supervised election. With this objective in mind, Pedro Altamirano moved into Jinotega and terrorized voters in hopes of dissuading them from going to the polls on November 4. A Legation cable to Washington recorded his actions: "Altamirano retreated toward the border plundering inhabitants, committing various other murders of a wanton, brutal character. Many people [were] captured, robbed, forced to act as burden bearers, (and) otherwise mistreated." But with this last act of vengeance, Sandino's army was forced out of the populated area by the increased U.S. presence.

Election day was quiet. Despite Sandino's intimidation, 130,004 votes were cast, with the Liberal candidate, General Moncada, easily defeating his Conservative rival. The conclusion of the election made good on a part of Stimson's original agreement with General (now President) Moncada. American policy was now faced with choices for the future, particularly that part of the agreement involving the maintenance of order. Policy had now reached a critical juncture. To a large degree, however, it was being forced by public criticism back home.

-12-

Nicaragua:
Protest and Withdrawal

The intervention of the Coolidge administration in Nicaragua brought forth a chorus of protest in Congress and among liberal and "anti-imperialist" segments of the general public. Mass demonstrations were held, the White House was picketed, and police had to forcibly remove the protesters. The disenchantment with guerrilla warfare against the Sandinistas was an important element in evolving relations with Nicaragua.

In the Senate, William H. Borah (R-Idaho), powerful chairman of the Senate Committee on Foreign Relations, became the most articulate and best-known congressional critic of the administration's policy. During the first landings of December 1926, he proclaimed, "the truth is, effort is being made to get this country into a shameless, cowardly little war with Mexico."[1] Other congressional critics soon fell in behind Borah. Early in January 1927 two resolutions were introduced in the Senate asking for a Marine withdrawal, but both were defeated.

Most Republicans in Congress remained loyal to the Coolidge administration while Democrats generally opposed the intervention. But the six-year congressional debate over Nicaragua was not exclusively confined to party lines. Time and again prominent Republicans (including Borah), in and out of Congress, rose to vigorously denounce the policies of both Coolidge and Hoover. The passion generated by the Nicaraguan debate sometimes blurred the distinction between party lines.

The situation in Nicaragua was discussed in open session in the Senate for the first time in mid-January 1927. Prominent "progressive" Republicans such as George Norris (Nebraska) and Robert La Follette

(Wisconsin), hammered away at the Coolidge administration. La Follette, in a fiery speech, summed up the opposition's case by pointing out that the Coolidge policy was (a) losing prestige for the United States, (b) unclear as to aims and objectives, (c) intervening in a civil war, (d) withholding information from the public at large, and (e) waging war without congressional consent.

These issues would remain the chief points used by congressional critics throughout the Nicaraguan debate. With varying degrees of emphasis and intensity, spokesmen for the opposition would continually confront both Republican presidents with similar arguments. Although the Senate and House were Republican-controlled, policy objection was so energetic and articulate that both administrations sometimes found it necessary to pursue policies by means of executive agreement in order to avoid congressional rejection. The training of the Guardia, supervision of Nicaraguan elections, and Marine combat against Sandino were all funded without congressional approval.

The reports of the Battle of Ocotal and the emergence of Sandino as an international figure greatly increased domestic protest. Congressional critics sharpened their attacks, and the volume of criticism during the next two years multiplied. The loss of American lives and the inability to bring the campaign to a conclusion added further fuel to the opposition fires. Senator Burton K. Wheeler wondered out loud: if the Marines were engaged against "bandits," could they not be put to better use in Chicago? Congressional attacks were sometimes emotional. Senator Clarence C. Dill, for example, labeled the intervention "one of the blackest and foulest crimes that has been committed against men." After the 1928 election in Nicaragua, pressure mounted steadily in Congress for removal of the Marines. Force reductions in 1929 and 1930 answered much of the criticism. These years saw a declining congressional opposition, as it appeared that President Hoover, as opposed to Coolidge, was moving steadily toward a withdrawal. The pace was slow, but it seemed as though the direction was correct.

The criticism of U.S. policies in Nicaragua on the part of the press and liberal groups in the nation was much less restrained than the congressional reaction. A rash of literature from a wide variety of left-wing, "anti-imperialist" sources flooded the country. Political groups sprang up overnight to harshly condemn the U.S. occupation, and many of them became emotionally pro-Sandinista. Academic, clerical, labor, and other groups signed petitions demanding an immediate U.S. evacuation.

Much of the press in the United States was opposed to the administration's policy. "The public certainly was stirred," wrote the *New York Times* correspondent, "but it was stirred against the State Department. A cry arose, from many conservative newspapers as well as the liberal ones, for light on what the administration was about in Latin America."[2]

The Battle of Ocotal and its aftereffects fanned into fresh flames the smoldering criticism of U.S. policy in Nicaragua. The great loss of Nicaraguan life at the hands of Marine aviation was interpreted by many policy critics as an example of American barbarism and cruelty. Even some congressmen referred to the Marines as the country's "ambassadors of death." Stories of Marines killing and bombing innocent civilians were disseminated during the remaining years of the occupation. Horrific pictures of the alleged results of Marine bombing attacks were printed.

The reports of Carlton Beals from *The Nation* probably had more influence among pro-Sandino groups than any other single source. After interviewing Sandino in Nicaragua, Beals returned to propagate the themes of U.S. imperialism, Marine blunderings, and Sandinista patriotism. Other journals, such as *Century, Outlook*, and *Nineteenth Century*, likewise played up this theme. *The Nation* sponsored "anti-Nicaraguan" conferences.

In January 1928 a demonstration against the intervention was attended by Mrs. Eleanor Roosevelt, William Allen White, Emerett Colby, Raymond B. Fosdick, and George Foster Peabody, all powerful figures of the day. During the summer and fall of 1928, the wave of adverse criticism refused to subside, and the Caribbean policy of the United States became an issue in the presidential campaign of 1928. Prominent Democrats, like Franklin D. Roosevelt, called upon the nation to renounce intervention "for all times."[3]

The Coolidge administration's critics were certainly smaller in number than its supporters, but the critics were louder and, hence, more visible. Like the congressional debate, however, dissent subsided after Marine withdrawals seemed to demonstrate that the country was on the right path. Much discontent lingered on, but the intensity of the debate was partially undercut by the Marine withdrawals of 1929 and 1930. The final withdrawal of all Marine units from the country in January 1933 was greeted by what one historian has called a "general rejoicing of the American press."[4]

The Battle of Ocotal also brought the issue to the rest of the world. It soon became impossible to explain the fiction of banditry in the face of an increasingly popular Sandinista international political and ideological movement. Indeed, the emergence of the Sandinistas as a political force beyond the borders of Nicaragua was as important as their military activities inside the country. Much of Sandino's international prestige was a direct outgrowth of Ocotal and the subsequent elusive guerrilla campaign he waged against the Marines. Like Fidel Castro, Che Guevara, and Commander "Zero" of a later generation, Augusto Sandino was a romantic folk hero, a political Robin Hood to the international left wing of the 1920s.

His cause was taken up throughout the Latin American left: by Argentina's socialist leader Alfredo Palacios, the Chilean poet Gabriela Mistral, the Mexican intellectual Jose Vasconcelos, the Peruvian revolutionary Victor Raul Saya de la Torre, etc. He was also seized upon by anti-U.S. governments in Latin America as a cause célèbre against growing U.S. influence.

The international reaction to U.S. intervention was almost universally hostile, particularly in Latin America. This was a regional movement, led by the Argentine government, and came to be much more than student and left-wing posturing. The second Marine intervention in Nicaragua happened to coincide with the emergence of an era of protest in Latin America against the continuing U.S. interference. The Sandino war became the focal point for this discontent. Throughout the entire episode, the Latin American press was nearly unanimous in its emphatic and constant denunciations of the continuing U.S. war against the Sandinistas.

At the Sixth Pan American Conference in 1928, the Nicaraguan intervention became the lead topic, putting U.S. diplomats on the defensive. Resolutions against the United States filled the air. Besides the Nicaraguan government, only Haiti and Cuba (both occupied by U.S. forces) defended the intervention. Indeed, the Sandino affair was the immediate prelude to the noninterventionist foreign policies, particularly the Good Neighbor policy, subsequently pursued by the Roosevelt administration.

The European reaction to the U.S. intervention was aloof and much more genteel, but hardly more sympathetic. Europe, as a whole, viewed the American difficulties with amused sarcasm. The intervention, however, according to the *New York Times*, caused more discussion in Europe than any action by Washington since the rejection of the Treaty of Versailles. American incursions into Nicaragua were thought to have "brought many chuckles in England, France, Germany, and Italy . . . [since, Europe felt] the United States has put herself on record in a fashion which will bind her to silence when the occasion presents itself to European powers to take analogous steps where their interests are at stake."[5] With America's tradition of anticolonialism in mind, Europe tactfully reminded the United States to mind its own business.

The early Sandinistas were crude but effective in exploiting this anti-American feeling. Sandinista propaganda agents distributed literature throughout the Western Hemisphere, and many of the leading newspapers regularly printed pro-Sandino statements. Sandino's propaganda arm regularly emphasized the themes of Hispanic nationalism and anti-Americanism and customarily exaggerated the success of his military operations against the Marines. His movement was given wide coverage and, in reality, represented a hemispheric propaganda war much greater in proportion than Sandino's actual military success within Nicaragua. In Guatemala a "Cigarrillo Sandino" was distributed, while "Nectar Sandino," a liquor, was sold in El Salvador. There was a Sandino Division in the Russian-advised Nanking Army during the 1927 Chinese civil war. Toribio Tijerino, one of Sandino's propagandists, started a new Central American publication called *Sandino*, explaining the ideals and goals of Sandinism. Demonstrations, lectures, and appeals for support were common in Central America and Mexico. Many of these were sponsored by communist and Marxist groups, such as the "Hands off Nicaragua" Committee, one of at least a dozen such groups that existed in Mexico alone.

The organizational chief for much of Sandino's propaganda was Pedro Zepeda, who used Mexico as a base to circulate a flood of Sandinista literature to Latin America. Jose Gonzales represented Sandino at the Second World Congress of Anti-Imperialists held in Frankfurt, Germany, in July 1929. The All-American Anti-Imperialist League in the United States circulated "Sandino" stamps until they were suppressed by the postmaster general. Subscription drives for funds to be sent to Sandino were successful in both Latin America and the United States. His brother, Socrates Sandino, became a Communist Party member and solicited funds inside the United States.

The *Communist International* originally backed his cause, and editorials in *The Daily Worker* solicited aid for him and encouraged support for the All-American Anti-Imperialist League. But Sandino was not a party member, and during his trip to Mexico in 1929 the Communist Party, apparently convinced that he was too nationalistic for them, labeled him a "traitor to the cause."[6] He remained, to the end, a home-inspired, nationalistic revolutionary.

American authorities certainly were not prepared for the propaganda arms of the Sandinista movement. But the emergence of Sandino as an international figure quickened efforts to eliminate him. The assistant secretary of state, for example, wrote, "He is . . . a figure of great international importance, especially in Latin America, and the inability of the Marines to get him so far has increased his international nuisance value and is causing us considerable annoyance in many ways."

A large part of Sandino's propaganda activity attempted to materially aid his military operations inside Nicaragua. The attempt to solicit funds, arms, food, and medical supplies was continent-wide. Early speculation as to the amount and degree of this aid was widespread in the press and Congress, but it was nearly impossible to be accurate. The following exchange, which took place in the U.S. Senate, is illustrative:

SENATOR JOHNSON: In your opinion is he receiving any outside aid?
GENERAL LANE: There are reports to that effect, and in my opinion he is; but it is just surmise.
SENATOR JOHNSON: Do you know when Sandino has received any other aid from outside countries?
ADMIRAL LATIMER: He had not when I left there, and I doubt whether he has since, except what he got from individuals across the border; not from any government.

While no Latin American government officially aided Sandino, a considerable number of supplies were privately purchased by the guerrillas in the United States and in Latin America during the last three years of the campaign. Many boatloads of munitions reached Sandino from Mexico. Other arms were either stolen or captured from Marines and Guardia or given to the guerrillas by Guardia deserters. Honduras was the chief "sanctuary" for Sandino. The U.S. minister there once related to those at home: "Honduras is used probably more than any other Central American country through which Sandino and the bandit leaders receive arms. . . . [A] barter trade in arms for products is carried on along the border . . . but this trade is difficult to control."

With the 1928 Nicaraguan elections safely behind them, U.S. authorities were no longer in a mood to continue the occupation indefinitely. "I fervently hope," wrote Assistant Secretary of State Francis White, "that we will have no more elections in Latin America to supervise." Washington, however, was reluctant to withdraw all U.S. troops immediately. For one thing, Sandino's inability to interrupt the elections had prompted the hope that he had given up. "It will not be long now," General Feland reported, "until we can say that they are cleaned up." More generally, U.S. officials were fearful of the consequences of an immediate withdrawal. The State Department noted that "a withdrawal which might be interpreted as weakness could very well lead to a very disagreeable situation."

By the beginning of 1929 American policymakers had reappraised the U.S. role in Nicaragua and decided on a gradual withdrawal of Marines, concurrent with a "Nicaraguanization" of the war against Sandino. During the spring and summer of 1929 over two thousand Marines were withdrawn from Nicaragua, and by early 1930 only about twelve hundred remained in the country.

This action was partly prompted by a lull in guerrilla activity. During most of 1929, Sandino was in Mexico soliciting support for his movement. His absence left the guerrilla war relatively quiet, a fact which prompted the brigade commander, Gen. Dion Williams, to comment that "this country has never been in such a peaceful state." This, however, was another deception. Sandino's absence was only a lull before the new storm.

During the first months of 1930, with Sandino back, guerrilla activity sharply increased. Sandinistas began again to raid the northern area and on several occasions were able to ambush combined Marine-Guardia patrols. Despite these signals of a possible return to full-scale insurgency, U.S. authorities continued reducing the Marines. The brigade commander was now writing pessimistically that to continue the occupation "would require many times the total available force of Marines and Guardia, and in addition, would produce no definite military results."

In the meantime, the Sandinistas mounted new and broader attacks. Sandino was now more aggressive, and the Guardia, which had taken over much of the responsibility in operations against him, was faring even worse than the Marines had before it. By late 1930 the U.S. minister in Nicaragua, Matthew Hanna, was reporting that "the disorder in Nicaragua is more widespread and threatening than it has been at any time during my residence here."

As the campaign dragged on, Sandino grew even more serious and deadly. Some of his lieutenants became relentless killers of both opposition and neutrals alike. The phrase "que sea pasado por las armas" (execute him) became a common ending of Sandino's circulars and letters.

The official Sandinista death came by machete—a much slower and torturous method than the firing squad. Minor offenses were also treated with the same instrument. These ranged from mutilations to grotesque *cortes*, methods of causing death by prolonged suffering. The most notorious of the cortes was the *corte de cumbo*, wherein the victim's head was severed at the top by a machete, leaving the base of the brain exposed. His death took long minutes, during which he usually spun around like a headless chicken.

Even slower was the *corte de chaleco* (waistcoat cut), where two slashes severed arm from shoulder while a third cut disemboweled the victim. Often the final blow beheaded the condemned in one stroke, ending his agony instantly. "Freedom is not conquered with flowers," Sandino wrote, "but with bullets, and this is why we have had to resort to the cortes."[7]

The violence of the Sandinistas had an immediate effect on U.S. policy when, on December 31, 1930, a patrol of ten Marines left their garrison at Ocotal to repair a broken telephone line. One of Sandino's "generals," Miguel Angel Ortez, ambushed the patrol near Achuapa, killing all but two. The remaining two, although severely wounded, managed to escape.

This massacre shattered American officials like nothing had since the Battle of Ocotal in 1927. It was also the first heavy U.S. loss in nearly two years. Minister Hanna cabled that the death of the Marines had "aroused public indignation and alarm, and greatly increased popular demand that energetic measures be adopted to terminate banditry and re-establish and restore peace in the Segovias." Nonetheless, order would have to be restored by the Guardia Nacional; Washington's determination to leave Nicaragua was irrevocable, despite worsening conditions. Throughout the summer and fall of 1931, the Guardia continued to be plagued by Sandino's hit-and-run tactics. It was obvious that he was getting stronger. The Guardia units, even with the aid of Marine aviation, could barely keep up with him, much less defeat him. The great chase was on again, but this time it was mostly Nicaraguans themselves chasing Sandino.

The only important combat activities of the Marine Corps during this time were led by Capt. Lewis B. "Chesty" Puller and his Company "M" (for "mobile"). With his gunnery sergeant, William A. Lee, Puller and his thirty enlistees from the Guardia scoured the hills against the guerrillas during 1932. In a lightning-quick movement lasting ten days, for example, Puller's company covered more than 150 miles of jungle and mountain terrain, fighting four pitched battles, and killing at least thirty enemy while destroying in the process over twenty-five of their camps. But Puller's swift pursuit came too late to save the intervention.

During the year 1932 the Sandinistas grew even bolder. The Guardia was unable to contain the new offensives. By mid-year Sandino's area of operations included all the provinces of the country except the lake district near Managua. Nevertheless, Washington stiffly adhered to its withdrawal policy. Herbert Hoover's new secretary of state, Henry Stimson—completely reversing his 1927 policy as a personal diplomat for Coolidge—privately wrote, "The more I think of it the more sure I am that I am right in regard to keeping the Marines from the center of Nicaragua." In doing so, however, he bitterly contrasted the intervention with the Philippine insurrection. "[T]he Marines haven't done their job . . . when one contrasts them with the way in which the Army handled similar problems in the Philippines, it simply hasn't been a good job well done. "

Stimson also had global problems in mind in withdrawing U.S. troops. By 1932 he felt embarrassed in his resistance to Japanese incursions in Manchuria because of the continued presence of Marines in Nicaragua. When asked by a reporter if he would ever land forces in Central America again, he responded, "Not on your life . . . it would undo all the labor of three years, and it would put me in absolute wrong in China, where Japan has done all of this monstrous work under the guise of protecting her nationals with a landing force."

Washington's revised estimate of Sandino was another factor in the policy reversal. Sandino had professed all along that the only rationale for his rebellion was the presence of American forces. By the late stages of the campaign, U.S. diplomats were beginning to accept this explanation. Charge Willard Beaulac cabled Washington that guerrilla disorders could well be "incidental to and derived from American assistance. In this connection it remains true that the avowed objective of Sandino . . . is to eject the American forces from Nicaragua." Minister Hanna later admitted that

> The possibility of eliminating Sandino will be greater if no Marines remain in Nicaragua and even if conciliation proved to be impossible, a united Nicaragua, having deprived Sandino of his principal excuse for belligerency, that is, the presence of American Marines on foreign soil, might be in a better position to eliminate banditry than the present government assisted by the Marines.

Assistant Secretary of State White himself noted that the "whole pose of Sandino . . . is that he is fighting Americans," thus a withdrawal would leave the guerrillas with "very little of a talking point left." By late 1932 State Department discouragement was so intense that White felt it "preferable to run the risk of revolutionary disturbances now and let the strong man emerge without further waste of time."

The mood of the United States had turned into grim frustration. Minister Matthew Hanna believed "that a disastrous turn of events after the withdrawal of the Marines is probable." The military had an equally pessimistic view of the Guardia: "It is not believed that the newly appointed native officers have had either sufficient time or experience to sufficiently conduct or maintain their organization after the guiding hand of the Marine Corps has been withdrawn." The U.S. military hierarchy, especially the Navy Department, had always been reluctant to withdraw. There was a general feeling that the Marines had not been given sufficient time or support to wage this strange guerrilla war properly. Admiral Pratt, chief of naval operations, expressed concern about "the good name of the Navy and Marine Corps, which would be getting out with the stigma of having failed in its job and withdrawing in the face of reverses." General Fuller, commandant of the Marine Corps, stated that "his acquiescence in the proposal to withdraw immediately was based on the failure of the Nicaraguan Government to give adequate financial support to the Guardia. He [Fuller] would welcome the opportunity to settle the situation with a sufficient force of Marines."

The last Marine departed Nicaragua on January 3, 1933, thus ending a six-year counterinsurgency that, in retrospect, posed a number of policy problems similar to the difficulties that the United States was to experience thirty years later in Vietnam and similar, in turn, to issues faced in past insurrections. While Sandino's troops were small in number and he lacked the technology to defeat the Marine Corps, his combination of political leverage and guerrilla war made him a true political revolutionary in the twentieth-century use of the term. A Marine Corps historian paid him at least this begrudging compliment:

Sandino was in every respect a wholly new phenomenon for the Marine Corps and the United States, and very much a man of the new century. Unlike Haiti's Charlemagne Peralte or the fiery bandits of Santo Domingo, Sandino was no local primitive on an island who could be isolated by control of the sea and removed from power by systematic police action. In his articulacy, his talent for agitation, his international connections, his exploitation of the press, his deft intrigue, his cynical disregard of political commitments, his vanishing across "neutral" frontiers, Sandino is far more readily recognizable in the 1960s than in the 1920s.[8]

Within the means at his disposal Sandino waged a classic guerrilla struggle. In principle, his tactics differed little from those espoused by more modern Communist revolutionary practitioners. The manner in which he rallied countrymen to his cause, blending nationalist attraction with terror, was summarized by a Marine communique in 1930:

> The natives throughout the countryside—through fear, often times blood relationship to bandits, resentment at presence of U.S. forces, and in some cases an ignorant sympathy for the perverted propaganda of their bandit leaders—seldom give timely information on bandits and their movements, but on the other hand, aid and assist and forewarn bandit groups of movements of Marine and Guardia patrols.

The problems posed to U.S. decision makers in Nicaragua bore a striking similarity to the cycle of policy syndromes observable in many other insurrections: the illusion that the U.S. role would be advisory and temporary, the "Americanization" of the war effort when the local army was seen as an auxiliary, and a U.S. withdrawal and de-escalation simultaneous with a dramatic revival of the local army's role. Most of these campaigns were conducted in a climate of hostile domestic and international opinion. Themes of aggressive "imperialism," accusations against American atrocities, and waging "unconstitutional" or "illegitimate" war were commonplace in the atmosphere of the Caribbean interventions, as they would be later regarding Vietnam and were earlier regarding the Philippines and other campaigns.

Most of the campaigns were fought in small, backward areas where the terrain and the enemy's tactics plagued conventional military strategies. In most cases, the presence of American forces helped stimulate the nationalistic appeals of the enemy and allowed him to enlist a sizeable portion of the countryside to his cause. Most important, however, the elusive guerrilla in the field usually understood that a defeat of the American military was impossible and that the strategic "center of gravity" was the American political culture and its tendency to grow weary of protracted and unproductive warfare in distant regions. Sandino's massacre of eight Marines in December 1931, for example, according to Marine historian Clyde Metcalf (who saw duty in Nicaragua), "was apparently made in the hope that such a disaster would create a demand in the United States for the immediate withdrawal of all the Marines from Nicaragua."[9]

If this was the case (Sandino left no records), Metcalf's political acumen was amazingly accurate. Metcalf had also summarized the U.S. problem in 1929, a problem very similar to the type of insurrections earlier generations faced from the swamps of Florida to the jungles of the Philippines:

By the beginning of 1929 it was becoming more and more evident to all concerned that the Marines in Nicaragua had been called upon to perform an almost impossible task, in the face of difficulties over which they had no control. They were expected to maintain order—taken to mean the eradication of banditry—without any control over the civil population, on whom they were almost entirely dependent for information, co-operation, and support. Neither the people nor their officials stood behind the Marines in their attempt to put down lawlessness. The bandits were able to intimidate the people into telling the Marines nothing about the bandits' movements and to keep them informed of all the movements of the Marines. The bandits were able to hide their weapons and disguise their identity, almost at a moment's notice, and pass as peaceful citizens. Notwithstanding all of their vigorous efforts, officers conducting the campaign were practically unanimous in the opinion that the military situation had reached a stalemate. So long as the people would not assist the Marines, the bandits could continue to operate in small groups and carry on their depredations in spite of everything the Marines could do.[10]

Despite these difficulties, the Marines gave an excellent account of themselves in Nicaragua. They were tactically energetic during the time when they were active against Sandino and, on occasion, displayed rare brilliance in the strict application of counterguerrilla war, as Puller's operations attest. Most U.S. Marines, however, were unprepared for either strict counterguerrilla war or for the sensitive relationship that was required in their dealings with the native Guardia. There were ten

Guardia mutinies during the occupation, plus many other incidents of sporadic friction between Marines and natives.

The most important legacy the American military derived from the Nicaraguan fighting was—not surprisingly—technological in nature. Establishing itself as the master in counterguerrilla aviation, the United States pioneered a number of combined air-ground military innovations, including dive-bombing attacks. In one year alone, the United States conducted eighty-four air attacks against the guerrillas on the ground. American-built airfields dotted the Nicaraguan terrain; eighteen were constructed between 1927 and 1928 alone. In 1930 Marine aviation made over 5,000 separate sorties, 1,275 being strictly military and the rest being logistical or miscellaneous (mail delivery, communications, etc.). The Nicaraguan war, from the American standpoint, was truly dependent upon airpower more than any other campaign to that time in history. The use of airpower was not only consistent with the traditional American emphasis on technological war but also set a precedent that would later realize its logical fulfillment over the skies of Vietnam.

For their part, Sandino's men had great respect for the American air arm. The Marines had twelve Falcon and Corsair observation-bomber planes in Nicaragua, in addition to seven amphibian observation-bombers and five Fokker transport aircraft. Together, these planes constantly scanned the skies, either in search of guerrillas or in assistance missions for Marine units. By mid-1928 the Sandinistas had become extremely wary of the planes, which often swooped down on them without warning, machine guns blazing. Their terrible defeat at Ocotal had been exclusively the result of U.S. airpower. "They [Sandinistas] move almost entirely at hours when the planes cannot reach them," Major Rowell of Marine Aviation noted. "They camouflage their camps and stables and confine their operations to terrain offering the best cover from aerial observation, and never fire on the planes unless they find themselves discovered and attacked."[11]

Some of the charges of Marine atrocities included the bombing of peaceful towns and the killing of innocent women and children from the air. Like other charges of Marine cruelty (mistreatment of prisoners, burning of villages, etc.), these contained elements of truth but were deliberately exaggerated by opponents of the intervention in order to discredit it. For the most part, the Marine command scrupulously dictated against indiscriminate bombing, despite the occasional abuses that occurred. Major Rowell deplored those journalists, such as Carleton Beals of *The Nation*, who played up these abuses while otherwise overlooking the more deliberate and systematic cruelty of the guerrillas. Rowell was ordered not to bomb towns or in any other way to terrorize the innocent. This often allowed the enemy a sanctuary inside the village, prompting Rowell to complain about "the restrictions of a political nature that crippled the morale and effectiveness of Marine airpower."[12] Identical complaints would repeat themselves throughout the Vietnam War.

Throughout the arduous guerrilla campaign, both the Nicaraguan and Washington governments variously classified Sandino as a "bandit" or "outlaw." When the Marines withdrew in January 1933, at the time Sandino's armed resistance ceased, the official classification of Sandino as a bandit was seriously eroded. By attacking U.S.-owned property and by clinging to the traditional revolutionary practice of looting, Sandino—to be sure—gave substance to the charges of banditry. But the credibility of the earlier view has to be judged against Sandino's unflinching opposition to both the American presence and to the Nicaraguan government. In truth, Sandino was a revolutionary guerrilla and much more than a mere bandit.

U.S. denunciation of Sandino as a bandit was motivated by its desire to convince the American public and the world that the United States was intervening in Nicaragua to preserve order and peace against illegality. With the civil war officially over in 1927, the United States refused to recognize the existence of a revolutionary third party in Nicaragua. The charges of banditry had become a U.S. effort against official recognition of the Sandinistas as a political party in Nicaragua. The United States was deceiving itself.

From a military perspective, it was logical for American authorities to view Sandino—the guerrilla—as only a bandit. This mindset had been ingrained in professional U.S. military thought for well over a century. In actual practice, furthermore, the charge had often enough been true. With the memory of William Quantrill, Jesse James, and others in mind, American officials had made a similar mistake in their initial judgment of guerrillas in the Philippines, Haiti, and the Dominican Republic. It is small wonder that their immediate reaction to the Sandinistas was the same. But by the close of the Sandino war U.S. officials had reversed their initial estimate of the Nicaraguan partisans as cowardly "bandits," begrudging the enemy a degree of popular support and a nationalist base. In effect, the United States reluctantly gave the Sandinistas a measure of strategic respect.

After the Marines left, a new era of politics began in Nicaragua. Using the U.S.-created Guardia Nacional, Anastasio Somoza inaugurated a dynasty of more than four decades of dictatorship over Nicaraguan political and economic life. Somoza was assassinated in 1956, but his two sons continued the family reign until 1979, when a second generation of Sandinistas, using modern guerrilla techniques and aided by Cuba and the Soviet Union, finally toppled the Somoza dynasty.

Sandino himself did not live to see the beginnings of the Somoza era. With the Guardia in the hands of Somoza, Sandino and his followers (then up to three thousand) retired to Nueva Segovia province, their weapons still with them. Hostilities between the Sandinistas and the Guardia flared up throughout the summer and fall of 1933.

In February 1934 the Nicaraguan president summoned both Sandino and Somoza to a peace conference in Managua. On the evening of the twenty-first, a dinner was held for Sandino, hosted by the president. After the festivities, Sandino and two compatriots were driven from the presidential palace toward downtown Managua. They were stopped at a Guardia roadblock at ten in the evening. All three were dragged from their car, lined up, and shot to death. Their bodies were quickly buried under the runway of Managua's airport.

As quickly as that, the original Sandinistas were finished in Nicaragua, Mafia-style victims of the Guardia and the intrigues of a political culture that knew only violence and revolution. Eight years of continuous warfare had finally brought a sort of truce to the infighting of Nicaragua's violent political system. For its part, the United States was through with intervention into Latin American guerrilla wars, a factor that led directly to the Good Neighbor policy of the 1930s and a whole new era of foreign policy.

The political lessons of continual interventions, particularly as absorbed by the leaders who had to supervise these events, was best summarized shortly after the last Marine had departed Nicaragua. In 1935 Albert K. Weinberg noted that the benefits of social progress imposed by force were not universally appreciated. The lesson is worth quoting at length and is equally worth remembering today:

> In point of fact the corrective enterprise on the island of Santo Domingo succeeded in everything better than in training for self-government. The authorities responsible for the political education of Haiti "twice dissolved her legislative assembly at the point of the gun, wrote a constitution and forced it upon the Haitian people, and set up on Haitian soil a government contrary to all the principles of political freedom." In the five years when Americans held the Dominican Re-

public under martial law, "public meetings were forbidden, the press censored, protesters court-martialed," and "every governmental function was taken over by American Marines." To be sure, these severities were due not to [the] design of the Government but to America's lack of preparation for such protectorates, limitations of the military mind in political administration, and the almost inevitable tendencies of militaristic reform itself. Moreover, these later acknowledged and regretted evils were perhaps overbalanced by substantial improvements in the external elements of civilization, such as sanitation, road-building, and security of life. Unfortunately, the more self-respecting natives were like Latin Americans in general in appreciating these material benefits less than the purely sentimental satisfactions of independent sovereignty.[13]

The United States was finished with Manifest Destiny and singular occupations. In his inaugural address of 1933, newly elected president Franklin D. Roosevelt reversed decades of American military interventions with the Good Neighbor policy, which began a new era of multilateral diplomacy between the United States and Latin America, subsequently developing the inter-American "system" and the Organization of American States.

-13-

World War:
Guerrilla Theaters

The withdrawal of U.S. Marines from Nicaragua in 1933 was, in retrospect, the end of an era. The modern American military that emerged after World War II was a much different instrument from the horse cavalry and volunteer infantry that had fought the hundreds of little battles during the many small wars against Indian tribes, Caribbean "banditos," and Asian guerrillas in the nineteenth and early twentieth centuries. The sophisticated U.S. military of the Cold War era was defined by technology: helicopters, tanks, missiles, long-range bombers, jet fighters, submarines, aircraft carriers, and nuclear weapons. The experience of winning the greatest wars in world history pushed U.S. military strategy further toward the type of large-scale, conventional, and technological dimensions that 1918 and 1945 symbolized. Despite the dominance of orthodox strategies and weapons, however, a number of practitioners began rediscovering guerrilla tactics in the jungles, mountains, and swamps of Japanese-occupied Asia.

During World War II, U.S. soldiers fought fringe campaigns of irregular warfare against the Japanese army in the Asian-Pacific theater. These were all small-scale compared to the amphibious campaign against Japanese-held islands in the Pacific, but these operations provide the only link between the irregular wars of the old military and the modern era of "counterinsurgency." Many of these guerrilla efforts against Japan, particularly in the Philippines, were the result of improvised strategies devised by a handful of adventurous soldiers, while others were loosely coordinated back in Washington by the Office of Strategic Services (OSS) and its flamboyant director, William "Wild Bill" Donovan. The United Stated also cooperated (and sometimes conflicted) with the parent British organization, the Special Operations Executive (SOE).

208

Donovan was a hero of the Great War and a Wall Street corporate millionaire. With the outbreak of World War II, the United States had no operational or institutional capacity for unconventional warfare. The history and culture of the subject was far beneath orthodox army thinking, which had grown to view anything beyond tradition as "un-American." This situation changed, however, on July 11, 1941, when President Roosevelt established the Office of Coordinator of Information (COI) and named Donovan as the first director. COI would later evolve into OSS.

The inspiration for the new American innovation, however, came more from the British than from anything Donovan himself had conceived. After wartime fact-finding trips to Britain and the Middle East, Donovan was so inspired by the British Secret Intelligence Service, with its creativity in psychological and irregular actions, that he recommended a similar organization for America, itself then only on the brink of war. In forming what was called "a new instrument of war,"[1] the COI sought to weaken enemy resolve through psychological penetration via radios and propaganda, followed up by "softening" operations such as commando and guerrilla raids, all in support of an advancing infantry. Thus, the first centralized U.S. agency in support of unconventional war defined its ultimate goals in terms that were almost exclusively conventional, and even these had to be hammered through the military bureaucracy. This reflected the American traditional faith in technology and conventional war, where irregular actions served only as adjuncts to the army.

The original COI was divided in two by Roosevelt in June 1942, with the psychological war function called the Office of War Information (OWI) and the paramilitary function now called the OSS and with Donovan as the director. From the beginning, Wild Bill was as unorthodox as the agency he was running. His initial recommendation to the president called for a revolution in tradition, "a guerrilla corps, independent and separate from the Army and Navy, and imbued with a maximum of the offensive and imaginative spirit."[2] It goes without saying that the professional military was not especially excited about a new, fledgling, largely civilian organization operating "independently and separately" from command hierarchy and led by a millionaire named Wild Bill. Nor did it help that Donovan enjoyed special and unusual access to the president. In providing independent, civilian leadership in an area scorned by most military and diplomatic professionals, Donovan was viewed by most observers as a dangerous loose cannon. So intense was the opposition to his movement that William Langer, head of Research and Analysis, within OSS, observed that "perhaps

Bill Donovan's greatest single achievement was to survive."[3] This was an understatement, as William R. Corson pointed out much later: "For Donovan to think, even with FDR's endorsement, that such an organization could be brought to pass in the face of the military's obvious objections was, charitably, an act of lunacy on his part."[4]

Corson was correct in the long run, but the OSS survived the duration of the war, and while the opposition of the military prevailed in the end, a postwar self-assessment by the OSS claimed, with a measure of self-endorsement, that the organization "undertook and carried out more different types of enterprises calling for more varied skills than any other single organization of its size in the history of our country."[5] At peak strength no more than thirteen thousand employees, half of whom never left U.S. shores, the OSS must still be considered the spiritual godfather of the unconventional warfare operations of the Cold War, the immediate ancestor of the Special Forces of the 1950s and the Green Berets of the 1960s. Alongside the OSS in this lineage were the U.S. Army Ranger battalions, which were organized under official army jurisdiction for commando operations in Europe and begun under Col. William O. Darby in June 1942.

Although they were short-lived, the OSS and other U.S. enterprises during World War II played an active role in the resistance movements against both Japanese and German occupations. "Modern" American unconventional warfare properly began in Burma during World War II. By early 1942 the Japanese had overrun all of Southeast Asia, including Burma on the western flank and the Philippines in the Pacific Ocean. In Burma, the United States had dispatched Col. W. R. Peers, Gen. "Vinegar Joe" Stilwell, and seven hundred men to organize guerrilla resistance behind Japanese lines. These Americans joined forces with British troops and native Burmese (mostly from the Kachin tribe) to harass and intimidate the Japanese. They formed a separate outfit under Col. Frank Merrill ("Merrill's Marauders"), which operated briefly with the Kachins in northern Burma. Together, these combined U.S. and Burmese irregulars killed or wounded thousands of Japanese troops and effectively prevented the enemy's freedom of movement. Eventually the Kachin tribe was placed under Stilwell's overall command. As Detachment 101 under an OSS command led by Colonel Peers, guerrilla companies, of about 125 Kachins each, fanned out in the Burmese theater to gather intelligence and harass the Japanese. They became legendary for their skills as guerrilla operatives under regular command, using the familiar tactics of jungle ambush, booby traps, and bamboo stakes. By guiding Merrill's

Marauders through enemy rear lines, the Kachins also proved invaluable as scouts, on one occasion leading troops through hundreds of miles of jungle canopy to capture a vital airfield, an event made into the movie *Merrill's Marauders*. Almost seven hundred U.S. Army officers and men contributed to the Burmese operation, with total guerrilla strength by 1945 at ten thousand. According to OSS historian R. H. Smith, Detachment 101 in Burma was "the most successful OSS guerrilla operation of the war."[6]

Roger Hilsman, who later helped President Kennedy form the Green Berets, has described the life of American-led guerrillas in wartime Burma:

> During World War II, our OSS guerrilla battalion operated behind the enemy lines in Burma. Nothing pleased us more in those days than to have a regular Japanese force take out after us. They operated in large unwieldy units that were easy to ambush. Their movements were simple to follow through the mountains and jungle. We felt that our own existence was well justified when the Japanese had to take regular forces from front line fighting to chase a guerrilla unit. At one stage, my outfit—consisting of four Americans and about 200 Burmese—kept a whole Japanese regiment of 3,000 men marching and countermarching over the mountains far away from the front lines. What we would have feared far more were smaller groups patrolling steadily—especially cavalry.[7]

By the spring of 1942 the regular Japanese army had driven the British out of Burma, and General Stilwell was ordered to take command of two Chinese armies and train them in commando tactics, to harass the enemy and eventually drive him out of Burma. Stilwell was thoroughly army and had little use for OSS irregulars, but his tactical operations still remain classically unconventional. With about sixty-six thousand Chinese organized into four divisions, Stilwell led this force through two hundred miles of jungle, swamp, and mountain terrain. His tactical maneuvers were masterpieces of irregular evasion, as he instructed his men to discipline themselves to engage Japanese forces in the jungle by brief frontal ambushes, only to envelope them on the flanks by fast-moving guerrilla attacks. Stilwell was then dispatched to China to assist the Nationalists under Chiang Kai-chek, an appointment that led to internecine political warfare between himself and Chiang and to Stilwell's ultimate removal.

Inside occupied China itself, over two thousand U.S. soldiers led by a naval officer, M. E. Miles, conducted sporadic raiding parties against the Japanese army. Miles's organization was heavily infiltrated by Nationalist Chinese secret police, and as a result, he found himself unwittingly involved in Chiang Kai-chek's political wars against the Chinese Communists. Nevertheless, Miles and his men were able to communicate weather and logistical information to the U.S. Pacific Fleet and, at least by his own account, killed thousands of Japanese. Miles's pro-Nationalist politics, however, ultimately led to his own downfall when official Washington moved toward a neutral position between Chiang and Mao Tse-tung. In 1945 his guerrilla organization was placed under an army command and he was forced to stop his clandestine and independent operations.

Similar political complications in China had earlier led to the dismissal of Stilwell, his replacement by pro-Chiang general A. C. Wedemeyer, and a four-part, confused political and military nightmare between the Chinese Nationalists (Chiang), the Communists (Mao), the Japanese, and the United States. The latter complicated this picture even more by a set of pocket factions, alternatively pro- and anti-Chiang. The long story of this tragedy—an American strategic disaster after World War II—cannot be told here, but it led to the collapse of the Nationalists and the Chinese Communist victory in 1949, to the eventual Vietnam debacle of the 1960s, and to the continuing legacy that the "fall" of China was caused by American ineptitude and, ultimately, even betrayal at the highest levels.

At the same time that Americans were organizing anti-Japanese resistance in Burma and China, similar teams were instrumental in the Philippine Islands, which soon became the scene of numerous contacts between American-led guerrillas and Japanese soldiers. After the fall of Corregidor, in early 1942, many U.S. soldiers retreated behind Japanese lines to remote areas of the Philippines, where they organized small guerrilla bands of natives. About fifty such groups emerged in the Philippines before the Japanese were able to consolidate their conquest. In a country of seven thousand islands and a land area of 115,000 square miles, these irregulars were as disparate and diverse as the terrain in which they operated. Many were simply bandits, others were Communists, but those who were led by Americans were the same Filipinos who would later line the beaches for General MacArthur's return. Ironically, forty years after their conquest of Aguinaldo's massive insurgent resistance, these Americans became guerrillas in their own right against the new conquerors from Japan.

General MacArthur, reflecting overall army opinion, refused to allow OSS to operate in the South Pacific, in spite of a plan advanced by Donovan for coordination of guerrilla resistance in the islands. But individual American officers, such as Navy commander Cliff Richardson and Army colonel Wendell Fertig, organized irregular armies of Filipinos. Scores of uprisings in the larger and more remote areas of Luzon and Mindanao kept the Japanese from a complete conquest of the archipelago. Viable guerrilla units sprang up elsewhere, and by 1943 the Philippines were a beehive of anti-Japanese irregular actions.

One such outfit, organized by Commander Richardson, was led by a Philippine army officer, Ruperto Kangleon. He aroused Japanese attention by organizing a vast area of the archipelago into a network of spies and informers, which, in turn, kept his quasi-army aware of the presence and movement of enemy forces and their constant regular infantry "sweeps." Kangleon was recognized by General MacArthur as the "official" guerrilla commander on Leyte Island, where American submarines kept his forces supplied with food, clothing, and arms. This guerrilla group was typical of hundreds in its methods, using classic partisans against armed and brutal occupiers from outside. As told by Ira Wolfert, they were able to develop: "a whole network of volunteer guards . . . civilians serving without pay, donating one day out of every four to act as sentinels or relay men for messages or lookouts. When Japanese approached, the civilians were warned, too, and in the hills many coastal barrio patrols found only empty houses and vacant towns."[8]

In northern Luzon, the guerrilla war was led by a thirty-year-old West Point captain by the name of Russell W. Volckmann. Later promoted to colonel for his success, Volckmann started from scratch in 1942 and by 1944 had organized over twenty thousand natives against Japan. By his own records, Volckmann estimated that his three years of intensive guerrilla warfare took about fifty thousand Japanese casualties.

Officers like Volckmann and Richardson, plus thousands of Filipino soldiers and civilians made it impossible for Japan to subdue the interior of the country. The Japanese army used relentless but conventional search-and-sweep operations, plus a huge informer and spy network, day and night patrolling, and cruel torture measures against nationalist insurgents. Despite massive Japanese countermeasures, they were almost completely frustrated by the experience. They simply could not defeat an aroused and united civilian populace. Colonel Volckmann has testified to the relentless and aggressive counterguerrilla operations of the Japanese army:

[T]he Japs retaliated in force and rushed thousands of troops into North Luzon. For eight months they conducted relentless mopping-up operations against the guerrilla forces and the loyal civilians supporting the resistance movement. Every town and city was garrisoned, and ten-day patrols which combed the surrounding country were kept out by each garrison. Entire civilian settlements suspected of supporting the "banditos" were destroyed. . . . The entire civilian population was organized into "Neighborhood Associations" in which fifteen families were placed under a head, the "Presidente," who in turn was held directly responsible to the mayor of the municipality for the families under him. The mayor was answerable to the local Japanese Garrison commander. The Neighborhood Associations were required to post around-the-clock guards on all trails and roads and to report all guerrilla activities.[9]

In the vast southern island of Mindanao the resistance was helped by the organizing genius of a mining engineer and reserve officer, Col. Wendell Fertig, who began with a guerrilla unit of five officers and 175 men. The unit faced an occupation army of about 175,000, which relied on the orthodox military "sweep" described above, a tactic that not only devastated the jungles around them but also succeeded in alienating the population within. By 1943 partisans under Fertig, and others such as Maj. Rex Blow, had grown to over ten thousand and were able to assume more aggressive tactics against the Japanese army. Small patrols were sent out in pursuit of isolated enemy columns and positions. Interisland communications were developed through the so-called bamboo telegraph, often employing women and children as field runners and informants. As described by Rex Blow:

When out on patrol we never carried anything but a change of clothes, a toothbrush and our arms. Every house we passed would offer us something to eat, whether it was a piece of corn or a fat chicken. The Japs were now offering quite a large reward for my head, dead or alive—the price being 5,000 yards of West Point khaki drill, valued at about 20 pesos a yard then. But there was never the slightest suggestion of earning that prize.[10]

So effective were the guerrilla movements in the Philippines that, by the time of the eventual American landings, many of the beachheads and airstrips needed for the invasion had already been seized and protected by partisan groups.

Unconventional U.S. operations during World War II were also extended to France, where the OSS sent several hundred Americans to assist the resistance in sabotage and commando operations against the German occupation. One specialist has labeled OSS action inside France as "the major OSS effort during the war,"[11] where three separate lines of operational duties coexisted. The first consisted of seventy-seven civilian operatives who worked as radio technicians and planned sabotage attacks against the German occupation. The second group of seventy-eight Americans, named the "jedburgh team," was parachuted into France beginning on D-Day and helped organize intelligence and guerrilla activities. As a young army lieutenant assigned to the OSS, Maj. Gen. John Singlaub later reflected on his involvement as a jedburgh in occupied France:

> As planned, we joined Wauthier and Jacques at a ruined forest church on the western side of the Corrèze valley. They were exhausted but quite pleased with themselves. It had taken all of Jacques's persuasive powers to convince the cautious Wauthier to split his unit into small ambush teams. But once he did, their ambushes between Ussel and Egletons had destroyed one armored car and knocked out six trucks. They counted at least twenty-five enemy dead and many wounded on the highway. The German relief column had not reached Egletons until dawn. Coriolan's agents reported that the enemy garrison in the school had loaded thirty casualties onto the convoy before the trucks departed for Tulle. The fortress we had struggled to take was now empty. But Hubert's troops had linked up with Antoine's ambush positions and together they continued to harass the German column.[12]

The third, and largest, OSS operation consisted of some 356 French-speaking Americans organized into "operational groups," who also parachuted into France and assisted the resistance with guerrilla attacks. "The principles that they embodied," Alfred Paddock has written, "were to significantly influence the Army's effort to develop a similar capability in later years."[13] In its *Summary of French Resistance, 6 June—31 August, 1944*, the army gave official, albeit grudging, credit to the OSS by noting that, "it is not at all out of place for OSS in general ... to take credit for its share in the planning and directing of the overall scheme of sabotage." General Eisenhower stated for the record that the French Resistance was worth fifteen divisions to him in the Normandy invasion.[14]

OSS operations and plans often conflicted with the more experienced and sophisticated British SOE, and—not unlike the greater war effort itself—the two organizations often operated at cross-purposes where bitter infighting and policy problems existed. But at least by one British account, the Americans earned their credentials as irregular partisans. A high-level SOE official, Bickham Sweet-Escott, once wrote, "By the end of the war their [OSS] bitterest detractors would be forced to admit that they had become quite as good as the British at getting secret intelligence and at carrying out special operations, and I personally thought that they were doing better."[15]

With the death of Franklin D. Roosevelt in April 1945, the OSS lost its godfather. On October 1 of that same year President Truman, bowing to various pressures, ordered that the OSS be disbanded. According to CIA historian Harry Howe Ransom, these pressures came from many quarters and, indeed, reflected part of American political culture as well.

> [A]pparently because of pressures from the armed services, the Federal Bureau of Investigation [FBI], the Department of State, and the Bureau of the Budget. Another influence was undoubtedly Mr. Truman's own apparent prejudice against cloak and dagger operations by the United States. To continue an international spying organization in peacetime seemed somehow un-American in the atmosphere of the immediate postwar period.[16]

Less than a month after the Japanese surrender, the only organized capability to wage irregular war in U.S. history was eliminated entirely. Another specialist on guerrilla war, Charles Thayer, places responsibility for this on American culture to be sure, but particularly as enshrined by the professional military, which "harbors a deep-seated aversion to guerrillas, apparently because they fit no conventional pattern and their underhanded clandestine tactics have little in common with the military code of honor and chivalry."[17]

By the end of World War II, the U.S. interest in unconventional operations had disappeared almost altogether. Communist guerrilla wars, however, were just getting off the ground. The Cold War had begun.

-14-

Cold War:
Aid and Advice

During the long and protracted era of history known as the Cold War, American soldiers were called into armed conflict as "cobelligerents" on two significant occasions, both on the peninsular "rimlands" of the Far East, geographically far removed from the center of the issue in western Europe. The final termination of the Cold War in Europe occurred between 1989 and 1991, with barely a shot fired in anger. Given the great destruction of European armies in both world wars, plus the enormous demolition of cities and civilians in World War II, this may well stand as the most powerful single fact of the entire twentieth century. The peaceful death of European Communism becomes even more remarkable given the destructive potential of the conventional and nuclear arsenals available to each of the Cold War antagonists. The exact nature and cause of the end of the Cold War, not unlike most of history's other great contests, will probably never find consensus among historians. Our purpose here is merely to note the irony, since almost all of American military deaths in the Cold War occurred in areas away from the global center, particularly in Vietnam where the historic incapacity of the American military to appreciate the nature of unconventional warfare led to perhaps the greatest strategic tragedy in U.S. history.

A major exception to this, largely unnoticed compared to Vietnam, was the victorious American aid and advice programs that helped arrest Communist insurrections in both Greece and the Philippines shortly after World War II. These counterguerrilla wars were also dwarfed by the Korean War (1950–53), a largely conventional contest reminiscent of the trench warfare in World War I. Korea contained a guerrilla sideshow, but it, too, was lost against the larger picture.

The U.S. intervention in Vietnam (1961–75), occurred within a true insurrection, beginning as a wholesale guerrilla operation and concluding with regular combat only after the United States had ruled out a lasting military victory. The differences are rooted both in the terrain of each peninsula (jungle canopy versus open plains and mountains), as well as in the politico-military strategies adopted by each of the two Communist opponents. The Korean War ended as the Truman administration wished it to, without the liberation of the North as demanded by General MacArthur. The results remain intact today: an independent and free South, a totalitarian and isolated North, and an area in between where the possibility of armed conflict is among the highest in the world. In this respect the Korean War has still not ended. Vietnam was a defeat for the United States by almost any definition. It is today a closed chapter of history, although, still, a Communist dictatorship rules in the long aftermath of America's only "lost" war. Both Korea and Vietnam offer stark and lasting testaments to the distinctions between strategic cultures: conventional war, in which Americans were able employ their weapons and infantry and hold a geographic line, versus unconventional war, in which Americans discovered that airpower and infantry tactics only prolonged the essential political and revolutionary nature of the contest. Geographic "lines" had little meaning in the midst of Vietnam's jungle and swamp terrain, and the real "front" existed in America's political backyard, amid the war-weariness and protests that the conflict had generated back home.

U.S. intervention into each of the two areas of the far eastern perimeter also reflects profoundly upon the ingrained American strategic *Weltanschauung* of political life as essentially two-dimensional, good versus evil, or in the latest incarnation, "either for us or against us." While this mindset has logical roots within the philosophical founding of the Republic, the "city on a hill," the particular characteristics that led U.S. entry into the Cold War were manifest in the leadership of each of the three political administrations that waged the early Cold War. President Harry S. Truman, a farmer and merchandise salesman from rural Missouri, found true strategic common ground with both Dwight D. Eisenhower, a West Point graduate and leader of history's greatest war, and John F. Kennedy, a wealthy Catholic Brahmin from Boston's Back Bay. Their cultural distinctions were overshadowed by the fact that they were Americans, who, in Kennedy's inspirational words, viewed the Cold War as a continuation of "the same revolutionary beliefs for which our forebears fought [which] are still at issue around the globe—

the belief that that the rights of man come not from the generosity of the state, but from the hand of God."

In announcing the Truman Doctrine in 1947, President Truman stressed the idea that U.S. foreign policy would "support free peoples who are resisting attempted subjugation by armed minorities or by outside pressures." In his inaugural address two years later, this same theme was repeated: U.S. policy would "provide unmistakable proof of the joint determination of the free countries to resist armed attack from any quarter." The origins of such a determined ideological and geopolitical policy from the American side rested, as Truman put it in the same address, "from the faith which has inspired this nation from the beginning . . . that all men have the right to freedom of thought and expression [and] that all men are created equal because they are created in the image of God." Truman's secretary of state, Dean Acheson, was even more expansive in private, once telling a congressional delegation that American power would determine the future of civilization:

> Only two great powers remained in the world . . . [the] United States and the Soviet Union. We had arrived at a situation unparalleled since ancient times. Not since Rome and Carthage had there been such a polarization of power on this earth. . . . For the United States to take steps to strengthen counties threatened with Soviet aggression or Communist subversion . . . was to protect the security of the United States—it was to protect freedom itself.[1]

The classic doctrinal clarification of this uniquely American worldview came in April 1950, three months before the Korean War, when Truman's National Security Council issued the definitive Cold War strategy paper (NSC 68), which set the stage for "brinksmanship" in a political globe defined in rigid bipolar terms. NSC 68 carried the distinctions between the two sides to a decidedly moral plane, noting that the fall of Czechoslovakia in 1948 was a moral blow to freedom as much as it was a geopolitical loss.

> [A] defeat of free institutions anywhere is a defeat everywhere. The shock we sustained in the destruction of Czechoslovakia was not in the measure of Czechoslovakia's material importance to us. In a material sense, her capabilities were already at Soviet disposal. But when the integrity of Czechoslovak institutions was destroyed, it was in the intangible loss of values

that we registered a loss more damaging than the material loss
we had already suffered.[2]

Although a more conservative strategic personality, Dwight
Eisenhower also endorsed the idea that the world was, as he put it in
his 1953 inaugural address, divided essentially into halves, where any
extension of one domain implied a corresponding loss for the other:

> Freedom is pitted against slavery; lightness against the dark.
> The faith we hold belongs not to us alone but to the free of all
> the world. This common bond binds the grower of rice in Burma
> and the planter of wheat in Iowa, the shepherd in southern
> Italy and the mountaineer in the Andes. It confers a common
> dignity upon the French soldier who dies in Indochina, the
> British soldier killed in Malaya, the American life given in
> Korea.

This early manifestation of the later phenomenon of "globaliza-
tion" was both primitive and implicit; Eisenhower was offering a Cold
War challenge to Americans that tied their future to the future of
peasants and guerrillas around the world. The epitome of Cold War
rhetoric, however, came in John F. Kennedy's stirring inaugural address, just prior to U.S. intervention in Vietnam, when he issued the
strongest challenge of the entire Cold War:

> In the long history of the world, only a few generations have
> been granted the role of defending freedom in its hour of maxi-
> mum danger. I do not shrink from this responsibility—I wel-
> come it. I do not believe that any of us would exchange places
> with any other people or any other generation. The energy, the
> faith, the devotion which we bring to this endeavor will light
> our country and all who serve it—and the glow from that fire
> can truly light the world.

These were the foundations of the beliefs that led American soldiers into the mountains of Korea in 1950, and the jungles of Vietnam,
beginning in 1961. But the Cold War neither began nor ended as a military contest. The initial U.S. reactions to what was defined as "Communist aggression" involved American aid and support, but decidedly
not American troops. These would come later, as the Cold War "heated
up" and as the stakes grew in proportion to the enveloping threat.

The United States experienced its first combat against Communist guerrillas, when, as a result of the Truman Doctrine, aid was dispatched to the Greek government in 1947. The Greek civil war, which had been ongoing since 1946, was led by the Communist-front EAM movement (National Liberation Front) and its twenty-three-thousand-strong guerrilla army, ELAS (National People's Liberation Army). The Soviet Union openly backed ELAS, which was able to operate with an open sanctuary over the borders of Yugoslavia, Albania, and Bulgaria, from which it could find both a supply route and an escape haven to use against the Greek army. Within the context of the "iron curtain" that Churchill had described to Americans a year earlier, the United States viewed the Greek civil war as an acid test against the expansionist ambitions of the Kremlin and its European satellites. The loss of Greece, Truman told Congress, would have "an immediate and serious effect" on neighboring countries such as Turkey and would also spread "confusion and disorder" throughout the region, including the Middle East. "Totalitarian regimes," he said, "imposed upon free peoples, by direct or indirect aggression, undermine the foundations of international peace and hence the security of the United States."

Thus, Truman implicitly announced the original "domino" theory subsequently defined explicitly by President Eisenhower and used openly by Presidents Kennedy and Johnson in support of the intervention in Vietnam a generation later. In the context of the Mediterranean theater, Truman was able to secure $300 million in economic aid to Greece and $100 million in military aid to Turkey. U.S. advisors were dispatched to Greece to assist Field Marshal Alexander Papagos in his conventional military sweeps against the Greek guerrillas, led by Marcos Vaphiadis, ensconced in the mountainous north. This time fortune favored the army.

In November 1948, in order to impose a quick solution against what it defined as a deteriorating situation, ELAS changed tactics from hit-and-run raids to the use of strictly conventional units, including brigades, divisions, and corps. The Communist rebels had thus far been unable to force the government to the defensive, and rebel reprisals and reckless terror had deprived their cause of significant popular support. ELAS was losing adherents while the army, bolstered by firepower, infantry, and airpower gained from U.S. aid, had greatly increased its strength. The government was able to launch a nationwide crackdown, including the arrest and deportation of fifteen thousand guerrillas to the Aegean islands. With over two hundred thousand well-armed recruits, the army went after the remaining ELAS units in 1949.

Noteworthy were two operations in August 1949, in the guerrilla strongholds of Vitsi and the Grammos mountains of northwestern Greece, where the Communist high command made the decision to hold and defend these areas against the army, already strengthened by American assistance and equipment. At the same time, Yugoslavia, now openly independent from Moscow, suddenly closed the border with Greece, depriving ELAS of its essential sanctuary. The result, predictably, was disaster for the guerrillas. By the end of the year the fleeing remnants of a few hundred guerrillas were either trying to survive in the mountains or were seeking asylum in Albania.

The Greek guerrilla crisis was over, but lessons drawn from the episode failed to dissuade military thinking from conventional codes of conduct. The failure of ELAS to pursue guerrilla strategies to their fullest and its brutality toward the population under its control helped seal its fate. The critical decision to launch regular infantry operations was equally stupid, and to the government and U.S. advisors, the victory seemed to support the idea that infantry tactics will invariably succeed if applied often enough and with sufficient firepower. ELAS lost the Greek civil war more than the Greek army won it, but this was a fortuitous circumstance rather than a pattern; the exception that proved the rule.[3] The subsequent insurrection in the Philippines would offer a better example of counterguerrilla operations.

After World War II the Philippines were again the scene of counterguerrilla operations in which Americans played major roles in leadership and assistance. The counterguerrilla war against the Communist Hukbalahap ("Huks" or "People's Army"), and their leader Luis Taruc, had strong similarities to the Greek war, but unlike the war in Greece, the contest against the Huks can accurately be defined as the first postwar counterinsurgency assisted by the United States in which police-style tactics and political stratagems were employed. U.S. soldiers were used in an advisory role only. The eventual defeat of the Huk insurrection in 1953 was largely the work of Filipinos, particularly the brilliant defense minister, Ramon Magsaysay. The U.S. advisory team, however, led by Air Force lieutenant colonel (later major general) Edward G. Lansdale was instrumental in tactical and technical assistance.

Not surprisingly, however, successful resistance to the Huks in the Philippines occurred only after the initial period of trial and error by conventional tactics had failed to produce results. Worse, the ponderous military sweeps conducted by Philippine armor, aircraft, and artillery—backed by U.S. aid—initially helped recruit more peasant sympathizers to the Communist cause and its land-reformist propaganda. Estimates of active peasant support of the Huks hovered around 10 percent of the population, with 10 percent opposed, leaving the vast middle 80 percent as fertile ground for either side. Peasant dissatisfaction with the government's incapacity to implement land reform initiatives was seized upon by Huk activists as proof of official complacency. Active military measures in peasant areas only made matters worse. Unable to obtain reliable intelligence from disaffected peasants, the government began the time-honored conventional tactic of isolating the insurgency through the type of "cordons" used in the Caribbean by the United States or the "blockhouse" tactic employed by the British in South Africa. In the Philippines they were called *zonas*, whereby targeted villages would be screened off from the outside by troops, the intention being to "isolate" the guerrilla "fish" from the "sea" of his support. These methods, awkward as they may have been, worked in other circumstances, but failed in the Philippines, principally because they reminded the peasants of identical policies used by Japan in the late war. Large-scale search-and-destroy operations, another favored army tactic, also backfired. As related by Huk guerrilla chief Luis Taruc, these operations rarely found sufficient numbers of Huks to justify their effort:

> [I]f we knew it was going to be a light attack, we took it easy. If it might give us more trouble than we could handle, we slipped out quietly in the darkest hours of the night, abandoning the area of operation altogether . . . it could be both amusing and saddening to watch the Philippine Air Force busily bombing and strafing, or to see thousands of government troops and civil guards cordoning our campsite and saturating, with every type of gunfire, the unfortunate trees and vegetation. Or we would watch them, worn and weary, scaling the whole height and width of a mountain, with not a single Huk in the area.[4]

After six years of such tactics by the army, Taruc estimated that exactly twelve guerrillas had been killed!

Other army methods only played into the hands of the irregulars. These included notorious "open area" firing techniques, whereby troops were instructed to shoot at anything that moved within certain field zones and road checkpoints; this allowed soldiers to rob peasants at will. Similarly, the "Nenita" units consisted of gangs of ruthless killers who murdered peasants at will, often without proof of Huk allegiance.

By 1950 Huk resistance, aided by clever agitprop political warfare tactics throughout central Luzon, had produced a steady growth of Huk support. With an active insurgent force of about 12,000, Huk strength in Luzon relied upon approximately 150,000 peasant villagers within a population of nearly two million people. But the tide of Huk power had peaked by 1950, when internal dissension and tactical confusions, including the lack of a sustained geographic sanctuary and poor overall coordination, began to see a decline in communist appeal. Heavy-handed terror also helped turn the course of the war against the insurgents. Most important, however, was not so much a loss of Huk resolve, but, rather, a remarkable surge in the popular approval and tactical sophistication of governmental countermeasures. Under the leadership of newly installed Defense Minister Magsaysay, the Philippines had finally found strategic solutions to the Huk riddle by 1950.

By then, both the U.S. team and the Philippine government were ready to wage authentic counterguerrilla war. After four years of trial and error, the government had begun to discover an ancient truth: that light infantry units, armed civilians and special scout squads operated best against guerrillas. Two of the Philippine government's best military leaders, N. D. Valeriano and C. T. Bohannan, have described how small patrols were able to keep the Huk guerrillas on the run:

> Regular patrols . . . passed through specified areas almost on a schedule, following roads or trails. There were unscheduled, unexpected patrols, sometimes following an expected one by fifteen minutes. There were patrols following eccentric routes, eccentric schedules, moving cross-country at right angles to normal travel patterns, which often unexpectedly intercepted scheduled patrols.[5]

With Magsaysay installed as defense minister, and with Lansdale constantly at his side, important reforms were made. Lansdale arrived in the Philippines in September 1950; the Huk rebellion would be over within two years. After surveying the wreckage that the military had left in its wake, Lansdale concluded that "the most urgent need was to construct a political base for supporting the fight. Without it, the Philippine armed forces would be model examples of applied military doctrine, but would go on losing."[6] Once a viable political base had been established, he believed, it would be able "to mount a bold, imaginative and popular campaign against the Huk guerrillas."[7]

The concept of civic action by the military was introduced and the army was instructed to improve troop behavior toward civilians. Corruption was cut down and discipline in both the army and government was improved. Magsaysay was running a tight ship. He eliminated "fire free" areas, a main tactic of conventional troops that inevitably resulted in civilian deaths. Interrogation techniques were made more civilized, and soldiers went into local "barrios" armed with food, clothing, and medical supplies. Magsaysay was beating the enemy on his own terms, offering hope of a better future and eliminating the source of Filipino grievances against the government. He also came to realize that local armies recruited from within the population, especially those with personal reasons to enlist, provided the best antiguerrilla personnel. The fact that Americans were *not* involved as ground troops, in fact, helped the cause immeasurably. As a Philippine lieutenant colonel wrote at the time,

> Foreign troops are certain to be less welcome among the people than are the regular armed forces of their own government. Local populations will shelter their own people against operations of foreign troops, even though those they shelter may be outlaws. For this reason, native troops would be more effective than foreign forces in operations against native communist conspirators. It would be rare, indeed, if the use of foreign troops would not in itself doom to failure an antiguerrilla campaign.[8]

Gradually, the civilian populace came over. Huk support eroded fast. An imaginative propaganda campaign—complete with loudspeakers, leaflets, and other technological devices—gained even more adherents. The institution of a system of rewards for information about suspected Huks helped turn the insurgents to the defensive. Land reform was instituted by the government and a generous amnesty program convinced thousands of Huks to abandon the war.

Within eighteen months of taking office, Magsaysay and his U.S. advisors had essentially stopped the Communist insurgency, but the final ending for the Philippines was not so positive. Magsaysay translated his popularity into electoral power, won the presidency in 1953, and began a series of long-overdue social reforms. These came to an abrupt halt with his tragic demise in an airplane crash four years later. The subsequent fourteen-year dictatorship of Ferdinand Marcos ran parallel with another surge in the historic Muslim uprisings in remote

Mindanao. Similar in type to that which came in the aftermath of the original insurrection against the United States generations earlier, the guerrilla/terrorist army of the Moro National Liberation Front (MNLF), plus another Communist resurgence by the Maoist National Democratic Front and its military wing, the New People's Army (NPA), have terrorized peasant areas of the Philippines in an insurrection now in its fifth decade, with no end in sight.

In retrospect, the Huk insurgency in the Philippines was a true popular rebellion that, like ELAS in Greece, had originated during the war to harass the occupation. Magsaysay and his U.S. advisors ended the war by employing even more popular measures, combined with police-style battle tactics. The example of the Philippine government victory and the role played by Edward Lansdale and the U.S. advisors had great influence among counterinsurgency experts in the years immediately prior to American intervention in Vietnam and represent to this day classic examples of the superiority of policies of attraction versus policies of suppression. The Philippine experience against the Huks, however, went generally unheeded within the U.S. military hierarchy. Most U.S. military leaders instinctively preferred conventional tactics and weapons, regardless of circumstances. The post–World War II U.S. Army *Field Service Regulations*, for example, had only eight paragraphs on guerrilla war. This attitude would find its most logical application in the Korean War.

The Korean War (1950–53) met the traditional American standard of the code of military operations. When North Korean armies mounted a massive assault across the 38th parallel on June 25, 1950, the United States viewed the invasion as another in a series of calculated Communist acts of aggression against the perimeter of the free world. To U.S. decision makers of that era, the enemy was a singular political unit, a "monolith," originating from "headquarters" in Moscow through Peking after 1949 and, subsequently, stretching to the outer edges of Eurasia, including Hanoi and Pyongyang. President Truman articulated this vision in his address to the nation two days after the initial attack:

The attack upon Korea makes it plain beyond all doubt that Communism has passed beyond the use of subversion to conquer independent nations and will now use armed invasion and war. It has defied the orders of the Security Council of the

United Nations issued to preserve international peace and security.

The Korean War was primarily a conventional war and, as such, it fit the historic American mold. Korea also saw, distinctly on the sidelines, a little guerrilla conflict between the two armies. Instead of a political revolution or an insurrection, however, Korean guerrillas on both sides fought as classic adjuncts to their respective ground armies. This fit the traditional and official U.S. military definition of the role of guerrillas in war.

American and South Korean guerrilla offensives sent as many as seven thousand men, almost all of them North Korean disaffected personnel, into the enemy's rear lines behind the 38th parallel. By early 1952 there were already three control organizations established for guerrilla operations, known as *Leopard*, *Wolfpack*, and *Kirkland*. All of these operations were based on the islands off the east and west coasts of Korea. Although U.S. soldiers often took part in tactical movements, they were seldom assigned permanently to the guerrillas located inside North Korea. Guerrilla tactics usually involved hit-and-run raids against enemy soldiers, reconnaissance, and infiltration. Offshore air and naval fire support frequently gave these "friendly" guerrillas their military cover. Indeed, the operation was—by and large—a simple conventional tactic inside a larger conventional war. Most U.S. staff officers, at least, never gave much credence to the idea of insurrection inside North Korea. The guerrilla "offensive"—if it can be called that—was considered little more than a nuisance war; an incidental activity almost completely overshadowed by the larger war down south. Brig. Gen. Robert McClure, chief of the army's Psychological Warfare Division, reflected most official opinion when he labeled the conduct of guerrilla warfare in Korea as "essentially minor in consequence and sporadic in nature."[9]

Few lessons on the true nature of insurrection and popular guerrilla warfare came out of Korea. North Korean partisans also were sent south to infiltrate, but they left no more of an impact on U.S. military strategy than most previous irregulars had throughout history. The North Korean partisans operated behind U.S. lines all the way from the 38th parallel to the southern tip of Korea. The following official U.S. Army account testifies to the harassing nature of these partisans. They harassed isolated villages, ambushed U.S. and South Korean patrols, ambushed troop trains, cut telephone lines, and attacked police stations. At peak strength, the North Koreans put as many as twenty-five thousand guerrillas into South Korea, to harass and frustrate the American soldiers. A typical action took place at Kowon, just a few miles from the 38th parallel:

> At the town of Kowon itself, before midnight, North Koreans attacked a northbound Marine Corps supply train. Thirty Marines were riding the train as guards. The night was dark, and snow flurries increased the poor visibility. After the train had stopped at a water tank, a North Korean soldier violently flung open the door of the front coach and burst inside. A Marine killed him instantly. Enemy burp gun and rifle fire now ripped into the coaches. Outside, enemy soldiers blew the track ahead and killed the engineer when he started to back the train. The North Koreans persisted in their efforts to enter the coaches despite heavy losses until they finally succeeded, shooting and clubbing every Marine they thought still alive. But 2 wounded Marines inside the coach successfully feigned death and escaped later. In this action the train engineer and 6 Marines were killed, and 8 Marines wounded.[10]

The U.S. and South Korean armies launched a counterattack, nicknamed Ratkiller, against enemy guerrillas in December 1951. By March 1952, Ratkiller had eliminated nearly twenty thousand North Korean guerrillas. Although the enemy irregulars were able to launch well-coordinated attacks against South Korean rail lines and installations, there was rarely sufficient troop strength to follow through and inflict major damage. The U.S. and South Korean command was able to deal with these enemy soldier-guerrillas as most other regular armies had dealt with similar opponents: they destroyed them through strength and firepower. The American high command made sharp distinctions between soldiers and guerrillas in Korea. Americans still had, in 1952, the same cultural prejudice toward unconventional warfare that their forebears had displayed. The same comparisons between "bandits" and guerrillas cropped up in official accounts as they had in past conflicts. The official U.S. Army record on this reaffirmed in Korea the "bandit" legacy of the old Caribbean and Central American guerrilla wars:

> In the rural areas guerrillas or bandits—it was difficult to distinguish one from the other—formed a constant threat to the lines of communication. In some sections the roads were un-

safe during the hours of darkness and many farmers were afraid to cultivate their land even under the protection of guards during the daytime. . . . ROK Army and police units waged a constant skirmish with these predators—whose chief objectives seemed to be food and clothing. But despite the toll that the ROK forces exacted, the guerrilla bands managed to gain new recruits and to carry out harassing raids. In July the ROK 1st Division was pulled out of the line and sent to southwestern Korea to help eliminate the nuisance. This had been tried before with only moderate success and the ROK 1st Division had to undergo a similar experience. As the division moved through the mountainous Chirisan region with National Police units attached, it met no organized resistance. The guerrillas followed the same pattern of dispersion and evasion that they used before. Breaking up into small groups until the ROK forces passed them by, they came together again afterwards and resumed their depredations.[11]

In Korea, U.S. officials generally preferred to keep American soldiers away from irregular actions as much as possible. Guerrilla war was implicitly considered to be a dirty nuisance, an internal problem between Koreans only. For the remainder of the 1950s, in the years just prior to U.S. intervention into Vietnam, this same distance between soldiers and guerrillas continued to direct most professional American military thought.

During this period the army began an official organization of guerrilla units with the creation of the Special Forces on June 20, 1952. The Special Forces came out of the old ranger battalions and the OSS of World War II fame and were the first such outfits to be formed by the United States during peacetime. The original Special Forces were commanded by Col. Aaron Bank and were activated at Fort Bragg, North Carolina. With an authorized maximum strength of twenty-five hundred men, Bank's outfit grew to one thousand within nine months. Many of the men in the ranks were the same personnel who had fought as rangers or with the OSS during World War II. They were trained in jungle fighting, airborne assaults, underwater operations, demolitions, and communications. The chief mission of these Cold War guerrillas was to support conventional operations in Europe should war with the Soviet Union breakout. They were trained to help organize irregular bands in Eastern Europe and to attack and harass Soviet communications, the main purpose being to slow or retard the westward progress of the Red Army. Their mission, therefore, was a direct outgrowth of U.S. experiences in Europe during the war.

In early 1953 the Special Forces were split in half. One group was sent to Bad Toelz, West Germany, where they moved into Flint Kaserne, a $13 million billeting complex formerly used by Hitler's SS troops. The other half remained at Fort Bragg as the Seventy-seventh Group, commanded by Lt. Col. Jack T. Shannon.

As an "elite" outfit of the U.S. Army, the Special Forces soon began to exhibit an individuality of their own. Distinctive clothing separated them from the conventional soldier. At Fort Bragg they increasingly took to wearing unique headgear—straw hats, cowboy hats, ski caps etc.—when they trained in the field. In Germany the troops began to don green berets. By 1955 the green beret became a permanent part of the Special Forces uniform, although efforts to stamp the beret as official headgear were refused by the U.S. Continental Army Command. Not until John F. Kennedy became president did the green beret win official recognition.

By the late 1950s the mission of the Special Forces underwent a subtle but dramatic change. Events in Southeast Asia were deteriorating rapidly from the U.S. perspective and the focus of unconventional warfare began shifting from a future world war in Europe to an actual guerrilla war in Asia.

-15-

Vietnam: Contradictions in Counterinsurgency

During World War II, the Vietnamese Communists, led by Ho Chi Minh, transformed an anti-Japanese coalition for national independence (the Viet Minh) into an elaborate organization geared toward seizing complete power. When the Japanese left in 1945 Ho proclaimed the Democratic Republic of Vietnam in Hanoi and made preparations for a showdown with the occupying French, who arrived back in the country in 1946. The resulting war lasted eight years. North Vietnam constituted the main theater of military action, while in the South a harassing and terrorist guerrilla war kept the French colonial forces off balance. The 1949 Communist victory in China had a profound effect on the eventual North Vietnamese victory, but inept French strategy and tactics simply failed to adequately address the dimensions of the revolution they were fighting. French commander general Henri-Eugene Navarre later admitted this fact,

> We had no policy at all [in Indochina]. . . . After seven years of war we were in a complete imbroglio, and no one, from private to commander in chief, knew just why we were fighting. Was it to maintain French positions? If so, which ones? Was it simply to participate, under the American umbrella, in the "containment" of Communism in Southeast Asia? Then why did we continue to make such an effort when our interest had practically ceased to exist?
>
> This uncertainty about our political aims kept us from having a continuing and coherent military policy in Indochina. . . . This rift between policy and strategy dominated the entire Indochina war.[1]

The key to North Vietnamese success was not just military strength but more important, political organization. The Viet Minh—and, later, the Viet Cong (VC)—were in fact one of the best led and organized paramilitary outfits in history. Thus, when the United States began to tentatively intervene in Vietnam in the early 1950s it was up against an insurgent body fighting on its own soil, already with the advantage of years of intense warfare—and victory—against the military powers of both Japan and France.

The Viet Cong political apparatus went down to the village level. It blended Vietnamese nationalism with Marxist ideology, Leninist organizational principles, and Maoist guerrilla tactics. It developed indigenous political roots within South Vietnam but depended upon Hanoi for central direction, leadership, and, eventually, personnel, equipment, and weapons. But the core element of the Viet Cong movement was its ability to organize a vast political machine within the history and culture of Vietnam. In this respect, it was remarkably similar to the Katipunan apparatus that Emilio Aguinaldo fashioned in the Philippines in 1899. According to guerrilla warfare expert Douglas Blaufarb, the Vietnamese Communist Party under Ho Chi Minh was

> able to convince many that it had inherited the "mandate of heaven" which conferred legitimacy in the traditional polity. Moreover, those features of Communist practice which were most offensive to Western values—its "monism" expressed in totalitarian control—were quite consistent with Vietnamese and indeed Confucian principles of society which saw the nation as a simulacrum of the patriarchal family, a unity mystically presided over by the emperor and his mandarins and which by definition, therefore, ruled out pluralism and the toleration of opposition and dissent.[2]

In effect, the Viet Cong constituted a government within a government in South Vietnamese society. The party was composed of full-time political cadres, who acted in secrecy with military discipline. It collected taxes and killed dissidents. It cowed whole villages and hamlets into strict obedience. Viet Cong terror was widespread but was still selective. It systematically tried to eliminate its "class" enemies, i.e., local leaders supportive of the South Vietnam government. A typical year would see thousands of local officials assassinated, four thousand in 1960, for example. Viet Cong terror had strong political overtones. There were mock trials for "punishment" against social "crimes." Great emphasis was placed on indoctrination and political propaganda. Terror and death were Viet Cong methods of administration; it was a true political army.

Numerically, the Viet Cong during the 1950s were a distinct minority in South Vietnam, rarely more than 10 percent of any local population. But party organization was the pillar of VC strength and the sine qua non for its operations. It began from a human base tested in the long and protracted struggle against France. After the 1954 Geneva Accords as many as seventy-five thousand southern cadres were brought north for further training—and were later sent back when guerrilla activities went full scale in 1959. Training and indoctrination were thorough, and in the Leninist tradition, membership in the Communist Party was a life commitment. As one VC paramilitary leader reminisced on his early political baptism,

> Cadres from the minorities were recruited usually through family or friendship ties, trained in short courses, and then sent back to their areas of work. When a cadre moved into a settlement, if he did not have any relatives or friends in the village, he set about winning the sympathy and trust of a villager, then contacted other families through this person.
>
> The most ardent sympathizers were trained to become cadres and to lead the local movement. After that the cadre moved on to another settlement where he could count on the kinship and friendship ties of the people he had recruited in the previous settlement to gain an entry into the area. At the same time, the villagers he had recruited would proselytize their own relatives, and friends scattered in various villages. In this way the network spread.[3]

The American Military Assistance Advisory Group (MAAG), which first went into this tempest in the mid-1950s, began preparing for a conventional assault, exactly as in Korea. U.S. military aid fashioned a South Vietnamese army with artillery, armor, and air units that could repulse the North Vietnamese if the latter tried to cross the 17th parallel (the dividing line). Gen. Sam Williams, MAAG commander, fashioned an army along traditional lines, as Frank Trager described it, "organized for conventional warfare in regiments, divisions, and corps. This military force was mechanized, motorized and road-conscious."[4]

By the time the French had been repulsed from Indochina after the climactic battle of Dien Bien Phu in May 1954, the United States was already financially committed to the anticommunist (and French colonial) position. Over $4 billion of U.S. aid had been dispatched to the French during the course of the long war in Indochina (1946–54), but this money failed to prevent the final disaster at Dien Bien Phu. Since late 1950 MAAG had been in Saigon, while the first U.S. military mission arrived in the spring of 1953. This was supplemented in February 1954 by a squadron of B-26 bombers, along with 250 U.S. Air Force technicians. Thus, the first U.S. troop commitment to Vietnam was already present while French combat forces were in the field. But during the Eisenhower administration U.S. officials were unwilling to supply combat troops. In the weeks immediately preceding the Battle of Dien Bien Phu, a debate on the use of American power to help the French took place at the highest levels. On one side was Admiral Radford, chairman of the Joint Chiefs of Staff, Vice President Nixon, and Secretary of State Dulles, all of whom urged the president to take forceful action to relieve the French garrison, including B-36 air strikes. But Eisenhower was not persuaded, nor were most U.S. allies, including Prime Minister Churchill of Britain. Gen. Matthew B. Ridgway, army chief of staff in 1954, closed the issue when he sent the president a copy of a report he had commissioned on U.S. intervention in Indochina. Coming as it did on the heels of the bitter experiences of the Korean War, Ridgway's report distilled the essence of the soldier's dilemmas in a guerrilla setting.

> Their report was complete. The area, they found, was practically devoid of those facilities which modern forces such as ours find essential to the waging of war. Its telecommunications, highways, railways—all the things that make possible the operation of a modern combat force on land—were almost non-existent. Its port facilities and airfields were totally inadequate, and to provide the facilities we would need would require a tremendous engineering and logistical effort.
>
> The land was a land of rice paddy and jungle—particularly adapted to the guerrilla-type warfare at which the Chinese soldier is a master.[5]

The French defeat in Indochina was formalized at an international conference held in Geneva, Switzerland, which divided the country into North and South Vietnam. But U.S. officials refused to even sign the final document and instead marshaled full political and military support for South Vietnam, which then was ruled by the fifty-four-year-old Catholic anticommunist Ngo Dinh Diem. Almost before the ink was dry on the Geneva Accords, however, unrest and disorder flared up all around Diem and his regime. The unified Communist government in the North still possessed one of the best and most experienced infantry armies in the world, while the Ho Chi Minh trail provided a covered infiltration route south. In addition, thousands of Communist cadres remained behind in the South to wage a campaign of guerrilla terror and subversion against Diem. The Cold War in Southeast Asia was becoming increasingly hot.

In the aftermath of Geneva, Diem's government was in a condition of near-anarchy. The army and civil service were rife with corruption. Nearly one million Catholic refugees had fled southward in order to escape Ho Chi Minh's totalitarian rule in North Vietnam. Local villages were beset with terror, assassination, and extortion from "liberation" forces led by Communist guerrillas. U.S. aid supplied Diem with artillery, aircraft, tanks, and vehicles for conventional warfare, while hundreds of South Vietnamese officers were enrolled in American professional military institutions, where they were taught how to organize an army to fight in the American style. But the Vietnamese guerrillas who were attacking Diem's shaky political structure were veterans of years of warfare against the French army and at peak strength numbered over three hundred thousand men. Indeed, the entire apparatus that began to tear apart South Vietnam in 1954 was the product of a whole generation of revolutionary organization and action. The Viet Cong (Vietnamese Communists) could trace their antecedents back to 1930, when the Vietnamese Communist Party was founded by Ho Chi Minh.

Diem's army, in reality, came more and more to resemble a "palace guard," an army that only reluctantly ventured far from the capital and played little part in combating the mounting guerrilla attacks in the countryside. Diem's political difficulties also increased the importance of U.S. aid and advice. His failure to hold a unifying election in 1956 (a mandate of the Geneva Accords) lost him a certain amount of credibility. More important, he grew increasingly isolated from his own people and came to rely more and more on the advice of his family kin. Local sects and tribes (particularly the Buddhist monks and Montagnard tribes) revolted against his rule. Despite honest attempts at land reform—which had partial success—and a vigorous repression of the Viet Cong, by the later 1950s Diem found himself growing more dependent upon the United States for the very life of his government.

The first Special Forces troops landed in South Vietnam in 1957. Within a year they had trained fifty-eight men of the Vietnamese army as the nucleus of the Vietnamese Special Forces. But official U.S. Army policy still looked upon these troops as auxiliaries, a sideline troop compared to the main force.

In 1959 the North Vietnamese created the National Liberation Front (NLF) to finally "liberate" South Vietnam from Diem and his American advisors. Guerrilla and terrorist acts escalated almost overnight, as hundreds of retrained irregulars infiltrated south through the triple-canopy jungle of Vietnamese terrain. The outgoing Eisenhower administration, which had projected the loss of Southeast Asia if Vietnam fell (the domino theory), increased aid and advisors. Nevertheless, Vietnam, a virtually unknown geopolitical location to most Americans, was still a low priority in U.S. policy. This would soon change, as America was about to enter the "counterinsurgency" era.

In the 1960 election John F. Kennedy captured the White House, and soon afterward, guerrilla war captured the imagination of his administration and of U.S. policy in Vietnam. Kennedy began the most concerted effort at organized counterguerrilla warfare in U.S. history; an effort contrary to the sum total of American military tradition. In retrospect, however, this would prove to be little more than a sideshow to professional military opinion and policy.

When Kennedy took office in 1961 there were 685 American troops in Vietnam; three had been killed. The war was virtually unknown to the American public and went unmentioned in the 1960 presidential election, which was dominated by the myth of a "missile gap" with the Soviet Union. President Kennedy's first few months in office, however, transformed national security policy and were crucial in the birth of the new perspective, labeled "counterinsurgency." The immediate stimulus for this was an inflammatory broadside delivered on January 6, 1961, even before Kennedy's inaugural by Soviet Premier Nikita Khrushchev, who declared bold Soviet support for "wars of national liberation" against the outposts of Western influence in third world trouble spots, Vietnam in particular. Kennedy was disturbed by the potential for Communist support of guerrilla movements (Castro had just come to power in neighboring Cuba the year before) and ordered a full-scale policy review on the subject. According to his biographer, Theodore Sorensen, the new president came to the sudden realization that unconventional war was "a low priority . . . the weakest point in the Western armor."[6] Under Kennedy's direction, the U.S.

national security system immediately became overwhelmed by the subject of guerrilla war, a true revolution in strategic thought.

A National Security Action Memorandum (NSAM) directed the secretary of defense to increase U.S. counterguerrilla "resources." In February Kennedy received a report on Vietnam prepared by Gen. Edward Lansdale, who had spent years in Vietnam following his duty in the Philippines. The recognized leading U.S. expert on the subject, Lansdale directed that the South Vietnamese shift their military and political structures toward dealing with Communist subversion in a reformist manner, much as Magsaysay had done in the Philippines in 1951 and 1952. Kennedy was frightened by the prospect of losing Southeast Asia to Communism and had a first-rate appreciation of the nature of the unconventional war threat to U.S. interests.[7]

The president soon adopted a personal enthusiasm toward the art of guerrilla warfare. The subject, in turn, became popular around the country, as lectures, articles, and books poured forth. A form of guerrilla "cult" rose up that romanticized the Special Forces as counterguerrillas, much as Che Guevara and Mao Tse-tung were being glamorized as guerrillas by the political left wing. Kennedy conferred the green beret as the official symbol of the Special Forces and in 1961 flew to their headquarters at Fort Bragg for a day of demonstrations. There he saw the latest in U.S. technology for antiguerrilla war. One soldier, with a rocket strapped to his back, flew across the treetops and streams in mock combat, a futuristic sample of modern U.S. counterguerrilla tactics.

Such theatrics aside, both Kennedy himself and the administration took the guerrilla threat very seriously. The president took time out to study the classic works personally. Combatting "wars of liberation" became the new Cold War focus. The unconventional war threat was internationalized by the Kennedy administration. In speeches before Congress and around the country, both the president and his men described the "new" enemy strategy in global terms. The Communists, the president told the country, "are exploiting the desire for change in the southern half of the globe. . . . Although the adversary did not create the revolution, he is seeking to capture it for himself . . . [a]nd in the contest we cannot stand aside."[8] Yet, alarm signals were beginning to sound. The most important, and historically one of the most prophetic, came from the French in the person of Charles de Gaulle himself, who warned Kennedy early on that Vietnam would be a "quagmire" by any definition. "We, the French, have experience [in Vietnam]. You, the Americans, wanted to take over our place in Indo-China. Now you want to take over where we left off and restart the war which we ended. I predict that you will sink bit by bit into a bottomless military and political swamp however much you pay in men and money."[9]

But de Gaulle was ignored, and the U.S. war machine moved ahead and optimistically. The best-known public articulation of the administration's thought on counterinsurgency came from Presidential Assistant Walt W. Rostow. At Fort Bragg, in June 1961, Rostow delivered what was considered to be the definitive American policy statement on guerrilla warfare in the 1960s. Entitled "Guerrilla Warfare in the Underdeveloped Areas," Rostow's speech was an American clarion call for action against Communist-inspired revolutions wherever they appeared. Reflecting the confidence and optimism of the new administration, Rostow concluded that "[t]he United States has a role to play in learning to deter the outbreak of guerrilla warfare, and to deal with it if necessary."[10]

Thus, in the early 1960s guerrilla war was a hot topic. In eighteen months alone, the military conducted nine counterinsurgency courses with over two thousand student officers. Over five hundred thousand enlisted men took special training in guerrilla fighting, including language training, civic action, and psychological operations. Unconventional warfare was integrated into standard military training. Civilian agencies had their own "guerrilla schools." The Foreign Service Institute provided training for State Department, AID (Agency for International Development), and USIA (U.S. Information Agency) personnel, while the CIA had its own training courses. The capstone of governmental instruction was the "National Interdepartmental Seminar," a six-week course that included such high-level administration figures as Robert Kennedy, Gen. Maxwell Taylor, Walt Rostow, and General Lansdale. At the end of the first session the entire student body was brought to the White House for a session with President Kennedy, who told them of his convictions on the importance of their studies:

> I was anxious to have you come to the White House because we want to emphasize the necessity for the experience which you are going through, that it be shared by all the people in the National Government who have anything to do with international relations. Every senior officer in all key departments must have a comparable experience to yours, have the knowledge that you have, have their attention focused on it. . . . They all must concentrate their energy on what is going to be one of the great factors in the struggle of the Sixties.[11]

The military bureaucracy was also harnessed to the unconventional war wagon. Maj. Gen. Victor B. Krulak, USMC, became special assistant to the Joint Chiefs of Staff for "Counterinsurgency and Special Activities." The army created several new offices for irregular operations, including a Special Warfare Directorate, which had responsibility for the Special Forces. The Green Berets became national symbols of the new American emphasis. A popular ballad written about them became a national hit. Their numbers were increased to over two thousand men, and new units and functions were created. Both the navy and air force created their own version of the army's Special Forces. The navy established the SEALs (Sea, Air, and Land Teams) and the air force the Air Commandos. "Civic action"—a term used to describe the use of the military for social improvement in less developed countries—was also integrated into army training as a counterguerrilla tactic. Military aid programs of the early 1950s stressed this role, not only in Vietnam, but also in Laos, Thailand, and in several Latin American countries. But beneath this veneer was a heavy dose of public relations and much transparent enthusiasm. In reality, the Special Forces remained a tiny fraction of the overall policy, and they continued as a small, elite guard, viewed with great suspicion by the regular army. The military was an old dog; new tricks were not entirely welcome.

The army's fascination with guerrilla warfare in 1961 and 1962, thus, remained a true flirtation: it disappeared almost as fast as it came and generated more passion and short-term brilliance than long-term strategic direction. This does not mean that the United States was fatalistically determined to fight only a main-force war. It means that the odds were decidedly against a transformation to counterinsurgency in the long term and that chosen tactics, when war came, would reflect the main strategic culture. Nor does it mean that elaborate preparations for counterinsurgency were not made throughout the foreign policy bureaucracy; they were, and they were many and conducted with the utmost dedication. Several study groups were formed in the government, new National Security Action Memorandums were prepared, blue-ribbon teams met, and a Special Group was organized wherein Attorney General Robert Kennedy attended in order to report back directly to his brother.

The common assumption that underlined all of this new bureaucracy and instruction was the idea that U.S. personnel should *supplement* the work of the host-country army; in particular, that U.S. troops would advise and not fight. The Kennedy administration made special efforts to highlight this point. Nevertheless, the caveat still remained:

if absolutely necessary, U.S. troops should be prepared for counter-guerrilla combat. The president admitted this in his 1962 commencement address at West Point, when he told the cadets that guerrilla wars "are the kinds of challenges that will be before us in the next decade if freedom is to be saved, a whole new kind of strategy, a wholly different kind of force, and therefore, a new and wholly different kind of military training."[12]

In some respects, ghosts of the past were pushing the United States into Vietnam. The view that the Truman administration had "lost" China in 1949 by refusing to commit troops or to support the Nationalist government with massive assistance had come back to haunt the Kennedy administration. The "loss of China" thesis was used effectively by the Republicans in 1952 and subsequent elections and had left an indelible stigma upon the conduct of foreign policy by the Democratic Party. No matter that the Truman administration made historic decisions to rescue Europe from Soviet Communism; Asia remained its Achilles' heel. Saving Europe, America's first line of defense in the Cold War, could not compensate for the loss of the world's most populous country to "international communism." Kennedy was determined that further loss wouldn't happen on his watch in Vietnam.

Thus we have the great irony that, because the United States refused unconditional support to save China from itself, it went on to commit millions of its own sons to save a tiny noncommunist enclave on China's southeastern border. This seeming geopolitical contradiction was waved aside by the famous "domino theory," which identified Vietnam as only one link in a greater chain, which, if not broken by U.S. power and resolve, would see all of Southeast Asia eventually fall to communism like a row of dominoes. Implications for the rest of the world, especially the Middle East and South Asia, were similarly drawn.

China played an equally important background role in the Kennedy administration's approach to guerrilla war. Those who believed that the United States "lost" China also blamed this on a handful of allegedly disloyal Foreign Service officers and their military co-conspirators inside China, who had repeatedly urged an accommodation with Mao Tse-tung and his Communist movement in northern China. This "stab in the back" interpretation had been used before in history, most notably by Hitler and the German Nazis to denounce the surrender in 1918 and, subsequently, the Weimar government of the 1920s. Such erroneous theories served only to confuse reality, leading to false assumptions and conclusions. The nature of the opposing sides in China, each with millions of followers, who had been at war for decades, received less attention in the United States than a handful of American bureaucrats and their political machinations.

Correspondingly, the powerful role that Mao's doctrines of revolutionary, guerrilla war had actually played in Chiang's defeat was misunderstood or ignored by a whole generation of American policymakers. In an era dominated by Senator Joseph McCarthy's anticommunist crusade in the United States, by the trials of Alger Hiss and of convicted spies such as the Rosenbergs and Klaus Fuchs, with China going down in 1949, followed by the Korean War shortly after, it is a small wonder that Americans looked for homegrown causations to explain foreign and military confusions. This not only led to a steeled defiance before Vietnam, with a determination for such reverses never to happen again, but it also contributed to the prevailing ignorance of revolutionary war theories and a superficial, albeit romantic, appreciation of how Americans would fight guerrillas twelve thousand miles from San Francisco.

The key question thus remained: if committed to warfare, how would the U.S. military fight? As subsequent events have demonstrably proved, once in combat, the American military performed in the best tradition of its own history and professional doctrine: as regular troops disposed to use massed strength and firepower to win a quick victory and a quick return home. Despite the administrative and popular fascination with guerrilla war, to most of the U.S. military command it remained little more than a passing fad. This was logical and consistent with everything important and lasting in the history of American strategic culture.

Even to its civilian publicists, the idea of antiguerrilla war was more glamour than reality. The chief public architect of this idea was Walt W. Rostow, who harbored an intrinsic belief in the efficacy of conventional airpower. Rostow had been an airpower enthusiast since his World War II days as a target analyst for strategic bombing surveys over Germany. He never lost his belief that airpower was the decisive weapon in World War II and that, if all else failed in Vietnam, air force bombing would still provide an unbeatable weapon against any enemy, guerrilla or otherwise. McGeorge Bundy, the president's special assistant for national security affairs, was of a similar mind with regard to the efficacy of conventional firepower and tactics, as were most, although not all, of the top U.S. chain of command. CIA chief John McCone, in line with the American orthodoxy, officially urged a sustained bombing campaign against Hanoi. His views were critical in the long and involved history of U.S. military action in Vietnam because they reflected both the dominant thinking that the war was "aggression" in the traditional (cross-border) sense and that it would and should be met primarily by a conventional response, airpower in particular:

We must hit them harder, more frequently, and inflict greater damage. Instead of avoiding the MIG's, we must go in and take them out. A bridge here and there will not do the job. We must strike their airfields, their petroleum resources, power stations and their military compounds. This, in my opinion, must be done promptly and with minimum restraint.[13]

High-level military opinion was likewise almost completely orthodox despite the training given for irregular action. Gen. Maxwell Taylor, Kennedy's special military representative, talked a great deal about guerrilla war, but in the end, he remained a conventional soldier at heart. An Army airborne commander in World War II, Taylor had long argued for a strong and mobile army. Tactically, he saw Vietnam as a conventional war, with Korea as the comparable example. Like Rostow and Bundy, Taylor favored a mobile infantry and airpower. North Vietnam, he cabled home from a late 1961 mission to Saigon, "is extremely vulnerable to conventional bombing, a weakness which should be exploited diplomatically in convincing Hanoi to lay off South Vietnam."[14]

In the aftermath of this trip, which Taylor made with Walt Rostow, the first decision to send large numbers of American ground troops to Vietnam was made. The Taylor-Rostow mission recommended an eight thousand–man task force, which would be used in an advisory role but with emergency instructions for self-defense. From the very beginnings, the U.S. military hierarchy thought of these men in traditional concepts. Gen. Lyman Lemnitzer, chairman of the Joint Chiefs of Staff, returned from Vietnam in 1961 and announced that "the new administration was oversold on guerrilla warfare and that too much emphasis on counterguerrilla measures would impair the ability of the South Vietnamese Army to meet a conventional assault like the attack on South Korea by the ten or more regular North Vietnamese divisions."[15] Later that year, army chief of staff Gen. Earle G. Wheeler told an audience in New York City

that what the United States was committed to support in Vietnam was military action, . . . despite the fact that the conflict is conducted as guerrilla warfare. It is nonetheless a military action. . . . It is fashionable in some quarters to say that the problems in Southeast Asia are primarily political and economic rather than military. I do not agree. The essence of the problem in Vietnam is military.[16]

By the middle of 1962, U.S. personnel and assistance were pouring into South Vietnam. Gen. Paul D. Harkins was appointed chief of the new Military Assistance Command Vietnam (MACV). Harkins was a tradition-bound soldier, with no experience either in guerrilla warfare or in the Far East. By this time the United States also had covert agents in North Vietnam and Laos, trying to organize an anticommunist resistance. But the main operations focused on the insurgency against the Diem government in South Vietnam. For the remaining years of the Vietnam War the United States would limit its ground incursions against North Vietnam to only small units while, at the same time, it would unleash history's greatest air bombardment against this same enemy. In the long run, both tactics failed.

By the end of 1962 it was obvious that the political and social reforms that Washington had earlier demanded of Ngo Dinh Diem would never come. His army, the Army of the Republic of Vietnam (ARVN), grew even more demoralized, and his administration became more corrupt and confused. At the same time, the Communist NLF and VC got bolder and more aggressive. By the end of the year they were in control of large areas of South Vietnam. The Communists were carrying on the propaganda war against Diem, and he was losing. They were also carrying on the terrorist war against him; by 1962 the government had to close over six hundred schools because of Communist terrorism.

The U.S. response was to fund a hefty increase in the ARVN, including the Civil Guard and Self-Defense Corps, and to help finance a "strategic hamlet" program. U.S. Army and Marine helicopters also began ferrying Vietnamese troops to and from battle, and—increasingly—to shoot back if shot at. Special Forces teams were busy in the central highlands and in the northern provinces trying to win the "hearts and minds" of Montagnard tribesmen.

In a rare example of counterguerrilla expertise, the Special Forces also created the Civil Irregular Defense Group (CIDG) program. The CIDG helped orient the allegiance of thousands of South Vietnamese toward the government and also supplied mobile guerrilla and strike forces into the combat arena. At the program's peak there were over eighty CIDG camps in South Vietnam, with sixty thousand local soldiers involved.

By early 1963 the U.S. presence had increased to ten thousand. The president told the country in his State of the Union message that "the spearhead of aggression had been blunted in South Vietnam." General Harkins reported to Secretary of Defense McNamara in March that the war might possibly be over by Christmas. By the middle of 1963 there were nearly sixteen thousand American troops in Vietnam and the U.S. ambassador, Frederick E. Nolting, told reporters in Saigon that "South Vietnam is on its way to victory over Communist guerrillas."[17]

Within months of these incredibly optimistic predictions both Presidents Kennedy and Diem were dead by assassination, and the course of history and the Vietnam War was on the verge of an abrupt and tragic new path. For the next twelve years the Vietnam War went on. It became the longest and the most controversial war in U.S. history. It cost over 57,000 American lives and another 350,000 wounded. It nearly tore apart the social fabric of American domestic life and helped foment a cultural and intellectual revolution among the young. In many respects it was a true guerrilla war with strong parallels in American history. But in the final analysis, Vietnam was much more than a guerrilla war, particularly in the battle tactics of both the professional U.S. military and the North Vietnamese Army.

Before it was over, Vietnam comprised at least four distinct military "wars": the original guerrilla revolt against the South Vietnam government, the U.S. conventional war against the Viet Cong and the North Vietnamese Army, the naval war, and the air war. In addition, there was the so-called "other" war of pacification efforts, favored by most civilian strategists but carried out only on the periphery of the main-line war. By any historic American standards, therefore, Vietnam was a very big war. At peak, the United States had 542,000 troops in Vietnam. The bombing campaigns were the greatest in history, dwarfing those of World War II. In 1965, air force bombing raids reached 4,800 a month. The next year they increased to 12,000 a month, some of them going as far north as the outskirts of Hanoi. The B-52 sorties, in particular, were awesome, with each plane capable of unleashing up to 60,000 pounds of bombs. By 1968 there were 800 B-52 raids per month; by 1972 there were 3,150. During the most intensive periods of air warfare, a time which lasted eight years, the B-52s flew an amazing 124,532 sorties and dropped 2,949,000 tons. In all, the United States exploded 14 million tons of ordnance over South Vietnam, half on the ground, half from the air. Over one million tons were dropped on North Vietnam by airplane, 1.5 million tons on Laos, and over half a million tons on Cambodia. By many times over, this was the most destructive physical force ever employed in the history of warfare.

The U.S. ground campaign relied on technology, helicopters, jeeps, trucks, and armored personnel carriers, in a strategy of endless attrition. This was conventional warfare supreme: a strategy designed to gain a military decision by quantitative, search-and-destroy tactics. The eventual commander of this powerful force was Gen. William C. Westmoreland—whose name would become synonymous, to millions of American television viewers, with nightly reports on "body counts" of "confirmed" enemy kills. Several years into this strategy, Westmoreland could still tell a news conference (April 14, 1967) that "We'll just go on bleeding them to the point of national disaster for generations. They will have to reassess their position."[18]

Such politically vacant reflections, far removed from the ideal models of Kennedy and Lansdale's "counterinsurgency" theories, recall the war of "attrition" employed at Verdun by German and French armies in 1916. That also stressed body counts but bled both sides to the point of mutiny and to the point of nearly one million dead soldiers by the close of the year 1916.

Perhaps the most telling symbol of the subsequent erosion of counterinsurgency in Vietnam came in 1967 when Defense Secretary Robert McNamara announced plans to construct an electronic anti-infiltration barrier to intercept Communist flow of arms and troops south through the demilitarized zone. This "McNamara line," as it became known, was to employ state-of-the art, high-tech listening devices to alert U.S. forces when Communist troops and logistics were crossing so that U.S. air and artillery strikes could be rained down upon them. At an estimated cost of $800 million per year, this modern-day version of the Maginot line met the same fate as its predecessor, as VC and North Vietnamese troops simply shifted their infiltration routes elsewhere. Once again, technology had failed to substitute for strategy, as the Vietnam conflict continued to defy the best of American total-war planners.

Like Verdun, and the general direction of American attrition strategies in Vietnam, the lives lost failed to produce the promised victory. The conduct of the war by the military hierarchy, and the ripple effects of this as it played out year after year in the domestic political base, led to a form of strategic "mutiny" on the home front and a gradual erosion of will and morale in the field, despite the greatest technological effort seen in the annals of warfare. Writing in 1971, Col. Robert Heinl, retired Marine turned author, described the American armed forces in

Vietnam as "wrenched by seemingly insurmountable problems within and without, [they] appear to have reached their lowest point in this century in morals, discipline and battleworthiness." Heinl quoted Gen. Matthew Ridgway, former army chief of staff, as describing the condition of the army in Vietnam as deteriorated to such a point that, Ridgway believed, "Not before in my lifetime . . . has the Army's public image fallen to such low esteem."[19]

During the Vietnam War, U.S. Marines blew up bunkers and tunnels used by the Viet Cong as part of the counterinsurgency strategy (above). The United States also used airpower, a recent tactical innovation, to attack Viet Cong structures (next page). However, these measures were insufficient to defeat the extensive and resourceful insurgents whose strength did not rely on tents but rather on their ability to recruit new members and take advantage of the dense jungle territory. *Department of Defense photos, National Archives at College Park*

-16-

Renewal: Vietnam
to the Persian Gulf

A lthough Americans may have thought that the last battle of Vietnam was played out in the jungles of Southeast Asia decades ago, the 2004 presidential election campaign has shown that neither the memories nor a forgiveness of that conflict have died out. Senator John Kerry spent much of the 2004 campaign defending his role as a swift boat officer in Vietnam, while reeling from the accusations that he considered the American soldier not much different than Genghis Khan in field conduct. These memories were used as political footballs in negative stereotypes during the campaign. Societies do not like to be reminded of lost campaigns, of dishonorable behavior, or of settings inconsistent with popular culture. Irregular war, of course, is certainly inconsistent with America's self-image. The key issue involved a flawed conceptual design, which produced an inappropriate strategic definition of the contest and a war which went on seemingly without end.

The great military theorist Carl von Clausewitz wrote that "the most important single judgment a political or military leader can make is to forecast correctly the nature of war upon which the nation is to embark. On this everything else depends." Strategic confusion, hesitation, or lack of direction, in the first place, will determine not only morale in war but, equally, cohesion and support at home. The notion that conventional power could win in Vietnam was the predominant mindset of the military hierarchy, despite the otherwise scholastic and historical doctrines stating that the contest was essentially political/revolutionary. Gen. Edward Lansdale, USAF, the most authoritative U.S. officer on the subject, reportedly told Secretary of Defense McNamara early in the Kennedy administration that if U.S. soldiers in Vietnam relied on weapons they couldn't carry by hand, then the war was already lost. Thus, airplanes, tanks, and artillery were not the priority weapons. As Lansdale later put it, the essence of the struggle was political, not military: "[T]he Communists have let loose a revolutionary idea in Vietnam and it will not die by being ignored, bombed or smothered by us. Ideas do not die in such ways." He then called for a political approach, in order to

> oppose the Communist idea with a better idea and to do so on the battleground itself, in a way that would permit the people, who are the main feature of that battleground, to make their own choice. A political base would be established. The first step would be to state the political goals, founded on principles cherished by free men, which the Vietnamese share; the second would be an aggressive commitment of organizations and resources to start the Vietnamese moving realistically toward those political goals. In essence, this is revolutionary warfare, the spirit of the British Magna Carta, the French "Liberté, Egalité, Fraternité" and our own Declaration of Independence.[1]

Writing before the heavy U.S. investment in Vietnam, Lt. Col. Joseph P. Kutger, USAF, reminded his readers how such failures of understanding have plagued conventional armies throughout history:

> The long list of unsuccessful operations conducted against guerrilla activities is a product of the inflexibility of many literary leaders as well as their intransigent attitude concerning the abandonment of conventional tactics. This military arteriosclerosis has existed down through the ages and is most evident toward the end of each epic period in the style of warfare, symbolized by a major transition of the conventional warfare of the day.[2]

As the battle-decorated warrior and author Lt. Philip Caputo wrote, American battle tactics in Vietnam were largely reminiscent of Verdun in World War I, where statistics and body counts defined results:

> Our mission was not to win terrain or seize positions, but simply to kill. . . . Victory was a high body-count, defeat a low kill-ratio, war a matter of arithmetic. The statistical measurements provided empirical accounts of success: pressure on unit com-

manders to produce enemy corpses was routine, and they in turn committed it to their troops. This led to such practices as counting civilians as Viet Cong. "If it's dead and it's Vietnamese, it's VC," was a rule of thumb in the bush.[3]

Col. David Hackworth lectured and taught after his tour of duty, which included rare and brilliant tactical excursions in Vietnam. In his view, the regular army seldom bothered to appreciate the nature of the situation.

[T]he average General that came to Vietnam did not have a good concept, good appreciation of the nature of guerrilla warfare. In most cases because of their lack of even reading in depth about guerrilla warfare, they were not prepared for the war and they had to fall back on Korea and World War II, and they used the thought process and the techniques that worked successfully there.[4]

While it may be easy to blame the politicians who ran the war, we must acknowledge that presidents, ambassadors, and congressmen rarely have either the knowledge or the experience to question the judgment of military professionals. But a major characteristic of the civilian leaders who have generally directed American wars has been their pronounced tendency to elevate contests into universalistic and moralistic crusades. This has been demonstrated to such a degree that it has become trite. But in Vietnam, as today in Iraq, the idea was developed that a guerrilla insurrection, even in locales remote to critical geopolitical interests, carried a burden that almost defined the future of humanity. This made the stakes all that much higher and fed the excesses of raw force. Few were better at elevating conflict with language than Lyndon Johnson. In April 1965, at Baltimore, for example, he laid down the gauntlet. We were in Vietnam, he thundered, for the cause of a peaceful world writ large:

Let no one think for a moment that retreat from Vietnam would bring an end to conflict. The battle would be renewed in one country and then another. The central lesson of our time is that the appetite of aggression is never satisfied. To withdraw from one battlefield means only to prepare for the next. We must stay in Southeast Asia—as we did in Europe—in the words of the Bible: "Hitherto shalt thou come, but no further."

Even Richard Nixon, ever the pragmatist, frequently lapsed into Wilsonian phrasemaking, telling the American Legion in 1966 that a loss in Vietnam meant World War III: "In the event that Vietnam is either lost at the conference table or on the battlefield, it will mean that the Pacific will become a Red Sea, that Communist China will become the dominant power in that area of the world, and that World War III will become inevitable."

Long before Vietnam, General Ridgway prophetically described the inherent dangers of such "open-ended" strategic obsessions:

A limited war is not merely a small war that has not yet grown to full size. It is a war in which the objectives are specifically limited in the light of our national interests and our current capabilities. A war that is "open-ended"—that has no clearly delineated geographical, political, and military goals beyond "victory" is a war that may escalate itself indefinitely, as wars will, with one success requiring still another to insure the first one.[5]

In Vietnam, thus, the United States fought an open-ended war minus a coherent strategic doctrine, in a largely conventional military manner. The analogy to the Korean War has been used by some professional military critics who have insisted that conventional war, with its machines, mass, and firepower, could have "won" in Vietnam, if only it had been applied in a near total-war scenario. One such critic, Col. Harry G. Summers Jr., USA, applied the traditional "Clausewitzian" principles of Napoleonic warfare to Vietnam. Summers, and others who viewed Vietnam in such a mold, held that the United States in Vietnam faced a war whose primary inspiration, as in Korea, came from an "outside" army. Summers acknowledged the insurgency but would have left this problem up to the Saigon regime, with American technology and doctrine left to face off against the North Vietnamese Army (NVA). "U.S. military operations in Vietnam . . . should have been focused on protecting South Vietnam from outside aggression, leaving the internal problems to the South Vietnamese themselves."[6] Under this strategy, the United States would have formally declared war against North Vietnam, leaving both Congress and the public with no choice but to support the war and the use of mass firepower and maneuver. Gen. John Singlaub, USA, also saw the failure in Vietnam as an improperly applied conventional war. His remedy was similar to that of Colonel Summers. He would have declared a national emergency, an extension of terms of service, mobilization of the armed services, a tactical "maritime quarantine" of North Vietnam, destruction of Haiphong harbor, and destruction of all rail and road links to China.[7]

The "soldier's" viewpoint is understandable and is derived from a professional and doctrinal heritage. As in medicine, if one consults a surgeon, the remedy is usually an operation. But operations also usually work. Thus, it is arguable that the total-war tactics urged in Vietnam may have arrested the developing quagmire, but we will never know, any more than we can imagine the consequences and implications of such an all-out approach. It is equally conceivable that even the best planned and implemented *political* strategy, such as the one used in the Philippines in the 1950s, might have failed. This would have meant that the revolutionary terrorism of totalitarian North Vietnam and its agents would have eventually overcome the U.S. efforts at creating genuine democracy in the authoritarian politics of South Vietnam.

The point, however, is not to overdo another Vietnam reconstruction, but simply to remind ourselves, as Clausewitz did as quoted above, of the critical importance of doctrinal definition. Absent this, the military flounders, the public questions, dissent rises, and "exit" strategies form and eventually bury what might have been honorable but misdirected intentions. Related to this central reminder is the corollary that such a scenario has developed in all cases in which the enemy presented a confusing profile and when the objectives became blurred and mired in paramilitary and unconventional situations. It began in North America when the British used redcoats against American revolutionaries in distant and unfamiliar terrain. It occurred subsequently, as this book has demonstrated in case after case, when American soldiers were sent out to arrest their own distant and unfamiliar insurgencies.

The aftermath of the Vietnam War in America is also reminiscent of how western Europe, especially Britain and France, reacted to the aftermath of four years of trench warfare during the Great War of 1914–18. The legacy of the slaughter on the western front, which took millions of innocent lives to no lasting avail, has been portrayed by Williamson Murray as responsible for the "appeasement" decade immediately preceding the Second World War:

> Beyond disillusionment, the 1920s brought literary outpourings of memoirs, novels and poetry underlining the horror of the trenches and the meaningless sacrifice of a generation of British youth. By 1930 much of Britain's elite, not merely the

intellectuals but the political and governing classes as well, had become convinced that no victors had emerged from the Great War; rather all had lost. The corollary to this view was that there would be no victors in a future war—that in fact there was no cause, no conflict that justified the sacrifice of a nation's youth.[8]

The so-called Vietnam "syndrome" permitted a similar cycle to play itself out in U.S. society during the war and especially after the collapse of South Vietnam in 1975. The belief that open-ended warfare generally and war casualties in particular could never again dominate societal goals became the accepted strategic norm. Politicians adhered to this rule, implicitly or explicitly, and the strategic and intellectual elite carefully adjusted to the new definition of the "rules" of war. Two significant books, with identical titles, recall the realities of that time.

The first, *No More Vietnams?* published by the Adlai Stevenson Institute in 1968, collected an assembly of more than twenty-five of the country's strategic elite as a postmortem of the war even as it was still raging. While the divergence of viewpoints permitted only a general consensus, two points expressed during the deliberations helped use the experience of the moment to outline future policies. The first, argued by Albert Wohlstetter of the University of Chicago, viewed the origins of the problem as derived from conventional war dominance in strategic thought:

[O]ne precedent that should make us thoughtful is the wrong lessons that were drawn in Vietnam from Korea. . . . U.S. decision-makers expected another conventional invasion across a parallel separating a communist north from a noncommunist south. To repel it they centered almost all our effort in organizing some 140,000 South Vietnamese into large conventional Army divisions . . . [which] reduced the chance that the Vietnamese, in spite of internal attack, would be able to advance in economic and political self-development and to operate under the rule of law. That, in turn, encouraged subversion, terror and counter-terror, and helped make a discriminate response unlikely. Our advisors were responding to a "lesson" of Korea.[9]

The second conclusion, summarized by former ambassador to Japan Edwin Reischauer and former State Department official James

C. Thompson Jr., projected a restrained future for American foreign policy:

> THOMPSON: With regard to the possibility of isolationism in today's world, Mr. Reischauer proposes the term "unconcern," which I think is a very useful way to put it. However, as my own policy prescription, "deactivism" or "disengagement," I think, would be more appropriate; actually the phrase I use is the Japanese term "low posture"—a "low posture" foreign policy.
> REISCHAUER: I think everybody would be for a low posture.[10]

The second book has the same title minus the question mark and revealed an evolved and opposite view. Writing in 1985, ten years after the fall of Saigon, former president Richard Nixon's take on "no more Vietnams" is an effort to rally the country from the strategic "low posture" described above. In Nixon's attempt at renaissance, he reminded Reagan-era readers, "Many of our leaders have shrunk from any use of power because they feared that it would bring another disaster like the one in Vietnam. Thus did our Vietnam defeat tarnish our ideals, weaken our spirit, cripple our will, and turn us into a military giant and a diplomatic dwarf in a world in which the steadfast exercise of American power was needed more than ever before."[11]

Thus, "no more Vietnams" had different meanings for different audiences at different times. Still, the lingering taste of the legacy of military interventionism continued to drive a cautionary and reactive wedge between the need to wield force abroad and the shared memory of the last war. From the end of the Vietnam War to the terror attacks of September 11, 2001, a period of twenty-six years, the United States sent armed forces into significant overseas missions on eleven occasions (many more were sent on covert missions).[12] Of all of these, the only one that could conceivably rise to the definition of "war," was the Gulf War, technically Desert Storm, an operation preceded by a thirty-eight-day air campaign and concluded by a ground campaign lasting precisely one hundred hours. After years of technological and tactical "transformation" of the military, the dreaded Vietnam syndrome had finally been cured.

The military campaigns of this period were highlighted not only by their brief duration but also by the streamlined and efficient use of force, strict adherence to defined missions, an almost universal popular support, and most important of all, a near-total avoidance of casualties. Major exceptions to casualty avoidance occurred in Lebanon on October 23, 1983, when a truck bomb exploded and killed 241 Marines, and in Somalia, October 3–4, 1993, when eighteen rangers were killed. In both cases, the U.S. response, even before public opinion could be mounted, was phased evacuation without further casualties. Remaining interventions of the decade, including the bombing sorties against Serb targets from above cloud-cover in the former Yugoslavia, stayed almost totally casualty-free. After 450 sorties, B-52s managed to drop only sixty-four bombs in Yugoslavia but escaped allied casualties altogether.

The strategic campaigns of the post-Vietnam period were summarized and directed during the Reagan administration by Secretary of Defense Caspar Weinberger in his six doctrinal "tests" governing the use of force overseas. Whether deliberately or not, these guidelines continued to direct the American military in an extraordinarily efficient and quick series of adventures. Groundswells of antiwar opposition never had an opportunity to coalesce, with the closest coming in 1991 against the Gulf War. President George H. W. Bush, unlike his son, cut these off almost immediately by bringing the troops home after the liberation of Kuwait (although air strikes went on for 15 years). This was a controversial decision, still being debated, but punctuated by a series of parades down main streets in the summer of 1991, the decision led President Bush to a (temporary) political high of 90 percent approval. He lost the presidency to Bill Clinton the following year, but this had nothing to do with his war performance. Saddam Hussein remained in power, but America avoided the type of occupation it fights today because Bush Sr. allowed Iraq to govern itself. At home, nobody seemed to care.

During the same time period, as the Cold War was waning, the United States became involved in several foreign insurgencies that, like the Greek war in 1947, were waged by Washington largely without the use of American soldiers. In retrospect, these may offer the prime examples of constructive counterinsurgency, for which the introduction of U.S. infantry is deliberately avoided. Taken together, these three examples—Nicaragua, El Salvador, and Afghanistan—fought primarily in the 1980s, offer classic lessons in the three "A's" of effective irregular operations minus American soldiers: aid, advice, and arms.

Since U.S. troops were not at issue, these cases are beyond the scrutiny of this book, but a retrospect of the outcome of these conflicts reveals that insurgencies can be overcome without large-scale force interventions, that is, the people involved can win or lose largely on their own. Lincoln's famous dictum, delivered at Gettysburg, has never been more accurate: in the last resort countries are won or lost "by the people [and] for the people." The United States may have provided important assistance to the local authorities in the cases mentioned above, but the critical elements remained within the responsibility and character of the principals themselves.

All three of these conflicts were topics of intense political debate inside the United States and one, the anti-Sandinista campaign in Nicaragua, nearly brought the Reagan administration to a standstill (with the Iran-Contra scandal). Yet, the administration survived intact and the Sandinistas were replaced in 1990 by a democratic government. At least in the short run, Oliver North and the Contra "freedom fighters" toppled the Communist government with much backchannel gunrunning and political theater but without significant American casualties.

In El Salvador both the Carter and Reagan administrations committed American interests to the defeat of the FMLN (Farabundo Marti National Liberation Front), a Marxist guerrilla group openly supported by Cuba, the Sandinistas of Nicaragua, and the Soviet bloc. With over ten thousand fighters threatening the Salvadorian government, the United States saw El Salvador as the test of pro-American stability in the Western Hemisphere. Salvadorian military officers were trained in counterinsurgency at Fort Bragg, and a small contingent of Americans was dispatched to supervise operations in-country. Efforts to promote political and social reform were preached by, among others, Vice President George Bush, who told his hosts in San Salvador in 1983, "Your cause is being undermined by the murderous violence of reactionary minorities."

Regardless, political violence in the tiny country was escalated by both the "death squads" of the right and by the leftist guerrillas. By the war's end in 1992 over 75,000 Salvadorians lay dead and a million were left homeless. Over this period the United States provided $2 billion in economic and $700 million in military assistance, while the security forces grew from 10,000 to 56,000, a ratio of 8 to 1 against the insurgents. Bases in Honduras and Costa Rica helped the United States support the home government's cause. In spite of painful setbacks, the democratic process in El Salvador inched along, helped immensely by the 1984 presidential election of Jose Napoleon Duarte and the subsequent ascension to power of his Christian Democrats. By 1989 international aid to the FMLN had dwindled substantially, while guerrilla terrorism in the rural countryside had turned the population decidedly toward the government.

It was a failed insurrection. In 1989 the last FMLN offensive was turned back. In 1992 a peace accord brought the twelve-year insurrection to an end, with a United Nations supervised disarmament regime and a pledge by FMLN leaders to the democratic process. The El Salvador conflict was a vicious and dirty war, with an outcome whose legitimacy may take years to determine. Yet the commitments of three American political administrations (Carter, Reagan, Bush) had finally realized the objective of a democratically elected government and the defeat of a communist-backed terror and guerrilla campaign. All of this, moreover, without the burden of American "boots on the ground." In an imperfect world, and considering the possibilities of even more tragic options, El Salvador was a war worth winning with a protracted strategy of considerable patience and reward.

In the Afghanistan insurgency against the Soviet Union the United States played a decisively distant but critical role. The full story of the Soviet defeat and departure, after eight years of massive, brutal, and clumsy intervention, is best told elsewhere. But with a supply of Stinger surface-to-air missiles late in the conflict, CIA training and assistance, plus annual aid payments of $80 to $400 million, the United States helped achieve what historian Anthony Joes has called "the most satisfying experience the Americans ever had with guerrilla war."[13] The reason for this simple but stark fact lay within the sacrifices and character of the Afghan mujahideen resistance coupled with Soviet Red Army indifference to authentic counterinsurgency. One State Department report summarized Afghanistan when the Soviets were about to withdraw: "[B]y 1987 the mujahideen had fought the Soviet regime forces to a stalemate; Moscow's Afghan policy had alienated it from the Islamic, Western, and nonaligned countries; and the Soviets failed to find a client leader in Kabul who could capture the loyalty of the Afghan people." In a haunting reflection on the implications of Afghanistan written in 1999, Anthony Joes projects that "Americans might further wish to ponder the great strength of the Afghan resistance derived from the lively religious faith of most of its members. What might happen if American forces ever find themselves confronting that kind of strength?"[14] Over five years past 9/11, the answer to this question remains both divisive and illusive throughout American society.

Epilogue

Does History Repeat?

Today, waging the war on terror and fighting against the Iraqi insurrection, America finds itself in precisely the dilemma articulated by Anthony Joes. Iraq heads the agenda, and the global campaign against al Qaeda has taken a backseat. The nation is consumed with intense, and often bitter, partisan debate on the Iraq question. As we have seen, this is common throughout the history of unconventional operations, but the occupation of Iraq represents a profound and abrupt transformation in America's national interests, political culture, and strategic history. For Bush Sr., there was no debate; he defended his 1991 decision not to stay in Iraq as derived from the reality of politics and history. Shrewd or expedient, Bush Sr. defined the situation in terms of political "realism." In *A World Transformed* (1998), Bush and his national security advisor, Gen. Brent Scowcroft, defended their actions in words that have come back to haunt us today:

> Trying to eliminate Saddam Hussein would have incurred incalculable human and political costs. . . . We would have been forced to occupy Baghdad and, in effect, rule Iraq . . . there was no viable exit strategy we could see, violating another of our principles. Furthermore, we had been self-consciously trying to set a pattern for handling aggression in the post–Cold War world. Going in and occupying Iraq, thus unilaterally exceeding the United Nations' mandate, would have destroyed the precedent of international response to aggression that we hoped to establish. Had we gone the invasion route, the United States could conceivably still be an occupying power in a bitterly hostile land.[1]

Bush might also have mentioned the much greater span of strategic history that preceded his political logic. While the Vietnam War was the most recent in this span, it was certainly not the only case available. As the historical record in this book has tried to show, Americans have *never* felt comfortable in unconventional situations. Success has always been the result of improvisation, failure the result of ignorance of the true nature of the enemy plus war-weariness all around. Those successes that did occur, in turn, were seldom passed on and they were not incorporated into official policy. They were simply forgotten, either conveniently or deliberately—or both.

The only military doctrine considered truly legitimate in American strategic culture is conventional, frontal war. The Vietnam War saw a series of formal training exercises in counterinsurgency that were probably the largest and most intense in history. They produced scores of programs in Vietnam and involved thousands of U.S. and Vietnamese officials. Nevertheless, despite this great effort, the only fully endorsed official doctrine of counterinsurgency ever accepted by the U.S. Army was the statement that a professionally managed conventional armed force could defeat insurgents as a "lesser included capability" of its own proficiency.[2] The Marine Corps did publish its *Small Wars Manual* in 1940, and this document has, belatedly, been updated by the army in October 2004. As one reviewer described the new manual, *Counterinsurgency Operations*, it shows "how much guerrilla warfare has changed in the last sixty-four years—while remaining strangely the same."[3] At about the same time, army historian Maj. Isaiah Wilson wrote an insider's critique of military planners who, he charged, suffered from "stunted learning and a reluctance to adapt." From his position as chief war planner for the 101st Airborne Division stationed in Iraq, Wilson noted the standard incapacity in doctrinal definition and recognition. "Reluctance in even defining the situation . . . is perhaps the most telling indicator of a collective cognitive dissidence on the part of the U.S. Army to recognize a war of rebellion, a peoples' war, even when they were fighting it."[4] As we have seen, this is an inherited problem.

In Vietnam, the U.S. military made concessions to the civilian concepts of pacification but remained unshakably wedded to the idea that the priority must go to the tradition of conventional military sweeps and the concentration of manpower and firepower against the enemy. Between the professional military and the policies of the civilian organizations such as AID and the State Department there was no reconciliation. The two went their own separate paths, with the military's being the dominant one. Seldom was there any real coordination between the pacification effort and the military effort—the "other" war versus the "real" war. Robert Komer headed CORDS (Civilian Operations and Revolutionary Development Support), which was the largest pacification program of the Vietnam War. Komer has made this conclusion on the subordination of counterinsurgency to the traditional military view in Vietnam:

> Counterinsurgency was never tried on a sufficient scale because it was not part of the institutional repertoire of most GVN, and U.S. agencies involved. . . . It fell between stools and was overshadowed from the outset by the more conventional approaches of the major GVN and U.S., institutions which were playing out their own institutional repertoires. The military institutions in particular knew how to mobilize resources, provide logistic support, deploy assets, [and] manage large efforts. So they employed all these skills to develop irresistible momentum toward fighting their kind of war.[5]

Today, after over three years combating insurrection inside Iraq, there is little evidence that the United States has learned basic lessons about guerrilla war: either occupy the country in a total sense or undermine guerrilla support with an efficient and progressive government. If you are unwilling to do the first or if the second is impossible, chances of success are remote. The case of the Philippines in the twentieth century offers examples of each of the two methods, both in the original insurrection and in the campaign against the Huks after World War II. Both were successful, and each offered a version of the two strategies.

On a domestic political level, chances for a lasting success decrease as the conflict grows longer and more protracted. The American political culture has little patience for drawn-out and inconclusive campaigns. Each day that passes without evidence of a conclusion becomes a tactical win for the insurgents. They can inch to victory day by day, month by month, year by year, without a single battle success. As the United States discovered in Vietnam and elsewhere, the true center of gravity in unconventional war is the domestic political system. The fact that the United States won every major battle in Vietnam proved irrelevant in the long term. The patience of the enemy on the ground proved more durable than the impatience of the public back home.

On a military level, it has been demonstrated that small, mobile, and swift units are able to keep insurgents on the run, while infantry and other large-scale, highly visible conventional units become targets for hidden insurgents. This often results in tactical overkill by the armies and bomber groups and can turn into strategic defeat. Orthodox tactics, numbers and massed firepower, to be sure, are able to smother rebellion, but these offer only temporary and misleading "victories." On a geopolitical level, it is important to deny guerrillas their sanctuaries since safe havens, either cross-border or within the locale, will prolong an insurrection indefinitely.

As protests on American streets, and in Congress, over U.S. policy in Iraq and the Middle East become more of a common occurrence, the lessons of the past bear studying. In terms of counterguerrilla warfare, it is worth remembering that there is not one single case in U.S. history that did not produce at least a measure of domestic protest. This protest played a significant role in many instances: it changed military tactics, it forced the nature of political strategies, and it affected the outcome and the timing of that outcome. Domestic criticism obviously varied from case to case. As a generalization, it is fair to say that the longer and more inconclusive the war, the more home dissension increased. The media also played a role, even a century ago. During the early years of the Philippine insurrection and in Nicaragua, for example, newspapers greatly fanned antiwar criticism. In the Caribbean during the Dominican Republic intervention, on the other hand, newspeople were kept away and there was little public debate. To do this today for any length of time would, of course, be inconceivable.

It is fairly safe to conclude, therefore, that counterguerrilla warfare in the American democracy will invariably be accompanied by a variety of domestic dissension. Conventional wars fought by the United States, on the other hand, have rarely produced such divisions among the populace. The politics preceding the great conflicts against other powers, to be sure, were riddled with debate and controversy. But once hostilities began, most discussion of the politics of the war came to a near-complete halt. The noninterventionist America First Committee, which bitterly opposed Franklin Roosevelt's activist foreign policies, shut down just four days after Pearl Harbor. There are several reasons for this important distinction between these two kinds of warfare.

In the first place, guerrilla conflicts tend to last longer, thus stretching the already-thin patience of the electorate. The war with Mexico lasted less than two years, the war with Spain only five months. U.S. participation in both world wars was also surprisingly brief, less than a year in World War I (combat time), less than four in World War II. The

Korean War went on for slightly over three years. Even the great Civil War lasted no more than four years. Contrast these to U.S. counterguerrilla campaigns: seven years for the Seminole War (much longer if we go to the real origins of the war in 1819), nineteen years in occupation of Haiti, over twenty years in Nicaragua, and eight years in the Dominican Republic. Prior to Vietnam, America's largest unconventional war was against the Philippine insurrection and went on for three and a half years of daily and intensive warfare, only to be renewed later in sporadic ambush attacks by the Philippine Moros, which lasted several more years.

The tactics used by the military, moreover, often prompted an ingrained American ideological sympathy with "liberation" wars against what were defined as repressive regimes. Often the military resorted to heavy-handed and aggressive tactics, which frequently allowed the political opposition to magnify the "romantic" aspects of the insurgents, exaggerating their political credentials into persecuted Davids against the American Goliath. The image of Ernesto "Che" Guevera remains a lasting symbol of this ideology almost forty years after his death.

Fighting against a national insurrection, therefore, is a tricky and intricate business. It requires great patience and political insight. Throughout most of its history, the professional American military has preferred to dismiss or ignore this trade. Rare has been the individual or unit that chose to discard its heavy baggage, wagon trains, trucks, planes, or artillery and to regroup in order to fight guerrillas. This would mean a true, if only temporary, conversion from soldier to guerrilla. George Crook and Lewis "Chesty" Puller were excellent examples of this ideal. So was Edward Lansdale, who had a rare insight into the political needs required to wage revolutionary war against revolutionaries. Most U.S. tacticians, on the other hand, disdained this side of irregular warfare and saw only a military enemy or criminals.

The political side of this enemy was invariably discovered, but only after long trial and error. Another reason for the length and unpopularity of guerrilla war lies within the actual tactics of the guerrilla army. The popular American preference has been for quick and decisive victory: "home before Christmas" or "on to Richmond," etc. But guerrillas almost always denied the regular army its victory. By eluding regular troops, by attacking them on their own schedule, by retreating when pursued, by avoiding battle, by melting into the population, the guerrillas often confused and frustrated the U.S. military command and the population back home. This led to longer wars, frayed nerves, occasional atrocities—which were often exaggerated by domestic protesters—and more dissension at home. The unpopularity of unconventional warfare, therefore, is not difficult to fathom.

Today, that unpopularity has surfaced again in the national debate over Iraq. On both sides, heavy casualties have occurred, atrocities have been committed, and Congress has debated the issue at length. Americans are turning on themselves and sharp divides have become emotional and intense. Patriotism is questioned and dissent is often equated with disloyalty. The role once played by such senators as George Hoar, Robert La Follette, and William Borah has been taken up by a new generation of congressional critics. Republicans and "neoconservatives," who originally lavished great praise on Defense Secretary Donald Rumsfeld, have come to question his ability and ask for his resignation. Rumsfeld is certainly not incompetent; he is only one of history's many political casualties of irregular warfare.

Where this will all lead is difficult to predict. Insurgents of the twenty-first century are better financed, better led, and better supplied than those of the past. The notion that they may have access to weapons of mass destruction makes the issue of survival a real concern. Increasing this difficulty is the vast growth in the power of the media— electronic and print—whose slant on an issue is capable of tipping support one way or another.

The real problem goes much deeper than news slants, talk radio, or political personalities. Much of the present turmoil has a familiar ring to it, reminiscent of times when soldiers and guerrillas fought over territory and issues long since forgotten by a nuclear generation. The fact that these sides are still engaged against one another in Iraq and in many other areas of today's turbulent and violent world should be a sufficient reminder that the ghosts of the past are still with us today. We should also remember that modern military technology, the information "battlespace," no matter how swift and powerful, has yet to replace the timeless necessity to understand the generic conflicts that have made guerrilla warfare and insurrection an enduring problem of history, politics, and culture.

This last point begs a question: is Iraq only another prime example of the history recorded throughout this book? The evidence strongly suggests that this is so and that future reflections on Iraq will note the profound similarities between this case and all of the others. This does not imply a fixed outcome in the Iraq case, only a sense of historical repetition. Without a final and definitive exit strategy the Iraq issue will continue to spark opinion, if not necessarily authority. But the history and nature of the subject of guerrilla warfare has an authority of its own, an autonomous record that deserves consideration for both the present and future. The aftermath of the Vietnam tragedy had its own autonomous record, one which produced its own "syndrome," broken only after the triumph of the Gulf War. We know that history, and the record of the forgotten and distant past. What will be history's verdict on our own conduct now? The prognosis is both uncertain and possibly ominous.

Finally, it is critical to remind ourselves that the essence of the problem of strategic culture, like most problems, is intellectual. Maj. Gen. Robert H. Scales, USA (Ret.), may have summarized it best in a 2005 editorial, noting the real origins of the "art" of war:

> During the opening battles of World War I, the Germans taught the British a lesson in blood: In war the intellectually gifted will win over practiced dullards every time. Just as the British failed to understand how to transition from small to large-scale combat, perhaps we are facing a similar intellectual challenge transitioning from large to small wars.[6]

Thus, in the last analysis, neither willpower, manpower, nor material resources are sufficient if we lack the mental agility and the imagination to appreciate and to master the art of unconventional warfare. Like the "practiced dullards" who charged over barbed wire and machine guns time and again in the Great War, we have also found ourselves repeating history over and again, chasing ghosts, while the source of our frustrations lies deeply within our own intellect and its corresponding strategic culture.

Notes

INTRODUCTION

1. James E. Dougherty, "The Guerrilla War in Malaya," *U.S. Naval Institute Proceedings*, September 1958, in Franklin Mark Osanka, *Modern Guerrilla Warfare* (New York: The Free Press, 1962), 302–303.
2. David P. Evans, "A Foreign Troop," *U.S. Naval Institute Proceedings*, June 1980.
3. Osanka, *Modern Guerilla Warfare*, xxii.
4. *Joint Army–Air Force Low Intensity Conflict Project Final Report* (Fort Monroe, VA: August 1986), 158.
5. Quoted in Russell Weigley, *The American Way of War* (New York: Macmillan, 1973), 221.
6. Maurice Matloff, "The American Approach to War, 1919–1945," in Michael Howard, ed., *The Theory and Practice of War* (London: Cassell, 1965), 235.
7. Quoted in R. Ernest Dupuy, *The Compact History of the United States Army* (New York: Hawthorn, 1956), 265.
8. Hanson W. Baldwin, "America at War: The Triumph of the Machine," *Foreign Affairs*, January 1946, 241.
9. Eric Larrabee, "Books on Guerrilla Warfare—Fifteen Years Overdue," *Harpers*, May 1964, 120.
10. W. W. Rostow, "Guerrilla Warfare in Underdeveloped Areas," in T. N. Greene, ed., *The Guerrilla—And How to Fight Him* (New York: Praeger, 1962), 59.
11. Robert B. Asprey, *War in the Shadows, The Guerrilla in History*, 1st ed., 2 vols. (Garden City, NY: Doubleday and Co., 1975); 2nd ed. (New York: William Morrow and Company, 1994).
12. Department of Defense, Joint Chiefs of Staff, *Dictionary of Military and Associated Terms* (Washington, DC: Joint Chiefs of Staff, June 1, 1979), 361.
13. Asprey, *War in the Shadows*, 1st ed., 1:xi.
14. Walter Laqueur, *Guerrilla: A Historical and Critical Study* (Boston: Little, Brown and Company, 1976), 3.
15. Quoted in Asprey, *War in the Shadows*, 2nd ed., 83.

PART I: HOME FRONTIERS: TERRORISM, GUERRILLA WAR, AND THE AMERICAN CAUSE

INTRODUCTION TO PART I: THE COLONIAL HERITAGE

1. Asprey, *War in the Shadows*, 1st ed., 101.
2. www.rogersrangers.org/rules/index.html, rule xxviii.
3. www.rogersrangers.org/rules/index.html, p. 2.
4. Asprey, *War in the Shadows*, 103–104.

CHAPTER 1: REVOLUTIONARY TERRORISM: WHIG vs. TORY

1. Wallace Brown, "Violence and the American Revolution," in Stephen G. Kurtz and James H. Hutson, eds., *Essays on the American Revolution* (Chapel Hill: University of North Carolina Press, 1973), 82.
2. Robert M. Calhoon, *The Loyalists in Revolutionary America, 1760–1781* (New York: Harcourt, Brace, and Jovanovich, 1973), 258.
3. Claude H. Van Tyne, *The Loyalists in the American Revolution* (New York: Macmillan, 1902), 46–47.
4. Bernard Bailyn, "Central Themes of the American Revolution," in Kurtz and Hutson, *Essays on the American Revolution*, 16–17.
5. North Callahan, *Royal Raiders: The Tories of the American Revolution* (Indianapolis, IN: Bobbs-Merrill, 1963), 100.
6. Van Tyne, *The Loyalists in the American Revolution*, 176.
7. North Carolina regulators. Free essays.com, 1.
8. Van Tyne, *The Loyalists in the American Revolution*, 74–75.
9. Calhoon, *The Loyalists in Revolutionary America, 1760–1781*, 368.
10. Van Tyne, *The Loyalists in the American Revolution*, 127, 103.
11. Howard Swiggett, *War out of Niagara: Walter Butler and the Tory Rangers* (New York: Columbia University Press, 1933), 126.
12. Stanley J. Adamiak, "The 1779 Sullivan Campaign," *The Early America Review*, Spring–Summer 1998, www.earlyamerica.com/review/1998/sullivan.html.
13. Adamiak, "The 1779 Sullivan Campaign," 9.

CHAPTER 2: SOUTHERN PARTISANS vs. BRITISH REDCOATS

1. Evans, "A Foreign Troop," 32.
2. Evans, "A Foreign Troop," 36.
3. Asprey, *War in the Shadows*, 122.
4. Don Higgenbotham, *The War of American Independence: Military Attitudes, Policies and Practices, 1763–1789* (New York: Macmillan, 1971), 384.
5. Theodore Thayer, "Nathanael Greene: Revolutionary War Strategist," in George A. Billias, ed., *George Washington's Generals* (New York: William Morrow and Co., 1964), 109.
6. In Kurtz and Hutson, *Essays on the American Revolution*, 142.
7. John Ellis, *A Short History of Guerrilla War* (New York: St. Martin's Press, 1976), 53.
8. Callahan, *Royal Raiders*, 72.
9. Jack Weller, "The Irregular War in the South," *Military Affairs*, Fall, 1960, 135.

CHAPTER 3: GRAY GHOSTS vs. UNION BLUECOATS

1. Carl E. Grant, "Partisan Warfare, Model 1861–65," *Military Review*, November 1958, 43.
2. Virgil C. Jones, *Gray Ghosts and Rebel Raiders* (New York: Henry Holt and Co., 1956), 3.
3. Jones, *Gray Ghosts and Rebel Raiders*, 308.
4. Grant, "Partisan Warfare, Model 1864–65," 48.
5. Jones, *Gray Ghosts and Rebel Raiders*, 313.
6. Jones, *Gray Ghosts and Rebel Raiders*, 286.
7. Jones, *Gray Ghosts and Rebel Raiders*, 294.
8. Jones, *Gray Ghosts and Rebel Raiders*, 309.
9. Jones, *Gray Ghosts and Rebel Raiders*, 341.
10. Grant, "Partisan Warfare, Model 1864–65," 45.
11. Grant, "Partisan Warfare, Model 1864–65," 46.
12. Jones, *Gray Ghosts and Rebel Raiders*, 356.
13 Bruce Catton, foreword to Jones, *Gray Ghosts and Rebel Raiders*, viii.

CHAPTER 4: OUTLAWS AND GUERRILLAS ON CIVIL WAR FRONTIERS

1. Michael Fellman, *Inside War: The Guerrilla Conflict in Missouri During the American Civil War* (New York: Oxford University Press, 1989), 85.
2. Fellman, *Inside War*, xvi.
3. Richard S. Brownlee, *Gray Ghosts of the Confederacy* (Baton Rouge: Louisiana State University Press, 1958), 36.
4. Brownlee, *Gray Ghosts of the Confederacy*, 70.
5. Brownlee, *Gray Ghosts of the Confederacy*, 139–140.
6. Benson J. Lossing, *The Civil War*, 3 vols. (Hartford, CT: T. Belmap, 1868), 2:499.
7. Lossing, *The Civil War*, 3:242.
8. Fellman, *Inside War*, 96.
9. Reid Mitchell, *Civil War Soldiers* (New York: Touchstone, 1988), 132.
10. Mitchell, *Civil War Soldiers*, 133.
11. Mitchell, *Civil War Soldiers*, 136.

CHAPTER 5: STRATEGIC CULTURES: INDIANS AND THE ARMY

1. Albert K. Weinberg, *Manifest Destiny: A Study of Nationalist Expansion in American History* (Chicago: Quadrangle, 1963), 74. (Originally published in 1935, by Johns Hopkins Press, Baltimore, MD.)
2. Weinberg, *Manifest Destiny*, 83.
3. Weinberg, *Manifest Destiny*, 73.
4. Robert M. Utley, *Frontier Regulars: The United States Army and the Indian, 1866–1891* (New York: Macmillan, 1973), 6.
5. Robert M. Utley, *Frontiersmen in Blue: The United States Army and the Indian, 1848–1865* (New York: Macmillan, 1967), 28.
6. Asprey, *War in the Shadows*, 2nd ed., 114.
7. Utley, *Frontiersmen in Blue*, 227.
8. Robert G. Athearn, *William Tecumseh Sherman and the Settlement of the West* (Norman: University of Oklahoma Press, 1956), 196.
9. Athearn, *Sherman and the Settlement of the West*, 206.
10. Athearn, *Sherman and the Settlement of the West*, 229.

11. Athearn, *Sherman and the Settlement of the West*, 236.
12. Athearn, *Sherman and the Settlement of the West*, 301.
13. Athearn, *Sherman and the Settlement of the West*, 160.

CHAPTER 6: TRIBAL IRREGULARS vs. ARMY IRREGULARS

1. Francis Paul Prucha, *The Sword of the Republic: The United States Army on the Frontier* (New York: Macmillan, 1969), 268.
2. Prucha, *The Sword of the Republic*, 281.
3. Prucha, *The Sword of the Republic*, 284.
4. Prucha, *The Sword of the Republic*, 283.
5. Utley, *Frontiersmen in Blue*, 241.
6. Douglas Porch, "Bugeaud, Gallieni, Lyautey: The Development of French Colonial Warfare," in Peter Paret, ed., *Makers of Modern Strategy* (Princeton, NJ: Princeton University Press, 1986), 378.
7. John G. Bourke, *On the Border With Crook* (Chicago: 1891), 213–214.
8. Clarence C. Clendenen, *Blood on the Border: The United States Army and the Mexican Irregulars* (New York: Macmillan, 1969), 79–80.
9. Utley, *Frontier Regulars*, 381.

PART II: FOREIGN FRONTIERS: EXPANSION, INSURRECTION, AND COUNTERINSURGENCY

●   ●   ●   ●   ●   ●   ●   ●   ●

INTRODUCTION TO PART II: IMPERIALISM

1. Weinberg, *Manifest Destiny*, 272.
2. Weinberg, *Manifest Destiny*, 145.
3. Weinberg, *Manifest Destiny*, 383.
4. Weinberg, *Manifest Destiny*, 385.
5. Weinberg, *Manifest Destiny*, 402.
6. "We are not going to the musty records of title archives to find our warrant for this war. We find it in the law supreme—the law high above the law of titles in lands . . . the law of man, the law of God. We find it in our own inspiration, our own destiny." (Weinberg, *Manifest Destiny*, 154.)
7. J. W. Pratt, "The Ideology of American Expansion," in J. Rogers Hollingsworth, ed., *American Expansion in the Late Nineteenth Century* (New York: Holt, Rinehart, and Winston, 1968), 9–17.
8. Weinberg, *Manifest Destiny*, 277.
9. Weinberg, *Manifest Destiny*, 304.
10. Weinberg, *Manifest Destiny*, 219.
11. Weinberg, *Manifest Destiny*, 219.
12. Weinberg, *Manifest Destiny*, 219.
13. Weinberg, *Manifest Destiny*, 265.
14. Weinberg, *Manifest Destiny*, 270.
15. Weinberg, *Manifest Destiny*, 261–262.

CHAPTER 7: THE PHILIPPINE INSURRECTION: INITIAL PHASE

1. Leon Wolff, *Little Brown Brother* (Garden City, NY: Doubleday, 1961), 221.
2. William T. Sexton, *Soldiers in the Sun* (Freeport, NY: Books for Libraries Press, 1939), 97.

3. Robert N. Ginsburgh, "Damn the Insurrectos," *Military Review*, January 1964, 62.
4. Sexton, *Soldiers in the Sun*, 136.
5. James E. LeRoy, *The Americans in the Philippines*, 2 vols. (Boston: Houghton-Mifflin Co., 1914), 2:54.
6. Sexton, *Soldiers in the Sun*, 184–185.
7. Sexton, *Soldiers in the Sun*, 198.
8. Wolff, *Little Brown Brother*, 289.
9. LeRoy, *The Americans in the Philippines*, 162.
10. J. R. M. Taylor, *The Philippine Insurrection Against the United States: A Compilation of Documents With Notes and Introduction*, 3 vols. (n.p.: 1906), 2:268–269.
11. LeRoy, *The Americans in the Philippines*, 216.
12. Sexton, *Soldiers in the Sun*, 248.
13. Sexton, *Soldiers in the Sun*, 249.
14. Wolff, *Little Brown Brother*, 311.
15. Wolff, *Little Brown Brother*, 311.
16. LeRoy, *The Americans in the Philippines*, 180–181.
17. Taylor, *The Philippine Insurrection*, 297–298.
18. LeRoy, *The Americans in the Philippines*, 260–261.
19. Usha Mahajani, *Philippine Nationalism* (Queensland, Australia: University of Queenland Press, 1971), 64–66.
20. LeRoy, *The Americans in the Philippines*, 285–286.
21. Taylor, *The Philippine Insurrection*, 227.
22. Op. cit.
23. Wolff, *Little Brown Brother*, 311.
24. LeRoy, *The Americans in the Philippines*, 245.

CHAPTER 8: THE PHILIPPINE INSURRECTION: PROTEST AND VICTORY

1. E. B. Tompkins, *Anti-Imperialism in the United States: The Great Debate, 1890–1920* (Philadelphia: University of Pennsylvania Press, 1970), 196.
2. Daniel B. Schirmer, *Republic or Empire: American Resistance to the Philippine War* (Cambridge, MA: Schenkem Publishing Co., 1972), 205–206.
3. Schirmer, *Republic or Empire*, 208.
4. Schirmer, *Republic or Empire*, 175.
5. Schirmer, *Republic or Empire*, 175.
6. Samuel Eliot Morison et al., *Dissent in Three American Wars* (Cambridge: Harvard University Press, 1970), 84.
7. W. Cameron Forbes, *The Philippine Islands* (Cambridge, MA: Harvard University Press, 1928), 60–61
8. Wolff, *Little Brown Brother*, 262.
9. Wolff, *Little Brown Brother*, 252.
10. Forbes, *The Philippine Islands*, 65.
11. Sexton, *Soldiers in the Sun*, 273.
12. Wolff, *Little Brown Brother*, 357.
13. Schirmer, *Republic or Empire*, 142.
14. Sexton, *Soldiers in the Sun*, 282.
15. Wolff, *Little Brown Brother*, 359.
16. Asprey, *War in the Shadows*, 1:211.

17. This citation and all others on pages 136–139 are from Donald Smythe, *Guerilla Warrior: The Early Life of John J. Pershing*, (New York: Scribner, 1973), 162, 165, 145, 147, 169, 195, 196, 199, 201.

CHAPTER 9: MEXICO: TEXAS RANGERS TO PANCHO VILLA
1. William Prescott Webb, *The Texas Rangers* (Austin: University of Texas Press, 1935), 201–202.
2. Webb, *The Texas Rangers*, 201–202.
3. Webb, *The Texas Rangers*, 172.
4. Webb, *The Texas Rangers*, 241.
5. Webb, *The Texas Rangers*, 319.
6. Webb, *The Texas Rangers*, 322.
7. U. S. Grant, *Personal Memoirs of U.S. Grant*, 2 vols. (New York: Charles A. Webster & Co., 1885), 1:53.
8. John S. D. Eisenhower, *So Far From God: The U.S. War With Mexico, 1846–1848* (New York: Random House, 1989), vvii.
9. Eisenhower, *So Far From God*, vvii.
10. Webb, *The Texas Rangers*, 115.
11. Justin H. Smith, *The War With Mexico*, 2 vols. (New York: Macmillan, 1919), 2:169.
12. Webb, *The Texas Rangers*, 115.
13. Smith, *The War With Mexico*, 172.
14. Smith, *The War With Mexico*, 172.
15. Webb, *The Texas Rangers*, 120.
16. Smith, *The War With Mexico*, 173.
17. Weinberg, *Manifest Destiny*, 161.
18. Weinberg, *Manifest Destiny*, 171.
19. Weinberg, *Manifest Destiny*, 176.
20. Weinberg, *Manifest Destiny*, 179.
21. Weinberg, *Manifest Destiny*, 180.
22. Weinberg, *Manifest Destiny*, 435.
23. Herbert M. Mason Jr., *The Great Pursuit* (New York: Random House, 1970), 83.
24. Clendenen, *Blood on the Border*, 230.
25. Smythe, *Guerilla Warrior*, 227.
26. Smythe, *Guerilla Warrior*, 220.
27. Smythe, *Guerilla Warrior*, 239.
28. Clendenen, *Blood on the Border*, 338.

CHAPTER 10: THE CARIBBEAN: THE DOMINICAN REPUBLIC AND HAITI
1. Weinberg, *Manifest Destiny*, 428.
2. Weinberg, *Manifest Destiny*, 432.
3. Clyde H. Metcalf, *A History of the United States Marine Corps* (New York: Putnam, 1939), 394.
4. Robert D. Heinl Jr., *Soldiers of the Sea: The United States Marine Corps, 1775–1962* (Annapolis, MD: U.S. Naval Institute, 1962), 189.
5. Marvin Goldwert, *The Constabulary in the Dominican Republic and Nicaragua* (Gainesville: University of Florida Press, 1962), 11.

6. Metcalf, *A History of the United States Marine Corps*, 357.
7. Sumner Welles, *Naboth's Vineyard: The Dominican Republic, 1844–1924*, 2 vols. (New York: Payson and Clarke, 1928), 2:804.
8. Metcalf, *A History of the United States Marine Corps*, 358.
9. Welles, *Naboth's Vineyard*, 806.
10. Welles, *Naboth's Vineyard*, 819–820.
11. James H. McCrocklin, *Garde d'Haiti* (Annapolis, MD: U.S. Naval Institute, 1956), 8.
12. Heinl, *Soldiers of the Sea*, 237.
13. Metcalf, *A History of the United States Marine Corps*, 396.
14. F. M. Wise, *A Marine Tells It to You* (New York: J. H. Sears and Company, 1929), 311.
15. Heinl, *Soldiers of the Sea*, 241.
16. Arthur C. Millspaugh, *Haiti Under American Control* (Boston: World Peace Foundation, 1931), 87.
17. Millspaugh, *Haiti Under American Control*, 95.
18. Millspaugh, *Haiti Under American Control*, 96.

CHAPTER 11: NICARAGUA: OPTIMISM TURNS INTO FRUSTRATION

Unless otherwise indicated, references and quotations in both chapters 11 and 12 are from my own Ph.D. dissertation, "The United States and Nicaragua, 1927–1933: Decisions for De-escalation and Withdrawal" (University of Pennsylvania, 1969), or from my article, "U.S. Intervention in Nicaragua, 1927–1933: Lessons for Today," *Orbis*, Winter 1971.

1. Harold N. Denny, *Dollars for Bullets: The Story of American Rule in Nicaragua* (New York: Dial Press, 1929), 9.
2. *New York Times*, January 11, 1927, 1.
3. Weinberg, *Manifest Destiny*, 400.
4. Dom Albert Pagano, *Bluejackets* (Boston: Meador Publishing Co., 1932), 136–137.
5. Clyde H. Metcalf, "The Marine Corps and the Changing Caribbean Policy," *The Marine Corps Gazette*, November 1937, 30–31.
6. Julian C. Smith et al., *A Review of the Organization and Operations of the Guardia Nacional de Nicaragua* (Quantico, VA: Marine Corps School, 1937), 23.
7. Heinl, *Soldiers of the Sea*, 273.
8. Neill Macauley, *The Sandino Affair* (Chicago: Quadrangle Books, 1967), 89.
9. Eduardo Crawley, *Dictators Never Die: A Portrait of Nicaragua and the Somoza Dynasty* (New York: St. Martins Press, 1979), 60.
10. *New York Times*, January 15, 1928, IX, 1.

CHAPTER 12: NICARAGUA: PROTEST AND WITHDRAWAL

1. *New York Times*, December 25, 1926, 2.
2. Denny, *Dollars for Bullets*, 249.
3. Franklin D. Roosevelt, "Our Foreign Policy," *Foreign Affairs*, July 1928, 11.

4. William E. Diez, "Opposition in the United States to American Diplomacy in the Caribbean, 1898–1932" (thesis, University of Chicago, 1948), 93.
5. *New York Times*, January 17, 1927, 4.
6. *New York Times*, May 30, 1930, 6.
7. Crawley, *Dictators Never Die*, 72
8. Heinl, *Soldiers of the Sea*, 288–289.
9. Metcalf, *A History of the United States Marine Corps*, 444.
10. Metcalf, *A History of the United States Marine Corps*, 439.
11. Ross E. Rowell, "Aircraft in Bush Warfare," *The Marine Corps Gazette*, September 1929.
12. Rowell, "Aircraft in Bush Warfare,"
13. Weinberg, *Manifest Destiny*, 437.

CHAPTER 13: WORLD WAR: GUERRILLA THEATERS

1. Alfred H. Paddock Jr., *U.S. Army Special Warfare: Its Origins* (Washington, DC: National Defense University, 1982), 6.
2. Paddock, *U.S. Army Special Warfare*, 26.
3. Paddock, *U.S. Army Special Warfare*, 31.
4. Paddock, *U.S. Army Special Warfare*, 26.
5. Paddock, *U.S. Army Special Warfare*, 24.
6. R. Harris Smith, *OSS: The Secret History of America's First Central Intelligence Agency* (Berkeley: University of California Press, 1972), 248.
7. Roger Hilsman, "Internal War: The New Communist Tactic," in Greene, *The Guerrilla*, 27.
8. Ira Wolfert, *American Guerrilla in the Philippines* (New York: Avon Books, 1945), 161.
9. R. W. Volckmann, *We Remained* (New York: W. W. Norton, 1954), 105–108.
10. Rex Blow, "With the Filipino Guerrillas," *Australian Army Journal*, 1966.
11. Paddock, *U.S. Army Special Warfare*, 27.
12. John K. Singlaub, *Hazardous Duty: An American Soldier in the Twentieth Century* (New York: Summit Books, 1991), 65.
13. Paddock, *U.S. Army Special Warfare*, 28.
14. Paddock, *U.S. Army Special Warfare*, 29.
15. Bickham Sweet-Escott, *Baker Street Irregulars* (London: Methuen, 1965), 126.
16. Harry Rowe Ransom, *Central Intelligence and National Security*, (Cambridge: Harvard University Press, 1948), 71–72.
17. Charles W. Thayer, *Guerrilla* (New York: Harper & Row, 1963), xxii, xxiii.

CHAPTER 14: COLD WAR: AID AND ADVICE

1. Quoted in Henry A. Kissinger, *Diplomacy* (New York: Touchstone, 1994), 452.
2. Kissinger, *Diplomacy*, 262.
3. For further reflections on the Greek civil war, see articles by Gen. Edward R. Wainhouse and Field Marshall Alexander Papagos in Osanka, *Modern Guerilla Warfare*, part 5.
4. Luis Taruc, *He Who Rides the Tiger*, (New York: Praeger, 1967), 42.

5. N. D. Valeriano and C. T. Bohannan, *Counterguerrilla Operations: The Philippine Experience* (New York: Praeger, 1962), 130.

6. *Joint Army-Air Force Low Intensity Conflict Project Final Report*, 160.

7. *Joint Army-Air Force Low Intensity Conflict Project Final Report*, 160.

8. *Joint Army-Air Force Low Intensity Conflict Project Final Report*, 160.

9. Paddock, *U.S. Army Special Warfare*, 107.

10. Roy E. Appleman, *The United States Army in the Korean War: South to the Naktong, North to the Yalu, June–November 1950* (Washington, DC: Department of the Army, 1961), 723.

11. Walter G. Hermes, *United States Army in the Korean War, Truce Tent and Fighting Front* (Washington, DC: U.S. Army, 1966), 345, 347.

CHAPTER 15: VIETNAM: CONTRADICTIONS IN
COUNTERINSURGENCY

1. Quoted in Phillippe Devillers and Jean Lacouture, *End of a War: Indochina, 1954* (New York: Praeger, 1969), 4.

2. Douglas S. Blaufarb, *The Counterinsurgency Era: U.S. Doctrine and Performance* (New York: The Free Press, 1977), 93–94.

3. Quoted in James Pinckney Harrison, *The Endless War* (New York: The Free Press, 1982), 165–166.

4. *Why Vietnam?* (New York: Praeger, 1966), 163.

5. Matthew B. Ridgway, *Soldier: The Memoirs of Matthew B. Ridgway* (New York: Harper & Brothers, 1956), 275–276.

6. Theodore Sorenson, *Kennedy* (New York: Harper & Row, 1965), 631–632.

7. Arthur M. Schlesinger Jr., *A Thousand Days: John F. Kennedy in the White House* (Boston: Houghton-Mifflin, 1965), 536–550.

8. Quoted in Blaufarb, *The Counterinsurgency Era*, 55.

9. Quoted in Asprey, *War in the Shadows*, 726.

10. Blaufarb, *The Counterinsurgency Era*, 58.

11. Blaufarb, *The Counterinsurgency Era*, 72.

12. Blaufarb, *The Counterinsurgency Era*, 80.

13. Quoted in Asprey, *War in the Shadows*, 798.

14. Quoted in David Halberstam, *The Best and the Brightest* (New York: Ballantine Books, 1992), 171.

15. Quoted in Roger Hilsman, *To Move a Nation* (New York: Doubleday, 1967) 415–416.

16. Hilsman, *To Move a Nation*, 426.

17. Quoted in Schlesinger, *The Bitter Heritage: Vietnam and American Democracy* (Boston: Houghton-Mifflin,1967), 25.

18. Quoted in Harrison, *The Endless War*, 256.

19. Quoted in Asprey, *War in the Shadows*, 1024.

CHAPTER 16: RENEWAL: VIETNAM TO THE PERSIAN GULF

1. "Vietnam: Do We Understand Revolution?" *Foreign Affairs*, October 1964, 76.

2. "Irregular Warfare in Transition," in Osanka, *Modern Guerrilla Warfare*, 52.

3. Philip Caputo, *A Rumor of War* (New York: Holt, Rinehart and Winston, 1977), xviii.

4. David Hackworth, *About Face: The Odyssey of an American Warrior* (New York: Simon & Schuster, 1989), 776.

5. Matthew B. Ridgway, *The Korean War* (Garden City, NY: Doubleday, 1967), 245.

6. Harry G. Summers, *On Strategy: The Vietnam War in Context* (Carlisle Barracks, PA: U.S. Army War College, 1982), 48.

7. Singlaub, *Hazardous Duty*, passim, especially, 273–283.

8. Williamson Murray, "The Collapse of Empire: British Strategy, 1919–1945," in Murray et al., *The Making of Strategy* (Cambridge: Cambridge University Press, 1994), 4.

9. Richard M. Pfeffer, ed., *No More Vietnams?* (New York: Harper Colophon, 1968), 4.

10. Pfeffer, *No More Vietnams?* 287.

11. Richard M. Nixon, *No More Vietnams* (New York: Arbor House, 1985), 13.

12. Peter Huchthausen, *America's Splendid Little Wars: A Short History of U.S. Engagements From the Fall of Saigon to Baghdad* (New York: Penguin, 2003).

13. Anthony James Joes, *America and Guerrilla Warfare* (Lexington: The University Press of Kentucky, 2000), 279.

14. Joes, *America and Guerrilla Warfare*, 323.

EPILOGUE: DOES HISTORY REPEAT?

1. George H. W. Bush and Brent Scowcroft, *A World Transformed* (New York: Alfred A. Knopf, 1998), 489.

2. Blaufarb, *The Counterinsurgency Era*, 100.

3. *New York Times*, November 28, 2004, Section 4, 7.

4. *Washington Post*, December 25, 2004, A18.

5. *Bureaucracy Does Its Thing: Institutional Constraints on U.S. GVN Performance in Vietnam*, R-967-ARPA (Santa Monica, CA: The RAND Corporation, August 1967), 145.

6. Robert H. Scales, *Washington Times*, February 17, 2005, A19.

Selected Bibliography

General Works

Asprey, Robert B. *War in the Shadows: The Guerrilla in History*. Garden City, NY: Doubleday and Co., 1975. 2nd ed., New York: William Morrow and Company, 1994.

Beckett, I. F. W. *Modern Insurgencies and Counterinsurgencies: Guerrillas and Their Opponents Since 1750*. London: Routledge, 2001.

Bell, J. Bowyer. *The Myth of the Guerrilla: Revolutionary Theory and Malpractice*. New York: Knopf, 1971.

Callwell, C. E. *Small Wars: Their Principles and Practice*. London: Her Majesty's Stationery Office, 1899.

Clutterbuck, Richard L. *Terrorism and Guerrilla War*. London: Routledge, 1990.

Ellis, John. *A Short History of Guerrilla War*. New York: St. Martin's Press, 1976.

Galula, David. *Counterinsurgency Warfare*. New York: Praeger, 1964.

Gann, Lewis H. *Guerrillas in History*. Stanford, CA: Hoover Institution, 1971.

Greene, T. N., ed. *The Guerrilla—and How to Fight Him*. New York: Praeger, 1962.

Grivas, George. *General Grivas on Guerrilla Warfare*. Translated by A. S. Pallis. New York: Praeger, 1965.

Guevara, Ernesto Che. *Che Guevara on Guerrilla Warfare*. New York: Praeger, 1961.

Joes, Anthony James. *Guerrilla Conflict Before the Cold War*. New York: Praeger, 1996.

———. *Resisting Rebellion: Inside Modern Revolutionary Warfare*. Lexington: University Press of Kentucky, 2004.

Kitson, Frank. *Low Intensity Operations*. London: Faber and Faber, 1971.

Laqueur, Walter. *Guerrilla: A Historical and Critical Study*. Boston: Little, Brown and Company, 1976.

———. *The Guerrilla Reader: A Historical Anthology*. New York: The New American Library, 1977.

Mao Tse-tung. *On Guerrilla Warfare*. Translated by Samuel B. Griffith. Champaign: University of Illinois Press, 2000.

275

McCuen, John J. *The Art of Counter-Revolutionary War*. London: Faber and Faber, 1966.

Merom, Gil. *How Democracies Lose Small Wars*. Cambridge: Cambridge University Press, 2003.

Moss, Robert. *Urban Guerrillas*. London: M.T. Smith, 1972.

Nasution, Abdul Haris. *Fundamentals of Guerrilla War*. New York: Praeger, 1965.

O'Neill, Bard. *Insurgency and Terrorism: Inside Modern Revolutionary Warfare*. Dulles, VA: Brassey's, Inc., 1990.

Osanka, Franklin Mark, ed. *Modern Guerrilla Warfare*. New York: The Free Press, 1962.

Paret, Peter, and John Shy. *Guerrillas in the 1960s*. New York: Praeger, 1962.

Payne, Robert. *Lawrence of Arabia: A Triumph*. New York: Pyramid Books, 1963.

Pimlon, John, ed. *Guerrilla Warfare*. New York: The Military Press, 1985.

Scott, Wimberly. *Special Forces Guerrilla Warfare Manual*. Boulder, CO: Paladin Press, 1997.

Standing, Percy Cross. *Guerrilla Leaders of the World: From Charette to Delvet*. London: Stanley Paul, 1912.

Sullivan, David S., and Martin J. Sattler, eds. *Revolutionary War: Western Response*. New York: Columbia University Press, 1971.

Taber, Robert. *War of the Flea*. Dulles, VA: Brassey's, 2002.

Thayer, Charles W. *Guerrilla*. New York: Harper & Row, 1963.

Thompson, Robert. *Revolutionary War in World Strategy, 1945–1969*. London: Secker and Warburg, 1970.

Trinquier, Roger. *Modern Warfare: A French View of Counter-insurgency*. New York: Praeger, 1964.

The American Experience

Alden, John R. *The American Revolution, 1775–1783*. New York: Harper and Brothers, 1954.

———. *The South in the Revolution, 1763–1789*. Baton Rouge: Louisiana State University Press, 1957.

Aleshire, Peter. *The Fox and the Whirlwind: General George Crook and Geronimo, A Paired Biography*. New York: John Wiley and Sons, 2000.

Anderson, Fred. *Crucible of War: The Seven Years' War and the Fate of Empire in British North America, 1754–1766*. New York: Alfred A. Knopf, 2000.

Appleman, Roy E. *The United States Army in the Korean War: South to the Naktong, North to the Yalu, June–November 1950*. Washington, DC: Department of the Army, 1961.

Athearn, Robert G. *William Tecumseh Sherman and the Settlement of the West*. Norman: University of Oklahoma Press, 1956.

Billias, George A., ed. *George Washington's Generals*. New York: William Morrow and Company, 1964.

Blaufarb, Douglas S. *The Counterinsurgency Era: U.S. Doctrine and Performance*. New York: The Free Press, 1977.

Boot, Max. *The Savage Wars of Peace: Small Wars and the Rise of American Power*. New York: Basic Books, 2002.

Bourke, John G. *On the Border With Crook*. Chicago: 1891.

Brant, Marley. *Jesse James: The Man and the Myth*. New York: The Berkley Publishing Group, 1998.

Brehan, Carl W. *Quantrill and His Civil War Guerrillas*. Denver, CO: Sage Books, 1959.

Brownlee, Richard. *Gray Ghosts of the Confederacy*. Baton Rouge: Louisiana State University Press, 1958.

Bush, George H. W., and Brent Scowcroft. *A World Transformed*. New York: Alfred A. Knopf, 1998.

Calhoon, Robert M. *The Loyalists in Revolutionary America, 1760–1781*. New York: Harcourt Brace Jovanovich, 1973.

Callahan, North. *Royal Raiders: The Tories of the American Revolution*. Indianapolis, IN: Bobbs-Merrill, 1963.

Callcott, Wilfrid H. *The Caribbean Policy of the United States, 1890–1920*. New York: Octagon Books, 1966.

Caputo, Philip. *A Rumor of War*. New York: Holt, Rinehart, and Winston, 1977.

Castel, Albert, and Thomas Goodrich. *Bloody Bill Anderson: The Short, Savage Life of a Civil War Guerrilla*. Mechanicsville, PA: Stackpole Books, 1998.

Clendenen, Clarence C. *Blood on the Border: The United States Army and the Mexican Irregulars*. New York: Macmillan, 1969.

Crawley, Eduardo. *Dictators Never Die: A Portrait of Nicaragua and the Somoza Dynasty*. New York: St. Martin's Press, 1979.

Crook, George. *General George Crook: His Autobiography*. Edited by Martin Ferdinand. Norman: University of Oklahoma Press, 1986.

Cummins, Lejeune. *Quijote on a Burro: Sandino and the Marines*. Mexico City: Impresora Azteca, 1958.

Denny, Harold N. *Dollars for Bullets: The Story of American Rule in Nicaragua*. New York: Dial Press, 1929.

Devillers, Phillipe, and Jean Lacouture. *End of a War: Indochina, 1954*. New York: Praeger, 1969.

Diez, William E. "Opposition in the United States to American Diplomacy in the Caribbean, 1898–1932." Thesis, University of Chicago, 1948.

Donovan, James A., Jr. *The United States Marine Corps*. New York: Praeger, 1967.

Dupuy, Ernest R. *The Compact History of the United States Army*. New York: Hawthorn Books, 1956.

Fall, Bernard. *The Two Vietnams*. London: Pall Mall Press, 1963.

Fellman, Michael. *Inside War: The Guerrilla Conflict in Missouri During the American Civil War*. New York: Oxford University Press, 1989.

Forbes, W. Cameron. *The Philippine Islands*. Cambridge: Harvard University Press, 1928.

Goldwert, Marvin. *The Constabulary in the Dominican Republic and Nicaragua*. Gainesville: University of Florida Press, 1962.

Goodrich, Thomas. *Black Flag: Guerrilla Warfare on the Western Border, 1861–1865*. Bloomington: University of Indiana Press, 1995.

Hackworth, David. *About Face: The Odyssey of an American Warrior*. New York: Simon & Schuster, 1989.

Halberstam, David. *The Best and the Brightest*. New York: Ballantine Books, 1992.

Harrison, Pinckney. *The Endless War*. New York: The Free Press, 1982.

Heinl, Robert D., Jr. *Soldiers of the Sea: The United States Marine Corps, 1775–1962*. Annapolis: U.S. Naval Institute, 1962.

Hermes, Walter G. *United States Army in the Korean War: Truce Tent and Fighting Front*. Washington, DC: U.S. Army, 1966.

Higgenbotham, Don. *The War of American Independence: Military Attitudes, Policies and Practices, 1763–1789*, New York: Macmillan, 1971.

Hilsman, Roger. *American Guerrilla: My War Behind Japanese Lines*. Washington, DC: Brassey's, Inc., 1990.

———. *To Move a Nation*. New York: Doubleday, 1967.

Huchthausen, Peter. *America's Splendid Little Wars: A Short History of U.S. Engagements From the Fall of Saigon to Baghdad*. New York: Penguin, 2003.

Hunt, Ray C., and Bernard Norling. *Behind Japanese Lines: An American Guerrilla in the Philippines*. Lexington: University Press of Kentucky, 1986.

Joes, Anthony James. *America and Guerrilla Warfare*. Lexington: University Press of Kentucky, 2000.

Jones, Virgil C. *Gray Ghosts and Rebel Raiders*. New York: Henry Holt and Company, 1956.

Karnow, Stanley. *In Our Image: America's Empire in the Philippines*. New York: Random House, 1989.

———. *Vietnam: A History*. London: Century Publishing House, 1983.

Komer, Robert. *Bureaucracy Does Its Thing: Institutional Constraints on U.S.-GVN Performance in Vietnam*. Santa Monica, CA: The Rand Corporation, 1967.

Kurtz, Stephen G., and James H. Hutson, eds. *Essays on the American Revolution*. Chapel Hill: University of North Carolina Press, 1973.

Lansdale, Edward G. *In the Midst of Wars: An American's Mission to Southeast Asia*. New York: Harper & Row, 1972.

Lapham, Robert, and Bernard Norling. *Lapham's Raiders: Guerrillas in the Philippines, 1942–1945*. Lexington: University Press of Kentucky, 1996.

LeRoy, James E. *The Americans in the Philippines*. 2 vols. Boston: Houghton-Mifflin Co., 1914.

Leslie, Edward E. *The Devil Knows How to Ride: The True Story of William Clarke Quantrill and His Civil War Raiders*. New York: Random House, 1996.

Library of Congress, Congressional Research Service. *U.S. Low Intensity Conflicts, 1899–1990*. Washington, DC: Government Printing Office, 1990.

Lossing, Benson J. *The Civil War*. 3 vols. Hartford, CT: T. Belmap, 1868.

Macauley, Neill. *The Sandino Affair*. Chicago: Quadrangle Books, 1967.

Mahajani, Usha. *Philippine Nationalism*. Queensland, Australia: University of Queensland Press, 1971.

McCrocklin, James H. *Garde d'Haiti*. Annapolis, MD: U.S. Naval Institute, 1956.

McCulloch, Ian, and Timothy J. Todish. *British Light Infantrymen of the Seven Years' War*. Oxford, UK: Osprey Publishing, 2004.

Metcalf, Clyde H. *A History of the United States Marine Corps*. New York: Putnam, 1939.

Millspaugh, Arthur C. *Haiti Under American Control*. Boston: World Peace Foundation, 1931.

Monaghan, Jay. *Civil War on the Western Border*. Lincoln: University of Nebraska Press, 1985.

Moore, Christopher. *The Loyalists: Revolution, Exile, Settlement*. Toronto: McClelland & Stewart, 1994.

Morison, Samuel Eliot, et al., *Dissent in Three American Wars*. Cambridge: Harvard University Press, 1970.

Mosby, John S. *Mosby's Memoirs*. Nashville, TN: J. S. Sanders & Co., 1995.

Munro, Dana G. *Intervention and Dollar Diplomacy in the Caribbean, 1900–1921*. Princeton: Princeton University Press, 1964.

———. *The United States and the Caribbean Area*. Boston: World Peace Foundation, 1934.

Nixon, Richard M. *No More Vietnams*. New York: Arbor House, 1985.

O'Donnell, Patrick K. *Operatives, Spies and Saboteurs: The Unknown Story of the Men and Women of World War II's OSS*. New York: The Free Press, 2004.

Paddock, Alfred H., Jr. *US Army Special Warfare: Its Origins*. Washington, DC: National Defense University, 1983.

Pagano, Dom Albert. *Bluejackets*. Boston: Meador Publishing Co., 1932.

Perkins, Dexter. *The United States and the Caribbean*. Cambridge: Harvard University Press, 1947.

Pfeffer, Richard M., ed. *No More Vietnams?* New York: Harper Colophon, 1968.

Pike, Douglas. *Viet Cong: The Organization and Techniques of the National Liberation Front of South Vietnam*. Cambridge: Harvard University Press, 1963.

Prucha, Francis Paul. *The Sword of the Republic: The United States Army on the Frontier*. New York: Macmillan, 1969.

Ramage, James A. *Gray Ghost: The Life of John Singleton Mosby*. Lexington: University Press of Kentucky, 1999.

Ransom, Harry Rowe. *Central Intelligence and National Security*. Cambridge: Harvard University Press, 1948.

Ridgway, Matthew B. *The Korean War*. Garden City, NY: Doubleday, 1967.

———. *Soldier: The Memoirs of Matthew B. Ridgway*. New York: Harper & Brothers, 1956.

Rippy, J. Fred. *Caribbean Danger Zone*. New York: Putnam, 1940.

Robinson, Charles M. *General Crook and the Western Frontier*. Norman: University of Oklahoma Press, 2001.

———. *The Men Who Wear the Star: The Story of the Texas Rangers*. New York: Modern Library, 2001.

Rogers, Robert. *The Annotated and Illustrated Journals of Major Robert Rogers*. Introduction by Timothy J. Todish. Fleischmanns, NY: Purple Mountain Press, 2002.

Schirmer, Daniel B. *Republic or Empire: American Resistance to the Philippine War*. Cambridge, MA: Schenlman Publishing Co., 1972.

Schlesinger, Arthur M., Jr. *The Bitter Heritage: Vietnam and American Democracy*. Boston: Houghton-Mifflin, 1967.

———. *A Thousand Days: John F. Kennedy in the White House*. Boston: Houghton-Mifflin, 1965.

Sexton, William T. *Soldiers in the Sun*. Freeport, NY: Books for Libraries Press, 1939.

Singlaub, John K. *Hazardous Duty: An American Soldier in the Twentieth Century*. New York: Summit Books, 1991.

Smith, Justin H. *The War With Mexico*. 2 vols. New York: The Macmillan Co., 1919.

Smith, R. Harris. *OSS: The Secret History of America's First Central Intelligence Agency*. Berkeley: University of California Press, 1972.

Smythe, Donald. *Guerrilla Warrior: The Early Life of John J. Pershing*. New York: Scribner, 1973.

Sorensen, Theodore. *Kennedy*. New York: Harper & Row, 1965.

Summers, Harry G. *On Strategy: The Vietnam War in Context*. Carlisle Barrack, PA: U.S. Army War College, 1982.

Sweet-Escott, Bickham. *Baker Street Irregulars*. London: Methuen, 1965.

Swiggett, Howard. *War out of Niagara: Walter Butler and the Tory Rangers*. New York: Columbia University Press, 1933.

Taruc, Luis. *He Who Rides the Tiger*. New York: Frederick A. Praeger, 1967.

Taylor, J. R. M. *The Philippine Insurrection Against the United States: A Compilation of Documents with Notes and Introduction*. 3 vols. n.p., 1906

Tompkins, E. B. *Anti-Imperialism in the United States: The Great Debate, 1890–1920*. Philadelphia: University of Pennsylvania Press, 1970.

Tierney, John J., Jr. *The Politics of Peace: What's Behind the Anti-War Movement?* Washington, DC: Capital Research Center, 2005.

———. *Somozas and Sandinistas: The U.S. and Nicaragua in the Twentieth Century*. Washington, DC: Council for Inter-American Security, 1982.

U.S. Marine Corps. *Small Wars Manual*. Washington, DC: Government Printing Office, 1940.

Utley, Robert M. *Frontier Regulars: The United States Army and the Indian, 1866–1891*. New York: Macmillan, 1973.

———. *Frontiersmen in Blue: The United States Army and the Indian, 1848–1865*. New York: Macmillan, 1967.

———. *Lone Star Justice: The First Century of the Texas Rangers*. New York: Oxford University Press, 2002.

Valeriano, N. D., and C. T. Bohannan. *Counterguerrilla Operations: The Philippine Experience*. New York: Praeger, 1962.

Van Tyne, Claude H. *The Loyalists in the American Revolution*. New York: Macmillan, 1902.

Volckmann, R. W. *We Remained*. New York: W. W. Norton, 1954.

Webb, William Prescott. *The Texas Rangers*. Austin: University of Texas Press, 1935.

Weigley, Russell. *The American Way of War*. New York: Macmillan, 1973.

Weinberg, Albert K. *Manifest Destiny: A Study of Nationalist Expansion in American History*. Baltimore: Johns Hopkins University Press, 1935. Reprint, Chicago: Quadrangle, 1963.

Welles, Sumner. *Naboth's Vineyard: The Dominican Republic, 1844–1924*. 2 vols. New York: Payson and Clarke, 1928.

Wert, Jeffery B. *Mosby's Rangers*. New York: Simon & Schuster, 1991.

Wills, Bruce Steel. *The Confederacy's Greatest Cavalryman: Nathan Bedford Forrest*. Lawrence: University Press of Kansas, 1998.

Wolfert, Ira. *American Guerrilla in the Philippines*. New York: Avon Books, 1945.

Wolff, Leon. *Little Brown Brother*. Garden City, NY: Doubleday, 1961.

Wood, Bryce. *The Making of the Good Neighbor Policy*. New York: Norton, 1967.

Younger, Cole. *The Story of Cole Younger, By Himself.* Introduction by Marley Brant. St. Paul: Minnesota Historical Society, 2000.
Zaboly, Gary. *American Colonial Ranger: The Northern Colonies, 1724–1764.* Oxford, UK: Osprey Publishing, 2004.

Index

About the Author

John J. Tierney Jr. is the Walter Kohler Professor of International Relations at the Institute of World Politics, Washington, D.C. He has also taught at Catholic University of America, the University of Virginia, and Johns Hopkins University. He has served in the U.S. House of Representatives and the U.S. Arms Control and Disarmament Agency. His Ph.D. dissertation at the University of Pennsylvania was on the Marine Corps counterinsurgency in Nicaragua against guerrillas led by Augusto C. Sandino ("Sandinistas"). Subsequently, he has researched and investigated material on related interventions, culminating in the present book. He lives in Washington, D.C.